¡Viva la gramática!

GCSE Spanish Grammar

Phil Turk and

Mike Zollo

HODDER
EDUCATION
AN HACHETTE UK COMPANY

Acknowledgements

The authors would like to thank the following people: Jenny Wake, Peter Bull and their pupils, and also the students of Britannia Royal Naval College for kindly trialling some of the materials, and for their helpful comments; José-Luis García Daza, Geneviève García Vandaele and Matilde Gutiérrez for their helpful comments on the original typescript and for monitoring the quality of the Spanish; Brenda Turk and Carol Zollo for their help with proof-reading and for their customary patience, support and encouragement.

Orders queries: please contact Bookpoint Ltd, 130 Milton Park, Abingdon, Oxon OX14 4SB. Telephone: (44) 01235 827720. Fax: (44) 01235 400454. Lines are open from 9.00–5.00, Monday to Saturday, with a 24 hour message answering service. You can also order through our website at www.hoddereducation.co.uk

A catalogue record for this title is available from The British Library

ISBN-13: 978 0 340 69705 4

First published 1998
Impression number   14
Year   2012

Typeset by Wearset, Boldon, Tyne and Wear.
Printed and bound by CPI Group (UK) Ltd, Croydon, CR0 4YY
338 Euston Road, London NW1 3BH.

CONTENTS

Chapter	Page
Introduction	v
1 PEOPLE AND THINGS nouns and articles	1
2 WHAT ARE THEY LIKE? adjectives	8
3 HOW DO THEY DO THAT? adverbs	17
4 'GOOD', 'BETTER', 'BEST' comparatives and superlatives	22
5 POINTING THINGS OUT demonstratives	29
6 WHO THINGS BELONG TO possessives	35
7 COUNTING numbers	43
8 HOW BIG AND HOW FAR? size, weight and distance	50
9 FIVE O'CLOCK, 1ST JANUARY Times and dates	54
10 THE WEATHER AND HOW YOU FEEL	61
11 'HE', 'SHE', 'HIM', 'HER' subject and disjunctive pronouns	70
12 'IT', 'TO ME' object pronouns	76
13 'THE PERSON WHO ...', 'THE THING WHICH ...' relative pronouns	82
14 ASKING AND EXCLAIMING interrogatives and exclamations	87
15 'NO!', 'NEVER!', 'NOBODY!' negatives	91
16 'FOR ME', 'WITHOUT YOU' prepositions	96
17 'PARA' OR 'POR'?	104
18 WHEN A PERSON IS THE OBJECT personal 'a'	111
19 MAKING IT SMALLER diminutives and other suffixes	113
20 TALKING ABOUT NOW the present tense of regular verbs	116
21 TALKING ABOUT NOW the present tense of irregular verbs	122
22 REFLEXIVE VERBS	131
23 LIKING, LOVING AND HURTING 'me gusta', 'me duele'	138
24 WHAT WILL HAPPEN? the future tense	143
25 WHAT WOULD HAPPEN? the conditional	148
26 WHAT YOU USED TO DO OR WERE DOING the imperfect tense	154
27 WHAT IS/WAS GOING ON? continuous tenses	162
28 WHAT HAPPENED? the preterite tense	167
29 WHAT HAPPENED? irregular verbs in the preterite tense	173
30 WHAT WERE YOU DOING WHEN I SAW YOU? the preterite and imperfect together	181
31 WHAT HAVE YOU DONE? the perfect tense	187
32 WHAT HAD ALREADY HAPPENED? the pluperfect and other compound tenses	194

¡Viva la gramática!

33 'DOING' AND 'DONE'   gerunds and past participles   198
34 INFINITIVES   203
35 'CAN', 'MUST' AND 'OUGHT'   209
36 DO'S AND DON'TS   the imperative   214
37 TO BE OR NOT TO BE?   'ser' and 'estar'   220
38 WHAT WAS DONE?   the passive   226
39 WHAT WAS DONE?   avoiding the passive   230
40 I WANT YOU TO DO THAT!   the present subjunctive   235
41 I WANTED YOU TO DO THAT!   the imperfect subjunctive   243
42 THE SPANISH ALPHABET   249
43 STRESS, ACCENTS AND PUNCTUATION   254
44 VERB TABLES   257
45 KEY TO EXERCISES   268

INTRODUCTION

To the teacher

This book follows the successful three-section format of our A level grammar *¡Acción Gramática!* and adapts it to the needs of the GCSE pupil. Each of the main chapters is divided into three sections: *¿Preparados?* explains the grammar point clearly in as simple English as possible; *¿Listos?* offers reinforcement exercises on each point; and *¡Ya!*, which offers a variety of oral and/or written activities in which the particular grammar point would occur naturally. As far as possible, the exercises and activities in the *¿Listos?* and *¡Ya!* sections are set in a context relevant to the Areas of Experience in the GCSE syllabuses. Vocabulary not found in the Foundation level lists provided by the Examination Boards is to be found in the *Glosario* at the end of each chapter.

Although the grammar explanation comes first, it is not intended that teaching should be 'grammar-led'; it is expected rather that pupils will have met most of the grammar points already in their main coursebook, and that this book will be used for consolidation, revision and reference. The self-check key at the end of the book for the *¿Listos?* section will enable pupils to work at their own speed and check their own progress. The *¡Ya!* section is there to provide enjoyment and to supplement the communicative activities of their coursebook, as well as helping to reinforce the grammar point in question. The exercises and activities are roughly graded in difficulty, with an **H** denoting those which are regarded as more suitable for Higher Level pupils only.

This book will provide pupils with the necessary grammatical support for their communicative abilities at both Foundation and Higher level, and for Higher level pupils, ease the transition from GCSE to A level.

To the pupil

This book is called *¡Viva la gramática!* because grammar is an important element in understanding how a language works, and because (contrary to popular belief!) learning grammar can be fun! You've probably had plenty of practice at speaking, reading, listening and maybe writing, but you may still be a bit shaky on those verb tenses, adjective agreements and other points of grammar that you need to get the highest grade you can. This book is designed to help you tidy up your grammar. Each chapter is divided into three sections, representing 'Ready?', 'Steady?', 'Go!'. First, a section called *¿Preparados?*, in which each grammar point is explained in simple English, with plenty of examples. Then there are some exercises – *¿Listos?* – to give you further practice – and a self-check key at the end of the book, so you can see for yourself what you have got right. Ask your teacher about what you didn't get right – and then have another go! Finally, there is a section of activities – *¡Ya!* – where you can work some role-plays with your classmates or do some written work to further practise your grammar. You should be pretty confident after all that! Even then, you can carry on using the *¿Preparados?* section to look up anything you are still not sure about, and for your final revision. *¡Suerte!*

1

PEOPLE AND THINGS
nouns and articles (the/a)

 ¿Preparados?

1 Nouns

What is a noun?

A noun is a name of something or somebody. It can be a thing, a person, an idea, a town or a country: cat, mountain, girl, Madrid, Spain, examination, success, failure.

a Gender

All Spanish nouns are either masculine or feminine, not only male and female people and animals, and the **article** – the word for 'the' or 'a' – changes accordingly: *el chico* 'the boy', *la chica* 'the girl'.

Of course, male people are always masculine and female people feminine:

el hombre	man	*la mujer*	woman
el panadero	baker	*la panadera*	baker (female)
el profesor	teacher (male)	*la profesora*	teacher (female)

In general, nouns which end in *-o* are masculine, and those which end in *-a* are feminine:

el libro	book	*la mesa*	table
el ojo	eye	*la oreja*	ear
el tío	uncle	*la tía*	aunt

 **¡Ojo!**

Important exceptions are: *el día* 'day', *el mapa* 'map', *la foto* (short for *fotografía*) 'photo', *la moto* (short for *motocicleta*) 'motorbike', *la mano* 'hand', *la radio* 'radio'.

¡Viva la gramática!

Sometimes endings other than *-a/-o* will tell you which gender a noun is:

■ All nouns ending in *-dad* (and also *-tad*, and *-tud*) are feminine: *la verdad* 'truth', *la ciudad* 'town', 'city', *la salud* 'health'.

■ There is a group of nouns ending in *-ma*, which are masculine: *el programa* 'programme', *el problema* 'problem', *el sistema* 'system', *el pijama* 'pyjamas'.

You could say that in Spanish, all *'dad'*s are feminine and quite a lot of *'ma'*s are masculine!

 ¡Ojo!

There are some other important groups to watch out for:

1. Nouns ending in *-ista* always end in *-a*, whether they are masculine or feminine: *el futbolista* (male) 'footballer', *la futbolista* (female) 'footballer'. In the same way: *el/la ciclista* 'cyclist', *el/la tenista* 'tennis player', *el/la taxista* 'taxi driver', and many others.

2. Almost all nouns ending in *-ión* are feminine: *la estación* 'station', *la ración* 'portion', *la excursión* 'excursion', 'trip'. They largely correspond to English words ending in *-tion* or *-sion*.
   Important exceptions: *el avión* 'aeroplane', *el camión* 'lorry'.
   Nouns ending in just *-ón* are masculine: *el cajón* 'drawer', *el rincón* 'corner', *el buzón* 'letterbox'.

3. Countries ending in *-a* (except *el Canadá*) are feminine. South American countries not ending in *-a* are masculine: *(el) Perú, (el) Uruguay, (el) Paraguay, (el) Chile, (el) Ecuador, (el) Brasil. Los Estados Unidos* 'United States', is masculine plural.

 ¡Consejo!

Although there are a few rather more complicated ways of telling gender, it is best to learn every new noun with *el* or *la* in front of it!

b Making nouns plural

When there is just **one** of something (a house, the dog), we say it is singular. When there are **more than one** (houses, the dogs), we say it is plural. In English we usually add *-s* or *-es* to a word to make it plural (dog/dogs, dish/dishes), and the rules are very similar in Spanish. There are in fact two simple rules:

■ If the noun ends in a vowel (*a, e, i, o, u*), you add *-s*: *el libro/los libros* 'book/books', *el kilómetro/los kilómetros* 'kilometre/kilometres'; *la casa/las casas* 'house/houses', *la mesa/las mesas* 'table/tables', *la zapatería/las zapaterías* 'shoe shop/shoe shops'.

■ If the noun ends in anything else, add *-es*: *el bar/los bares* 'bar/bars', *el reloj/los relojes* 'clock/clocks'; *la ciudad/las ciudades* 'town/towns'.

 **¡Ojo!**

Watch out for two groups of nouns when you make them plural:

1. There are a lot of nouns ending in *-án*, *-én* and *-ón*: these lose the accent in the plural: *el alemán/los alemanes* 'German' (man)/'Germans', *el andén/los andenes* 'platform/platforms', *el buzón/los buzones* 'letterbox/letterboxes', *la estación/las estaciones* 'station/stations'.

2. Nouns ending in *-z* change to *-ces*: *cruz/cruces* 'cross/crosses', *lápiz/lápices* 'pencil/pencils', *una vez/dos veces* 'once/twice'.

2 Articles
What is an article?
This is the name given to 'the' and 'a'. 'The' is the **definite** article because we know the one or ones we are talking about, and 'a' is called the **indefinite** article, because we are not referring to a definite thing or person.

In Spanish the word for 'a' changes according to whether the noun is masculine or feminine:

    un *hermano*   a brother
    una *hermana*   a sister

and the word for 'the' also changes to show singular or plural as well:

el *hermano*	the brother	**los** *hermanos*	the brothers
la *hermana*	the sister	**las** *hermanas*	the sisters

¡Viva la gramática!

 **¡Ojo!**

1. Before a few feminine nouns beginning with stressed *a* or *ha* you use *el* not *la* in the singular only: *el agua* 'the water', but *las aguas* 'the waters'.

2. Remember that *a + el = al* 'to the', and *de + el = del* 'of the'/'from the'. These are the only two occasions when two words merge into one in Spanish.

3. You don't use *un/una* after *ser* 'to be', or *hacerse* 'to become', with professions and occupations:

Quiero ser programador(a) de ordenadores.	I want to be a computer programmer.
Por fin Mercedes se hizo profesora.	At last Mercedes became a teacher.

4. You don't use a word for 'some' before a singular noun (don't try to copy the French *du/de la*: *du lait/de la crème* etc.)

¿Quieres leche?	Would you like some milk?
Voy a tomar pescado.	I'm going to have fish.

In the plural, as a rough guide, use nothing where we use nothing or 'any' in English, and use *unos* (masc.) or *unas* (fem.) where we use 'some':

¿Quieres gambas?	Do you want prawns?
¿Quieres unas gambas?	Would you like some prawns?
¿Vamos a tomar patatas fritas?	Shall we have chips?
¿Vamos a tomar unas patatas fritas?	Shall we have some chips?
¿Tiene usted (Vd.) helados?	Do you have any ice creams?

 ¡Ojo!

You don't use *un/una* as a general rule after *no hay* or *no tener*:

No hay helados. / No tenemos helados.	There aren't any. / We don't have any ice creams.

But you do use *el/la/los/las* when talking of things in general:

Me gusta el chocolate.	I like chocolate (in general).
Los españoles son muy simpáticos.	Spaniards (in general) are very friendly.
La limonada es bastante barata.	Lemonade (in general) is quite cheap.

4

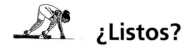 **¿Listos?**

1 ¿El o la?

Escribe el artículo *el* o *la* delante de estos sustantivos. Puedes utilizar un diccionario.
Write *el* o *la* in front of these nouns. You may use a dictionary.

salida	lápiz	avión	tienda	hombre
toro	esquina	bolígrafo	seguridad	noche
reunión	vaca	espejo	Canadá	clima
tomate	museo	mujer	tocador	China

2 ¡No vale!

En estos grupos, ¿qué sustantivo no vale **por su género**?
Which noun is the odd one out **because of its gender**?

1. problema, crucigrama, programa, goma, sistema.
2. césped, ciudad, salud, humedad, verdad.
3. pie, brazo, mano, dedo, codo.
4. día, noche, tarde, mañana, hora.
5. excursión, avión, distracción, estación, recepción.

3 Los hermanos gemelos

Quieres comprar un regalo de cumpleaños para tu mejor amigo/a, y te acuerdas de que tiene un hermano gemelo/una hermana gemela ¡y tendrás que comprar dos regalos iguales!

You've made a list of possible birthday presents for your best friend, when you realise you'll have to buy the same present for his/her twin. Convert your list to two of everything!

un par de calcetines	dos pares de calcetines
una caja de caramelos	....
una camisa	....
una barra de jabón	....
un monedero	....
un libro	....
un pendiente	....
una pulsera	....
un reloj	....
un cinturón	....

4 *En el restaurante*

Estás cenando en un restaurante con un grupo de amigos y estáis escogiendo del menú. Rellena los espacios en blanco en lo que dice cada persona con una palabra que aparece en el recuadro. ¡Un espacio debe quedar sin rellenar!

You are eating in a restaurant with a group of friends, and you are deciding what to choose. Fill the gaps in what each person says with a word chosen from the box. One gap must remain empty!

Pepa: Yo voy a tomar ....1.......... gambas.
Miguel: Para mí ....2.......... macarrones.
Carmen: Yo quisiera una ....3.......... de cerdo.
Fede: ¿Son españoles los ....4.......... ?
Marisol: No me gusta ....5.......... carne, prefiero ....6.......... pescado.
Esteban: ¿Está fresca la ....7.......... ?
Montse: ¿Hay ....8.......... agua mineral?
Pablo: Yo no voy a tomar ....9.......... .

quesos	unas	el	trucha	postre	la	unos	chuleta

¡Ya!

5 *¿Qué es?*

La clase o grupo se divide en dos equipos. Un miembro del equipo A tiene que señalar un objeto, preguntando *¿qué es?* o *¿qué son?* Un miembro del equipo B tiene que responder *es un/una*, o *son unos/unas* con el nombre del objeto.

The class or group divides into two teams. One member of team A points to an object and a member of team B has to say what it is, using *Es un/una . . .*, or *Son unos/unas . . .* with the name of the object. If the answer is correct, **with the correct gender**, the team scores a point.

Ejemplo:
A.   **¿Qué es?**   **¿Qué son?**
B.   **Es una silla.**   **Son unas tijeras.**

6 *Clase de geografía*

En un mapa español de Europa o del mundo, busca todos los países masculinos.

On a Spanish map of Europe or the world, look for all the countries which are masculine. Remember that the majority of countries end in *-a* and are usually feminine.

7 *Menús y mapas*

Pide a tu profesor(a) un documento en español (por ejemplo un menú, un plano de una ciudad, un folleto de hotel) e indica si los sustantivos que contiene son masculinos o femeninos, poniendo *el/la/los/las*.

Ask your teacher for a document in Spanish, (e.g. a menu, a town plan, or a hotel brochure) and say whether the nouns it contains are masculine or feminine, writing in *el/la/los/las*.

Ejemplo:

TORTILLAS	**LAS TORTILLAS**
PLAZA MAYOR	**LA PLAZA MAYOR**
ASCENSOR	**EL ASCENSOR**

8 *¡Más! ¡Dame más!*

Tu compañero/a de clase escribe el nombre de un objeto. Tú le devuelves el papel cambiando *un/una* a un número más grande (¡máximo 10!) y cambiando el objeto al plural.

Your partner writes down the name of an object. You return the paper, changing *un/una* to a bigger number (maximum 10!), not forgetting to make the noun plural. You could choose nouns in general or from a particular area you have studied: ask your teacher.

2

WHAT ARE THEY LIKE?

adjectives

 **¿Preparados?**

What is an adjective?
An adjective is a word used to describe or give more information about a noun: 'a **large** house', 'my **little** brother', 'your **best** friend', '**Spanish** food', '**fast** trains'.

1 Making adjectives agree

You already know that all Spanish nouns are either masculine or feminine, and that the ending often tells you which. Spanish adjectives differ from English ones, in that they also change their ending according to the noun they describe, as follows:

■ Adjectives ending in -*o* (the vast majority) have four endings:

Masculine singular	Masculine plural	Feminine singular	Feminine plural
un sombrero blanco a white hat	*sombreros blancos* white hats	*una camisa blanca* a white shirt	*camisas blancas* white shirts
un cinturón nuevo a new belt	*cinturones nuevos* new belts	*una chaqueta nueva* a new jacket	*chaquetas nuevas* new jackets

■ Adjectives ending in a consonant or -*e* only change in the plural; they don't have a feminine singular ending. Add -*s* to those ending in -*e*, and -*es* to others (that is, those that end in a consonant):

Masculine singular	Masculine plural	Feminine singular	Feminine plural
un sombrero azul a blue hat	*sombreros azules* blue hats	*una camisa azul* a blue shirt	*camisas azules* blue shirts
un sombrero verde a green hat	*sombreros verdes* green hats	*una camisa verde* a green shirt	*camisas verdes* green shirts

 **¡Ojo!**

There are some objectives which don't behave exactly according to these rules:

1. Adjectives denoting nationality or a region have a separate feminine form, both singular and plural, and the masculine plural ends in *-es* not *-os*. This also applies to adjectives ending in *-án*, *-ón*, and *-or* (except *marrón* 'brown', *mayor* 'older/elder/bigger', *menor* 'younger/smaller', *mejor* 'better', and *peor* 'worse'):

   ■ Nationality and regional adjectives do not use a capital letter.
   ■ Watch out for the spelling changes (e.g. no accent needed when an ending is added; *z* becomes *-ces*).

Masculine singular	Masculine plural	Feminine singular	Feminine plural
un chico inglés an English boy	*chicos ingleses* English boys	*una chica inglesa* an English girl	*chicas inglesas* English girls
un río andaluz an Andalusian river	*ríos andaluces* Andalusian rivers	*una ciudad andaluza* an Andalusian town	*ciudades andaluzas* Andalusian towns
un profesor gruñón a grumpy teacher	*profesores gruñones* grumpy teachers	*una profesora gruñona* a grumpy teacher	*profesoras gruñonas* grumpy teachers
un alumno hablador a talkative pupil	*alumnos habladores* talkative pupils	*una alumna habladora* a talkative pupil	*alumnas habladoras* talkative pupils

2. Adjectives already ending in *-a* never change to *-o*, they just add *-s* in the plural. The many adjectives ending in *-ista* and *belga* 'Belgian' come into this category. *Cada* 'each/every', only has a singular form.

Masculine singular	Masculine plural	Feminine singular	Feminine plural
un jugador belga a Belgian player	*jugadores belgas* Belgian players	*una jugadora belga* a Belgian player	*jugadoras belgas* Belgian players
un concurso ciclista a cycling competition	*concursos ciclistas* cycling competitions	*una carrera ciclista* a cycle race	*carreras ciclistas* cycle races
cada día every day		*cada noche* every night	

3. A small group of adjectives shorten ('apocopate' is the technical term) when they come before a noun.

¡Viva la gramática!

- The following do it in the **masculine singular only**: *bueno* 'good', *malo* 'bad', *primero* 'first', *tercero* 'third', *alguno* 'some', *ninguno* 'no/not any', and *Santo* 'Saint'.

*hace **buen/mal** tiempo*	It's good/bad weather
*¡**buen** viaje!*	have a good trip!
but: *¡**buena** idea!*	good idea!
*el **primer/tercer** edificio a la derecha*	the first/third building on the right
*la **primera/tercera** calle a la izquierda*	the first/third street on the left
*¿Hay **algún** problema? No, no hay **ningún** problema.*	Is there some problem? No, there's no problem.
*¿Tienes **alguna** idea? No, no tengo **ninguna** idea.*	Have you any idea? No, I've no idea.

San *Sebastián* 'St Sebastian', but always **Santo** *Tomás*. All female saints are *Santa*: **Santa** *Teresa* 'St Teresa'.

- *Grande* becomes *gran* before any singular noun:

*Un **gran** hombre y una **gran** mujer.*	A great man and a great woman.

2 Position of adjectives

- As you will have seen in most of the above examples, in general adjectives come **after** the noun in Spanish. Here are a few more examples:

*la calle **principal***	the main street
*a mano **derecha***	on the right hand side
*un coche **alemán***	a German car
*una persona **muy fea***	a very ugly person

- A few common adjectives can come before the noun, especially the 'shortened' ones described above.

 ¡Ojo!

Sometimes an adjective can have a different meaning, depending on whether it comes before or after the noun:

*un **viejo** amigo*	an old friend (one you've known a long time)
*un amigo **viejo***	an old friend (an elderly one)
*una mujer **pobre***	a poor woman (with no money)
*una **pobre** mujer*	a poor woman (in a sad state)

10

3 Using adjectives after *ser, estar* and *parecer*

■ Adjectives often occur after both verbs 'to be', *ser* and *estar*, and agree in the usual way:

> *¿Eres **española**, Beatriz? No, soy **mejicana**.*
> Are you Spanish, Beatriz? No, I'm Mexican.
> *Nuestra profesora no está **muy contenta** hoy. Está **cansada**.*
> Our teacher isn't very happy today. She's tired.

(For the difference between *ser* and *estar* see Chapter 37.)

■ You also find adjectives after *parecer* 'to seem':

> *Los niños parecen **cansados**, ¿no?*
> The children seem tired, don't they?

4 Where you don't use an adjective

To tell you what things are made of in Spanish, you usually use *de* + a noun:

una corbata de seda	a silk tie
un bolso de plástico	a plastic handbag
una silla de madera	a wooden chair

 **¡Ojo!**

You can't use another noun as an adjective, as in 'tennis match'. Again you have to use *de* + noun:

un partido de tenis	a tennis match
una cuchara de sopa	a soup spoon
el tren de Barcelona	the Barcelona train

---

5 *Lo* + adjective

You meet this quite often, and it is best explained by some examples:

*Lo **malo** es que . . .*	The bad thing is that . . .
*Dime **lo interesante**.*	Tell me the interesting bit.
*Has olvidado **lo importante**.*	You've forgotten the important part.

It has the meaning of 'the (adjective) part/thing/bit'.

¡Viva la gramática!

¿Listos?

1 El cumpleaños de Pedro

Pedro recibió mucho dinero por su cumpleaños. El sábado siguiente fue a la ciudad y compró estas cosas. Haz concordar los adjetivos.

Pedro received a lot of money on his birthday. The following Saturday he went to town and bought these things. Make the adjectives agree where necessary.

un reloj
(*nuevo*)

una radio
(*japonés*)

unas gafas
(*negro*)

una guitarra
(*español*)

una bicicleta
(*moderno*)

una camisa (*rojo*)

unos vaqueros
(*azul*)

unos pañuelos
(*blanco*)

unos zapatos
(*marrón*)

una chaqueta (*de cuero*)

2 Una tarjeta postal

Tracy está de vacaciones con su familia y escribe una tarjeta postal a su amiga española, Susana. Rellena los espacios en blanco con una de las palabras del recuadro.

Tracy is on holiday with her family and writes a postcard to her friend Susana. Fill the gaps with a word chosen from the box.

fría	española	rica	cómodas	contenta	ingleses	buen
	blanca	enfadado	azul			

¡Hola Susana! Hace muy .... tiempo.
Estoy sentada en la playa en Benidorm.
La arena es .... y el mar es ....
Bebo una limonada muy ....
Papá está .... porque no hay periódicos .... Yo he comprado una revista .... La comida en el hotel está muy .... y las camas son muy .... ¡Yo estoy muy ....!
Un beso de tu amiga Tracy

3 Lista de bodas

José e Isabel van a casarse. Están preparando su lista de bodas, pero los materiales de que están hechos los regalos están un poco mezclados. ¿Puedes ponerlos en orden?

José and Isabel are getting married. They are preparing their wedding list, but the materials the presents are made of have got mixed up. Can you sort them out?
(Make up the most likely match, using each phrase once only!)

1. una alfombra	a. de plástico para la ducha
2. una bandeja	b. de plata para el comedor
3. una cortina	c. de algodón para la cama
4. cuchillos y tenedores	d. de madera para la cocina
5. un espejo	e. de cuero para la sala de estar
6. una estatua	f. de lana para esquiar
7. un par de sábanas	g. de nylón para el suelo del vestíbulo
8. un sofá	h. de porcelana para el comedor
9. dos sombreros	i. de cristal para el cuarto de baño
10. seis tazas	j. de piedra para el jardín

4 ¿De qué nacionalidad?

Tienes que escoger una palabra de cada recuadro para completar estas frases, y hacer concordar los adjetivos.

¡Viva la gramática!

Choose a word from each box to complete these sentences and make the adjectives agree.

1. Ejemplo: Nápoles es . . . **una ciudad italiana**.

2. El BMW es un . . .

3. Barcelona y Tarragona son . . .

4. El Támesis y el Severn son . . .

5. Washington es la . . .

6. Mitsubishi es una . . .

7. Ben Nevis es una . . .

8. Benidorm es una . . .

9. Francia es un . . .

10. Calais es un . . .

11. El café es un . . .

12. Los canguros son . . .

ríos	playa	coche	**ciudad**	animales	montaña	país	puerto	capital
	producto	ciudades	compañía					

australiano	japonés	colombiano	inglés	escocés	francés	alemán
	catalán	**italiano**	español	norteamericano	europeo	

 ¡Ya!

Nota
En todas estas actividades tendrás que emplear muchos adjetivos: **¡no te olvides de hacerlos concordar!**

In all these activities you will need to use a lot of adjectives: **don't forget to make them agree!**

5 *¿De quién hablo?*

Un miembro de la clase tiene que describir a una persona y los otros tienen que adivinar a quién describe. Puede ser otro/a alumno/a, un(a) profesor(a) o un personaje conocido de la televisión, del cine, de la historia, etc.

A member of the class has to describe a person and the others have to guess who he/she is describing. It can be someone in the class, a teacher, or a well-known personality from television, cinema, history, etc.

Ejemplo: **Es una chica bastante alta y delgada. Tiene el pelo negro y los ojos castaños. Tiene la nariz bastante larga. Lleva el uniforme escolar hoy, pero los sábados le gusta llevar vaqueros azules y una camisa roja y blanca. ¿Quién es?**

6 *Mi dormitorio*

Describe tu dormitorio a tus compañeros/as de clase. Describe el color y el tamaño de las cosas que hay. Habla de las paredes, las cortinas, la alfombra, la cama, el tocador o escritorio, y si los tienes, el televisor, el vídeo, el ordenador, los pósters, etc. Ellos te pueden hacer preguntas.

Describe your bedroom to your classmates. Describe the colour, size, etc. of the walls, and furnishings and equipment that you have in it. Your classmates can ask you questions.

7 *¡Interrogación!*

Trabajo en grupos. Hay que hacer preguntas a un(a) compañero/a acerca de sus familiares, su casa, su colegio.

Pair or groupwork. You have to ask a classmate questions about his/her family members, house, school, etc.

Emplea frases como/Use phrases such as: *¿Cómo es/son . . . ?*, *¿De qué color es/son . . . ?*, *Descríbeme . . . .* El/ella tiene que contestar usando varios adjetivos. He/she should reply using a number of adjectives. A 'secretary' could be chosen to take down what he/she says and then report back. After a few questions change 'victim'!

Ejemplos:
A.   **¿Cómo es tu hermana menor?**
B.   **Es pequeña y delgada, con los ojos negros.**
A.   **¿De qué color son las cortinas de tu sala de estar?**
B.   **Son verdes y amarillas.**

¡Viva la gramática!

A. **Descríbeme la calle donde vives.**

A.   **Descríbeme la calle donde vives.**
B.   **Es larga y recta pero no muy ancha.**

Reportaje: 'La hermana menor de Emma es pequeña y delgada, etc. . . .'

8 ¿Cómo soy?

Vas a viajar solo/a a España a trabajar de *au pair* en casa de una familia que no conoces. Van a recogerte en el aeropuerto y tú les escribes para describirte y la ropa que vas a llevar puesta para el viaje, para que te reconozcan.

You are going to travel alone to Spain to work as an *au pair* in a Spanish family. You write to them describing yourself and the clothes you will be wearing that day so that they will recognise you at the airport.

> Estimados Sres Jiménez:
> Les escribo para decirles que llegaré al aeropuerto de Madrid-Barajas
> el 15 de setiembre a las 16.30 en el vuelo IB3175 de Iberia.
> Para que me reconozcan fácilmente,
> llevaré . . . .
> Soy . . . .

Glosario

australiano	Australian
bandeja	tray
canguro	kangaroo
japonés	Japanese
norteamericano	(North) American (i.e. from USA)
porcelana	china
póster	poster

3

HOW DO THEY DO THAT?
adverbs

 **¿Preparados?**

What is an adverb?
You already know that adjectives describe or tell you more about nouns. Adverbs tell you more about verbs, adjectives and other adverbs.

Adverbs can be single words or groups of words (phrases), or can be made up from adjectives.

1 Adverbs in their own right
These are often of:

a place, which tell you **where**:

allí	there	*aquí*	here
por todas partes	everywhere	*delante*	in front
detrás	behind	*encima*	on top

b time, which tell you **when**:

ahora	now	*entonces*	then
hoy	today	*mañana*	tomorrow
pronto	soon	*después*	afterwards
tarde	late	*a menudo*	often
siempre	always	*a veces*	sometimes
muchas veces	lots of times, often		

c degree, which tell you **how much** or **to what extent**:

muy	very	*bastante*	quite, fairly
un poco	a little	*poco*	not very
más	more	*menos*	less

17

d manner, which tell you **how**:

de prisa	quickly	*despacio*	slowly
a pie	on foot	*con cuidado*	carefully
de repente	suddenly		

Many of this last category, which tells you **how** something is done, end in *-mente*: see section 2 below.

*¡Ponlo **allí**, no **aquí!***	Put it **there**, not **here**!
*Eso es todo **por ahora**. Continuaremos **mañana**.*	That's all **for now**. We'll continue **tomorrow**.
*Miguel estaba **muy** cansado y **un poco** nervioso.*	Michael was **very** tired and **a little** nervous.

2 Adverbs formed from adjectives by adding *-mente*

In English we make adjectives into adverbs by adding '*-ly*': glad – gladly, easy – easily, independent – independently.

In Spanish, you first make the adjective feminine (if possible) and then add *-mente*: *perfecto – perfectamente* perfect – perfectly, *rápido – rápidamente* quick – quickly, *furioso – furiosamente* furious – furiously, *igual – igualmente* equal – equally, *independiente – independientemente* independent – independently. (The last two examples don't have a feminine form.) Any accent on the adjective remains on the adverb.

*Los españoles hablan muy **rápidamente**.*	Spanish people speak very **quickly**.
*Hablas español **perfectamente**.*	You speak Spanish **perfectly**.
Probablemente** lo escribes **bien también	You **probably** write it **well too**.

(*Probablemente*, *bien* and *también* are all adverbs!)

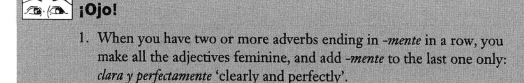 **¡Ojo!**

1. When you have two or more adverbs ending in *-mente* in a row, you make all the adjectives feminine, and add *-mente* to the last one only: *clara y perfectamente* 'clearly and perfectly'.

2. The adverb for *bueno* (good) is *bien* (well):

   *La señora Dickens es una profesora muy **buena**. Enseña muy **bien**.*
   Mrs Dickens is a very **good** teacher. She teaches very **well**.

 **¿Listos?**

1 ¡Positivamente!

Todos estos adjetivos tienen un significado positivo. Cámbialos a adverbios, añadiendo *-mente*.

All these adjectives have a positive meaning. Change them to adverbs by adding *-mente*. Don't forget to make them feminine first if you can. Look them up if you don't know them!

| feliz | afortunado | alegre | agradable | cortés |
| nuevo | primero | útil | válido | verdadero |

2 Alternativamente

Muchas veces hay dos o tres maneras de expresarse. ¿Cuáles de los adverbios con *-mente* de la segunda columna corresponden a las frases de la primera?

There are often two or more ways of saying the same thing. Match the adverbs ending in *-mente* in the second column with the adverb phrases in the first. Use a dictionary if there are words or phrases you don't know.

1. despacio	a. especialmente
2. de prisa	b. súbitamente
3. en seguida	c. excesivamente
4. sobre todo	d. gradualmente
5. a menudo	e. lentamente
6. sin ruido	f. cuidadosamente
7. de repente	g. rápidamente
8. poco a poco	h. inmediatamente
9. con cuidado	i. frecuentemente
10. demasiado	j. silenciosamente

3 ¿Cómo lo hacen?

Mira los dibujos y rellena los espacios en blanco, escogiendo un adverbio del recuadro.

Look at the drawings and fill the gaps, choosing an adverb from the box.

Ejemplo:
1. **Juan toca el piano muy mal.**

¡Viva la gramática!

1. Juan toca el piano muy ....

2. Anita toca la guitarra muy ....

3. El tren AVE va muy .... ,

4. pero el tren tranvía va muy .... y se para ....

5. Esta clase trabaja ....

6. pero esta clase trabaja .... ,

7. .... Carlos no ha aprobado sus exámenes,

8. pero Adela lee sus resultados ....

9. Paco juega al fútbol ....

10. Esta revista sale ....

tristemente	mal	diariamente	a menudo	ruidosamente	con alegría
	semanalmente	despacio	bien	rápidamente	en silencio

¡Ya!

4 ¡Sin mirar!

Sin mirar tus libros ni en el diccionario, haz una lista de todos los adverbios que sepas con *-mente*. ¡A ver quién hace la lista más larga!

Without looking at your books or in a dictionary, make a list of all the adverbs you can think of ending in *-mente*. Who can make the longest list?

5 ¿Cuántas maneras de hacerlo?

Usando adverbios, busca maneras de hacer estas acciones.
Using adverbs, try to find as many ways as possible of doing the following actions.

Ejemplo: **¿Cómo se puede nadar?**
            Se puede nadar bien / mal / un poco / estupendamente / de prisa / con cuidado, etc.

hablar español	cocinar
jugar al tenis	cruzar la calle
levantarse por la mañana	hacer los deberes
comer	comprar la ropa
trabajar	gastar dinero

4

'GOOD', 'BETTER', 'BEST' comparatives and superlatives

 ¿Preparados?

1 The comparative
What is the comparative?
We call it the comparative when you are **comparing** two or more things, people, ideas, ways of doing something, etc. You can say 'a small**er** car', 'a **more** interesting film', 'a **less** comfortable house'. You can also make comparisons by saying, for example that somebody/something is '**as** good **as**' or '**not as** nice **as**' somebody/something else.

a 'more . . . than'
In English we make the comparative by adding *-er* to short adjectives (short – shorter, long – longer) or by using 'more' with the longer ones (more beautiful, more frightening). In Spanish, you use *más* with all adjectives and adverbs +*que* for 'than':

*Isabel es **más lista que** su hermana.*	Isabel is **cleverer (more clever) than** her sister.
*El español es **más fácil que** el francés.*	Spanish is **easier than** French.
*Daniel trabaja **más rápidamente que** yo.*	Daniel works **quicker (more quickly) than** I (do).

 ¡Ojo!

Note the following special comparative forms: *mejor* 'better', *peor* 'worse', *mayor* 'elder/older', *menor* 'younger'.

*En España el café es **mejor que** el té.*	In Spain the coffee is better than the tea.

22

> *Paquita habla inglés **mejor que** su madre.* Paquita speaks English better than her mother.
>
> *Mi hermana **mayor/menor*** My elder/younger sister

b 'less than'

This so-called 'negative comparative' works in the same way, using *menos que* 'less than':

> *Javier es **menos listo que** su hermano.* Javier is **less clever than** his brother.
>
> *Merche juega al tenis **menos bien que** Ramón.* Merche plays tennis **less well than** Ramón.

 **¡Ojo!**

When you use *más* or *menos* with a number, use *de* not *que*:

> *Había **más de** seis mil personas en el concierto.* There were **more than** 6,000 people at the concert.

c 'as ... as', 'not as ... as'

You can compare two equals by using *tan ... como*:

> *Esta camisa es **tan barata como** aquélla.* This shirt is **as cheap as** that one.
>
> *Yo escribo **tan claramente como** tú.* I write **as clearly as** you.

And you can make a contrast by making this negative:

> *Esta camisa **no** es **tan barata como** aquélla.* This shirt is **not as cheap as** that one.
>
> *Yo **no** escribo **tan claramente como** tú.* I **don't** write **as clearly as** you.

 ¡Ojo!

You can't say *tan mucho*: use *tanto ... como* for 'as much/many ... as':

> *Esta tienda no tiene **tantas camisas como** la otra.* This shop doesn't have **as many shirts as** the other one.

Use this also with weather expressions (see Chapter 10):

> *Hace **tanto calor** aquí **como** en Sevilla.* It's **as hot** here **as** in Seville.

¡Consejo!

You don't necessarily have to include *que* 'than' or *como* 'as':

*Ahora el trabajo es **más fácil**.*	Now the work is easier.
*Ahora estoy **menos cansada**.*	I'm less tired now.
*Ahora **no** estoy **tan cansada**.*	I'm not so tired now.

2 Superlatives

What is a superlative?

The superlative is 'the most' or 'the least'.

In English we add *-est* to short adjectives and use **'most'** with the others: 'the **shortest** route', 'the **most beautiful** view'; you can also say 'the **least interesting** film'.

a 'the most' / 'the least'

You simply use *el/la/los/las* + noun + *más/menos* + adjective:

la playa más popular *de la región*	**the most popular beach** in the area
la calle más concurrida *de la ciudad*	**the busiest street** in the town
*la profe **menos simpática*** *del colegio*	the **least pleasant** teacher in the school

 ¡Ojo!

1. If you are also learning French, note the difference: in Spanish you **don't** repeat the definite article (*el/la/los/las*) before the adjective!

2. Have you noticed that you always use *de* for 'in' after a superlative?

*Cristina es la chica más alta **de** su clase.*	Cristina is the tallest girl **in** her class.

b *-ísimo*

If you want to say that someone is, for example, 'very, very pretty' or 'extremely rich', you can add *-ísimo* to the adjective after removing the ending.

 **¡Ojo!**

Watch out for spelling changes:

*¡Montse es **guapísima**!*	Montse is **very, very pretty**!
*¡Este hombre es **riquísimo**!*	This man is **extremely rich**!

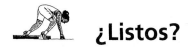 **¿Listos?**

1 En mi ciudad
Haz comparaciones con estas frases.
Make comparisons with these phrases.

Ejemplo:
Cine – es – moderno – museo
El cine es más moderno que el museo.
El cine es menos moderno que el museo.
El cine es tan moderno como el museo.
El cine no es tan moderno como el museo.

1. La iglesia es – antigua – el ayuntamiento

2. El río es – ancho – el canal

3. El centro está – concurrido – las afueras

4. El mercado es – barato – las tiendas

5. Los supermercados son – caros – las tiendas pequeñas

6. Los monumentos son – interesantes – las discotecas

7. La sala de fiestas es – pequeña – el cine

8. Los habitantes son – simpáticos – los turistas

9. El estadio de fútbol es – grande – el polideportivo

10. Los autobuses son – frecuentes – los trenes

2 Comparaciones
Mira los dibujos y luego decide si las siguientes frases son verdaderas o falsas.
Corrige las falsas.

Look at the drawings and then decide whether the following sentences are true or
false. Correct the false ones.

1. Miguel es más alto que Pablo.

2. Juanita juega mejor al hockey que Dolores.

3. Mi padre es menos gordo que mi madre.

¡Viva la gramática!

4. Juanita es más joven que Dolores.

5. La sala de estar es menos grande que la cocina.

6. Pablo escribe tan bien como Miguel.

7. Mi gato es más cariñoso que mi perro.

8. Mi dormitorio no es tan cómodo como el dormitorio de Pablo.

9. Pablo nada mejor que Dolores.

10. Mi madre no es tan vieja como mi abuela.

3 En clase
Todos sobresalimos de alguna manera. He aquí unos miembros de la clase.

We all excel in some way. Here's how some members of the class do it.

Ejemplo:
María – chica – habladora – clase
María es la chica más/menos habladora de la clase.

1. Esteban – chico – vago – clase

2. Conchi – chica – lista – todas

3. Isabel – chica – simpática – clase

4. Federico – joven – sobresaliente – su grupo

5. Emi – chica – delgada – mis amigas

6. La señora Pérez – profesora – popular – colegio

7. Luis – chico – guapo – la ciudad

8. Enrique – chico – deportivo – colegio

9. Anita – alumna – trabajadora

10. El director – profesor – estricto – colegio

 ¡Ya!

4 En mi ciudad

Haz el ejercicio 1 otra vez, pero esta vez, compara cosas de tu propia ciudad o pueblo.

Do exercise 1 again, but this time compare things in your own town or village.

5 Mi compañeros de clase

Explica cómo los alumnos de tu propia clase sobresalen, utilizando los superlativos del ejercicio 3 y otros.

Explain how the pupils in your own class excel, using the superlatives in exercise 3 and others.

6 España

Mira un mapa de España y haz comparaciones entre las ciudades, montañas, ríos, etc.

Look at a map of Spain and make comparisons between the towns, mountains, rivers, etc. You could make deliberately incorrect statements, for your partner or classmates to correct.

¡Viva la gramática!

Ejemplo:

A. **Madrid no es tan grande como Santander, ¿verdad?**

B. **¡No es verdad! Madrid es más grande que Santander. (Santander no es tan grande como Madrid.)**

Glosario

estricto	strict
frecuente	frequent
el polideportivo	sports centre

5

POINTING THINGS OUT
demonstratives

 **¿Preparados?**

What is a demonstrative?
As their name implies, these are adjectives and pronouns which **demonstrate** which object you are referring to. They are used to point out exactly what you are talking about:

I want **this** book, not **that** book! **That one** is more expensive than **this** one. **These** apples are fresher than **those**, but I prefer **those** ones.

In Spanish, just like other adjectives and pronouns, demonstratives have to change their endings to match the noun they refer to. So there are forms for masculine and feminine singular and masculine and feminine plural.

■ 'This', 'these': *este, esta, estos, estas,* used to point out something close to you, or something you have just mentioned.

>   *Este libro es muy interesante, pero estas revistas son aburridas.*
>   **This** book is very interesting, but **these** magazines are boring.

■ 'That', 'those': *ese, esa, esos, esas,* used to point out something further away from you.

>   *Esa chica no estudia nada, pero esos chicos son majos.*
>   **That** girl does not study at all, but **those** boys are hardworking.

■ That, those: *aquel, aquella, aquellos, aquellas,* used to point out something even further away from you.

¡Viva la gramática!

> *Este coche es caro, ese coche es más caro, ¡pero aquel coche es el más caro de todos!*
> **This car is expensive, that** car is more expensive, but **that one over there** is the most expensive of all.

All three demonstratives can either be used **with** a noun (demonstrative adjective) or standing alone to **replace** a noun (demonstrative pronoun). If the demonstrative doesn't have a noun with it, it is a pronoun and has an accent on the first *e*.

> *¿Cuál de estos melones prefieres, éste, ése o aquél?*
> Which of these melons do you prefer, this one, that one or the other one?

So, the full range of demonstratives is:

Singular

adj.	*pron.*	*adj.*	*pron.*	*adj.*	*pron.*
este	éste	ese	ése	aquel	aquél
esta	ésta	esa	ésa	aquella	aquélla

Plural

estos	éstos	esos	ésos	aquellos	aquéllos
estas	éstas	esas	ésas	aquellas	aquéllas

■ You may also meet a special form ending in *o* which relates to a general idea and not to anything in particular. This form has no gender – it is neither masculine nor feminine, and so is used when you don't know the gender of what it is referring to.

> esto eso aquello

> *Esto es algo que no me gusta nada.*
> This is something I do not like at all.

■ Finally, *éste/a/os/as* and *aquél/la/os/as* are often used as 'the latter' and 'the former'.

> *María vive en Madrid y José vive en Málaga; éste habla inglés, pero aquélla no.*
> María lives in Madrid and José lives in Málaga; the latter speaks English, but the former does not.

30

8. torre alta que menos edificio esta ese es

9. es profesora de todas menos antipática de colegio este esta la las

10. aquel esta ésa gordo gorda cerdo vaca pero más que es es aún más

 ¡Ya!

5 ¡Indecisión!

Visitas a una tía muy simpática (tu compañero/a de clase). Te ofrece varias cosas, pero siendo indeciso/a, no sabes qué escoger. Inventa otras conversaciones como en el ejemplo.

You visit a very kind aunt (your classmate). She offers you various things, but being indecisive, you don't know which to choose. Invent other conversations like the one in the example.

Ejemplo:

Tía: **¿Quieres uno de estos pasteles?**

Tú: **¡Gracias, tía! Pero, ¿cuál prefiero, éste o ése? Creo que prefiero aquél.**

Tía: **Pero vamos, chico/a, ¡decídete!**

Otras sugerencias

manzanas	bizcochos	tartas	caramelos	tebeos	helados	vídeos
		cassettes	naranjas			

6 Vamos de compras

Estás en una boutique con un(a) amigo/a. Tienes que comprar la ropa necesaria para ir de vacaciones, pero todo es demasiado grande o demasiado pequeño. Tenéis que inventar conversaciones como la siguiente.

You are in a boutique with a friend. You need to buy the necessary clothes to go on holiday, but they are all too big or too small. Invent conversations like the following one.

Tú: **¿Debería comprar esta camiseta?**

Amigo/a: **No, es demasiado pequeña, pero aquélla te queda muy bien.**

Tú: **Sí, pero prefiero ésta.**

¡Viva la gramática!

H 7 *El arte de vender*

Tú y tus amigos trabajáis en un mercado. Tenéis que persuadir a los clientes de que tus productos son los mejores de todos.

You and your friends work in a market. You have to persuade the customers that your products are the best of all.

Ejemplo:
Vendedor 1: Estos plátanos son los mejores.
Vendedor 2: No, éstos son mejores que aquéllos.

Otros productos posibles:

fruta	queso	jamón	camisas	calcetines	etc.

H 8 *Rivalidad*

Tus amigos siempre te llevan la contraria. Cuando tú dices algo, siempre te desmienten, como en el ejemplo.

Your friends are always contrary. Whenever you say something, they always contradict you, as in the example:

Ejemplo:
Tú: ¡Qué coche más bonito es éste!
Amigo 1: ¡Qué va! Este coche no es tan bonito como ése.
Amigo 2: No, hombre, ¡aquel coche que está ahí es el más bonito de todos!

6

WHO THINGS BELONG TO
possessives

 **¿Preparados?**

What are possessives?
Possessives are words which tell us who owns something, whose it is or to whom it belongs; in this chapter we cover all the ways of expressing possession.

1 Saying whose something is using *de*
In English we say **whose** something is by adding –*'s* to a name or a word describing a person. Spanish has no similar way of expressing possession, but instead uses the preposition *de* (see Chapter 16 for a full explanation of prepositions.)

*Es el amigo **de** Juan.*	He is Juan**'s** friend.
*¡Mira la moto **de** aquella chica!*	Look at that girl**'s** motorbike!
*Son los hijos **del** señor González.*	They are Señor González**'s** sons.
*¿Quién tiene las fotos **de** Maribel?*	Who has got Maribel**'s** photos?

 ¡Ojo!

Take care when using *de* in front of *el*, *la*, *los*, or *las* (the) – see Chapter 16 on prepositions: *de* + *el* = **del**).

2 Possessive adjectives: 'my', 'your', 'his', 'her', 'our', 'their'
Being adjectives, these words in Spanish change their ending to match the noun they describe as follows: (See Chapter 2 for an explanation of adjectives)

	Singular	Plural
my: *mi(s)*	***mi** libro* my book	***mis** lápices* my pencils

¡Viva la gramática!

	Singular	Plural
your: *tu(s)* (familiar – *tú*)	**tu** *hermano* your brother	**tus** *padres* your parents
your: *su(s)* (formal – *usted*)	**su** *casa* your house	**sus** *amigos* your friends
his, her: *su(s)*	**su** *coche* his/her car	**sus** *zapatos* his/her shoes

 **¡Ojo!**

1. These three have NO separate feminine forms.

2. *su(s)* is used for formal 'your' as well as 'his', 'her', 'its', and 'their'.

	Masc sing	Fem sing	Masc plural	Fem plural
our: *nuestro/a* *nuestros/as*	**nuestro** *hijo* our son	**nuestra** *hija* our daughter	**nuestros** *hijos* our sons/children	**nuestras** *hijas* our daughters
your: *vuestro/a* *vuestros/as* fam. *vosotros*	**vuestro** *tío* your uncle	**vuestra** *tía* your aunt	**vuestros** *tíos* your uncles (and aunts)	**vuestras** *tías* your aunts
your: *su(s)* formal *ustedes*	**su** *padre* your father	**su** *madre* your mother	**sus** *padres* your fathers/ parents	**sus** *madres* your mothers
their: *su(s)*	**su** *sobrino* *their nephew*	**su** *sobrina* *their niece*	**sus** *sobrinos* *their nephews* (and nieces)	**sus** *sobrinas* *their nieces*

 **¡Ojo!**

1. The adjective always agrees with the thing possessed, NOT the owner!

2. Again, *su(s)* has no separate feminine forms, and is used for 'their' as well as for 'his', 'her', 'its' and formal 'your'.

3 Possessive pronouns: 'mine', 'yours', 'his', 'hers', 'ours', 'theirs'

Why pronouns? Because they **replace** the noun referred to, while possessive adjectives go just in front of the noun.

(See Chapters 11 and 12 for a full explanation of pronouns.)

Compare the following sentences:

*Esta es **mi** moto, y aquélla es **tu** moto.*	This is my motorbike. (adjectives)
***La mía** es más rápida que **la tuya**.*	Mine is faster than yours. (pronouns)

Here are the possessive pronouns, followed by a few examples of them in use.

mine	el mío	la mía	los míos	las mías
yours (familiar *tú*)	el tuyo	la tuya	los tuyos	las tuyas
yours (formal *ustedes*)	el suyo	la suya	los suyos	las suyas
his/hers	el suyo	la suya	los suyos	las suyas
ours	el nuestro	la nuestra	los nuestros	las nuestras
yours (familiar *vosotros*)	el vuestro	la vuestra	los vuestros	las vuestras
yours (formal *ustedes*)	el suyo	la suya	los suyos	las suyas
theirs	el suyo	la suya	los suyos	las suyas

*¿De quién son estos libros? **El mío** es más interesante que **el tuyo**.*
Whose are these books? **Mine** is more interesting than yours.
*Nos gustan nuestras hermanas. **La mía** es muy simpática, y **las suyas** también.*
We like our sisters. **Mine** is very nice, and so are **his/hers/yours/theirs**.
*Esos gatos son menos gordos que **los nuestros** pero me gustan más que los **vuestros**.*
Those cats are less fat than **ours** but I like them more than **yours**.
*Deberíamos cuidar de los animales, aunque no sean **nuestros**.*
We should look after animals, even if they are not **ours**.
*¿De quién es? No es **mía** ni **suya** . . . Ah, sí, es **vuestra**.*
Whose is it? It isn't mine or **his/hers/yours/theirs** . . . Oh yes, it is **yours**.

As you can see, these are similar in some ways to the adjectives, and have to match the noun in the same way. They are almost always used with *el*, *la*, *los*, or *las*, but you will sometimes find them without, as in the last two examples.

4 What you do to yourself: parts of the body and clothes

Where in English we often say things like 'I put on **my** coat' and 'she washed **her** hair', Spanish does not express possession in any of the ways described above. Instead Spanish uses a reflexive verb as in the following examples:

(See Chapter 22 for more information on reflexive verbs.)

*El juez **se puso** el abrigo*	The judge put **his** coat on.
*Las chicas **se lavaron** las manos.*	The girls washed **their** hands.

In both examples, somebody is doing something to him/herself involving a part of the body or an item of clothing. The idea of possession is expressed by the reflexive pronoun (*me*, *te*, *se*, *nos*, *os*).

 ¿Listos?

1 ¡Listas!

Mañana te vas en un viaje escolar. Con la ayuda de tu madre/padre has preparado una lista de las cosas que tienes que poner en tu maleta, para no olvidar nada. Las primeras cosas tienen un adjetivo posesivo, las otras no. Rellena los espacios en blanco.

Tomorrow you are going on a school trip. With the help of your mother/father you have prepared a list of the things to pack in your suitcase so that you don't forget anything. The first objects have a possessive adjective, the rest haven't. Fill in the gaps.

Ejemplo: *Mi traje de baño, **mis** toallas*

1. .... pasaporte

2. .... cheques de viaje

3. .... máquina fotográfica

4. .... sombrero

5. .... camisetas nuevas

6. .... calzoncillos/bragas

7. .... calcetines

8. .... vaqueros

9. .... pantalón corto

10. .... walkman

11. .... gafas de sol

12. .... fotos de mamá

13. .... cepillo de dientes

14. .... pasta de dientes

15. .... jabón

Luego, escribe la misma lista para un amigo que también hace el mismo viaje.

Then write the same list for a friend going on the same trip.

Ejemplo: *Tu traje de baño, **tus** toallas*

¡Tu madre olvidó varias cosas! Tienes que añadirlas.

Your mother forgot a few things! You have to add them.

Ejemplo: *Mi monedero/cartera, **mis** casetes*

2 ¿De quién es?
Rellena cada espacio con el adjetivo posesivo que mejor convenga para el significado de estas frases.

Complete each gap with the possessive adjective which best fits the meaning of these sentences.

Ejemplo: **La mayoría de .... amigos van a .... cole.**
La mayoría de *mis* amigos van a *mi* cole.

1. .... mejor amigo se llama Manolo; estamos en la misma clase.

2. .... familia vive al lado de la casa donde vivimos nosotros.

3. Tiene muchos hermanos: ¡............... padres tienen mucho trabajo!

4. Mañana vamos juntos a ver a .... amigas, que son hermanas.

5. .... madre murió el año pasado.

6. Por eso tienen que cuidar de .... hermanos menores.

7. También ayudan mucho a .... padre, ¡que es profesor y trabaja mucho!

8. Y tú, ¿ayudas mucho a .... padres?

9. ¿Te gusta estar con .... mejor amigo/a?

10. Tú y tus amigos/as, ¿qué pensáis de .... profesores, o es un secreto?

3 Es de

Contesta las siguientes preguntas, usando 'de' para escribir que cada objeto pertenece a la persona cuyo nombre viene en paréntesis.

Answer the following questions, using 'de' to write that each object belongs to the person whose name is in brackets.

Ejemplo: **¿De quién es el gato? Es *de* Juan/Es el gato *de* Juan**

1. ¿De quién es el perro? (Pepe)

2. ¿De quién es la moto? (Pablo)

3. ¿De quién es el coche? (el profesor)

4. ¿De quién es el balón? (Marita)

5. ¿De quién es la foto? (Conchi)

6. ¿De quién son los lápices? (la profesora)

7. ¿De quién son las gafas? (el director)

8. ¿De quién son estas cartas? (Jorge)

9. ¿De quién son los anillos? (Pepa)

10. ¿De quién son estas llaves? (mi madre)

4 ¡Demasiada rivalidad!

Un joven español viene a pasar una semana en tu casa. Quiere saber algo de tu país, y te hace varias preguntas. ¡Qué buena oportunidad para un poco de rivalidad! Tienes que contestarle como en el ejemplo.

A Spanish youngster comes to stay with you for a week. He wants to know a few things about your country and asks you several questions. What a good opportunity for a bit of rivalry! Answer him as in the example.

Ejemplo:
A. Mi pueblo tiene un cine muy bueno. ¿Y el tuyo?
B. ¡El mío tiene un cine mejor que el tuyo!

1. Mi país tiene un equipo de fútbol muy bueno. ¿Y el tuyo?

2. Mi región tiene unos panoramas magníficos. ¿Y la tuya?

3. Mi casa tiene una piscina fabulosa. ¿Y la tuya?

4. Nuestra ciudad es muy hermosa. ¿Y la vuestra?

5. Nuestros ríos son muy largos. ¿Y los vuestros?

6. Nuestras playas son buenísimas. ¿Y las vuestras?

7. Nuestra calle es muy ancha. ¿Y la vuestra?

8. Mis padres son muy simpáticos. ¿Y los tuyos?

9. Mis abuelos son muy generosos. ¿Y los tuyos?

10. Mi hermano/a es guapísimo/a. ¿Y el tuyo/la tuya?

 ¡Ya!

5 ¡Otra lista!

Escoge una de las siguientes situaciones:

- Mañana te vas de vacaciones con tus amigos/as.
- Esta tarde vas a la discoteca.
- Mañana será tu primer día en el nuevo colegio.
- Te preparas para el nuevo trabajo.

Con la ayuda de tu amigo/a, prepara una lista de las cosas necesarias.

Choose one of the following situations:

- Tomorrow you are going on holiday with your friends.
- This evening you are going to the disco.
- Tomorrow will be your first day at your new school.
- You are getting ready for your new job.

¡Viva la gramática!

With the help of your friend, make a list of the things you need.

Ejemplo:
A. **Bueno, tengo que llevar *mi* chandal y *mis* zapatillas.**
B. **Sí, ¡y no olvides *tu* barra de labios y *tus* pendientes!**

6 *Posesión equivocada*

Después de lavarlas y plancharlas, tu madre/padre (un(a) amigo/a de clase) ha puesto varias prendas de vestir en tu cama, pensando que son tuyas. Dile que no son tuyas y de quién son.

After washing them and ironing them, your mother/father (a classmate) has put various items of clothing on your bed. Tell her/him they are not yours and whose they are:

Ejemplo:
¡Esta camisa no es *mía*! Es *de* David.
¡Estos calcetines no son *míos*! Son *de* papá.

7 *La primera carta*

Escribe una carta a un(a) amigo/a español(a) en la que describes a tu familia, tu casa, tus amigos y tu pueblo. Claro, ¡tienes que utilizar muchos posesivos!

Write a letter to a Spanish friend. Describe your family, your home, your friends and your town or village. Of course, you have to use lots of possessives!

Glosario

el juez	judge
el viaje escolar	school trip
los calzoncillos	underpants
las bragas	briefs

7

COUNTING
numbers

 **¿Preparados?**

1 Counting 1, 2, 3 . . .: 'cardinal' numbers

You can't get far without numbers! You need them for dates, addresses, telephone, distances, directions, and perhaps above all, for shopping! So make sure you learn them thoroughly!

Here are the Spanish numbers from **1** to **30**. Note how 16–29 are spelt!

1	*uno*	11	*once*	21	*veintiuno*
2	*dos*	12	*doce*	22	*veintidós*
3	*tres*	13	*trece*	23	*veintitrés*
4	*cuatro*	14	*catorce*	24	*veinticuatro*
5	*cinco*	15	*quince*	25	*veinticinco*
6	*seis*	16	*dieciséis*	26	*veintiséis*
7	*siete*	17	*diecisiete*	27	*veintisiete*
8	*ocho*	18	*dieciocho*	28	*veintiocho*
9	*nueve*	19	*diecinueve*	29	*veintinueve*
10	*diez*	20	*veinte*	30	*treinta*

From **30** to **99** those not ending in 0 are written as three words:

31	*treinta y uno*
35	*treinta y cinco*
40	*cuarenta*
47	*cuarenta y siete*
50	*cincuenta*
52	*cincuenta y dos*

¡Viva la gramática!

60	*sesenta*
66	*sesenta y seis*
70	*setenta*
78	*setenta y ocho*
80	*ochenta*
83	*ochenta y tres*
90	*noventa*
94	*noventa y cuatro*

 **¡Ojo!**

sesenta is to seis: 60
    as
setenta is to siete: 70

100 *cien* (when counting or before a noun): *cien kilómetros*, but when you go on counting 'a hundred and something' it is *ciento*.

 **¡Ojo!**

There is no *y* between the hundreds and the tens.

101	*ciento uno*
110	*ciento diez*
125	*ciento veinticinco*
199	*ciento noventa y nueve*

200–999

There are special words for 200 to 900.

 **¡Ojo!**

500, 700, 900!

200	*doscientos*	217	*doscientos diecisiete*
300	*trescientos*	326	*trescientos veintiséis*
400	*cuatrocientos*	438	*cuatrocientos treinta y ocho*
500	***quini**entos*	542	***quini**entos cuarenta y dos*
600	*seiscientos*	653	*seiscientos cincuenta y tres*
700	***sete**cientos*	766	***sete**cientos sesenta y seis*
800	*ochocientos*	875	*ochocientos setenta y cinco*
900	***nove**cientos*	999	***nove**cientos noventa y nueve*

 **¡Ojo!**

200 to 900 also agree with their noun:

Doscientos veinte mejicanos   220 Mexican pesos (masculine)
Doscientas veinte libras esterlinas   220 pounds sterling (feminine)

Thousands

You need these for dates, which are said in full:

1.000 *mil*   1998 *mil **nove**cientos noventa y ocho*
2.000 *dos mil*   2001 *dos mil uno*
10.000 *diez mil*   10.481 *diez mil, cuatrocientos ochenta y uno*
1.000.000 *un millón*

 **¡Ojo!**

Some more points to watch:

1. *uno* always becomes *un* before a masculine noun, even when it is on the end of a bigger number: ***un*** (1) *coche, veinti**ún** (21) coches, novecientos treinta y **un** (931) coches.*

2. when you write figures, in common with continental European practice, you divide the thousands with a dot.
   4.587 (*cuatro **mil** quinientos ochenta y siete* four thousand five hundred and eighty seven)

   and write a comma for a decimal point:
   4,587 (*cuatro coma quinientos ochenta y siete* four point five eight seven).

2 Putting things in order: 'ordinal' numbers

The bad news is that there is no set pattern for 'fifth', 'twentieth', etc., in Spanish, you just have to learn the form for each one. The good news is that you only normally use the 'ordinals' up to 10. Above that you use the 'ordinary' (cardinal) number. You need ordinals for addresses (e.g. '3rd floor') and directions ('4th street on left', etc.).

1st   *primero*
2nd   *segundo*
3rd   *tercero*
4th   *cuarto*
5th   *quinto*

¡Viva la gramática!

6th	*sexto*
7th	*séptimo* or *sétimo* (you don't sound the *p*)
8th	*octavo*
9th	*noveno*
10th	*décimo*

 **¡Ojo!**

Don't confuse *cuarto* = 4th with *cuatro* = 4!

 **¡Ojo!**

1. These are adjectives and agree with their noun: *la tercera calle a la derecha*.

   Primero and *tercero* drop the *o* before a masculine singular noun: *el primer/tercer piso*.

2. Above 10, use the cardinal numbers: *mi dieciséis aniversario*, 'my 16th birthday'; *el siglo veintiuno* 'the 21st century'.

3 Maths: the four rules!

*Dos **más** dos **son** cuatro.*	Two **plus** two **are** four.
*Ocho **menos** tres **son** cinco.*	Eight **minus** three **are** five.
*Tres **por** cuatro **son** doce.*	Three **times** four **are** twelve.
*Quince **dividido por** cinco **son** tres.*	Fifteen **divided by** five **are** three.

 # ¿Listos?

1 ¿Qué número?

Escoge el número del recuadro que corresponda con el número escrito.

Choose the number from the box which corresponds to the number written out in full.

1. tres

2. diecisiete

3. treinta y cinco

4. sesenta y uno

5. setenta y dos

6. ciento noventa y ocho

7. trescientos cuarenta y cuatro

8. quinientos cuarenta y cuatro

9. mil ciento cincuenta y siete

10. dos mil doscientos ochenta y uno

61	1.157	344	3	2.281	35	544	72	17	198

2 ¡Aritmética mental!

He aquí unas soluciones y unos problemas. Tienes que decidir qué solución pertenece a qué problema.

Match the answers on the left to the sums on the right!

1. 21   a. veinticinco por cuatro

2. 15   b. once por diez

3. 54   c. mil dividido por cuatro

4. 41   d. quince más seis

5. 35   e. cuarenta y cinco dividido por cinco

6. 8   f. veinte más diecinueve más dos

7. 100   g. veinticuatro menos nueve

8. 250   h. siete por cinco

9. 9   i. seis por nueve

10. 110   j. sesenta y cuatro dividido por ocho

3 ¿Cuántos chicos y cuántas chicas?

Escoge la forma correcta del número.
Choose the correct form of the number.

1. En mi colegio hay **cuatrocientos / cuatrocientas** chicas.

2. Yo estoy en el **tercer / tercero / tercera** curso.

¡Viva la gramática!

3. En el colegio de mi hermano hay **sietecientos / setecientos / setecientas** chicos.

4. Ayer compré un ordenador por **mil seiscientos / seiscientas** euros,

5. pero mi amiga Pili sólo pagó **mil quinientos / mil cincocientos** euros.

6. Si vas a mi casa, toma la **primera / primer** calle a la derecha,

7. llama a la **cuarta / cuatra** puerta,

8. y toma el ascensor hasta el **cinco / quinto** piso.

4 ¡Pisos mezclados!

En la placa de los botones del ascensor del piso de Conchi, se han mezclado los números de los pisos. ¡Ponlos en orden!

On the button plate of the lift in Conchi's block of flats, the floor numbers have been mixed up. Put them in the right order – going up, of course!

¡Ya!

5 *¡Más aritmética!*
En un papel escribe un problema de aritmética en cifras. Tú compañero/a de clase tiene que leerlo en voz alta – ¡con la solución!

On a piece of paper write down a sum in figures. Your partner has to read the figures aloud in Spanish – and give the answer!

Ejemplo:
A.　　4 × 4 = ?
B.　　Cuatro por cuatro son dieciséis.

6 *Mi número de teléfono es . . .*
Cada alumno tiene que decir su número de teléfono (o el de un(a) amigo/a). Los otros tienen que escribir los números en un papel.

Each pupil in turn says their telephone number (or that of a friend). The others have to jot the number down in figures as it is said.

Ejemplo:
A.　　Diego, ¿cuál es tu número de teléfono?
B.　　Es el ochenta y seis, treinta, veintinueve, con prefijo cero uno, dos, veinticinco (86 30 29 code 01 2 25).

7 *¿Dónde está . . . ?*
Con tu compañero/a de clase, imaginad que estáis en un sitio del centro de tu ciudad o pueblo. Uno pregunta al otro: *¿Dónde está . . . ?* y el otro tiene que contestar, utilizando los números ordinales.

With your partner, imagine you are somewhere central in your town or village. One asks *¿Dónde está . . . ?* and the other has to give directions using ordinal numbers.

Ejemplo:
A.　　Por favor, ¿dónde está el banco NatWest?
B.　　Tome la *segunda* calle a la izquierda. Es el *tercer* edificio a la derecha.

8

HOW BIG AND HOW FAR?
size, weight and distance

 **¿Preparados?**

Metric measures are, of course, used in Spain and other Spanish-speaking countries. The most frequently used ones are:

■ Size and distance

un centímetro	centimetre
un metro	metre
un metro sesenta	one metre sixty (centimetres)
un kilómetro	kilometre

■ Liquid capacity

un litro	litre
medio litro	half a litre

■ Weight

un gramo	gram
doscientos gramos	200 grams
un kilo	kilo(gram)
medio kilo	half a kilo

1 Size
a Dimensions

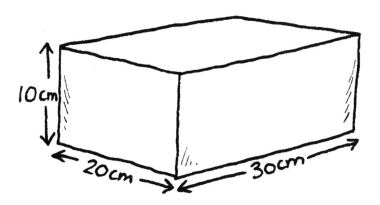

*¿**Cuánto mide** esta caja?*	**What** does this box **measure**?
*¿**Cuánto tiene** esta caja **de largo**?*	**How long is** this box?
de ancho	wide ?
de alto	high/tall ?

*Esta caja **tiene/mide** treinta centímetros **de largo**, veinte centímetros **de ancho** y diez centímetros **de alto**.*
This box **is** 30 cm **long**, 20 cm **wide** and 10 cm **high/tall**.

You usually use *tiene* as the verb in giving dimensions, but you can also use *mide* 'measures'.

If the object is round, you say:

*Esta pelota tiene cinco centímetros **de diámetro**.*	This ball is 5 cm **in diameter**.

b Personal height

*¿Cuánto **mides**? **Mido** un metro cincuenta y nueve.*	How **tall** are you? I'm 1 metre 59.
*Mi hermano **mide** un metro sesenta y cinco.*	My brother **is/measures** 1 metre 65.

2 Weight

*¿Cuánto **pesas**? **Peso** sesenta kilos.*	How much do you **weigh**? I weigh 60 kilos.

¿Cuánto pesa este paquete? Pesa setecientos gramos.

How much does this parcel **weigh**? It **weighs** 700 grams.

3 Distance

When you want to say how far away something is, you must use *a*:

¿A qué distancia / A cuántos kilómetros está Sevilla de Madrid?
How far / How many kilometres is Seville from Madrid?
Sevilla está a quinientos cuarenta kilómetros de Madrid.
Seville is 540 kilometres from Madrid.
Correos está a unos trecientos metros, a dos minutos andando.
The Post Office is about 300 metres, two minutes away on foot.

 ¿Listos?

1 *¿Cuánto mide?*

¿Cuáles son las dimensiones aproximadas de las siguientes cosas?
What are the approximate dimensions of the following things?

1. un terreno de fútbol

2. una pista de tenis

3. un autobús de dos pisos

4. un paquete de 250 gramos de mantequilla

5. la pantalla de un ordenador típico

6. un disquete de ordenador

7. una pelota de tenis

8. un reloj de pulsera

 ¡Ya!

2 *¿Cuánto mides?*

Se escoge a un(a) alumno/a y los otros tienen que adivinar lo que mide.

A pupil is chosen and the others have to guess his/her height. The nearest guess scores a point.

Ejemplo:

A.   **Martín, mides un metro sesenta y tres.**

B.   **Incorrecto. / Correcto.**

3 *¿A qué distancia . . . ?*

a. En parejas o en clase haced preguntas unos a otros según el ejemplo.

In pairs or as a class, ask each other questions based on the examples. Ask about things within reasonable distance in your town or village.

Ejemplos:

A.   **¿Dónde está la iglesia?**

B.   **Está a quinientos metros.**

A.   **¿A qué distancia está la estación?**

B.   **Está a cinco minutos andando.**

b. Tu compañero/a de clase es un(a) turista español(a) que no habla inglés. Con un mapa de Gran Bretaña te hace preguntas sobre la distancia de una ciudad a otra.

Your partner is a Spanish tourist who speaks no English. With a map of Britain he/she asks you about distances from one town to another. Change roles frequently.

Ejemplo:

A.   **¿A cuántos kilómetros está Manchester de Londres?**

B.   **Está a doscientos setenta kilómetros. (Está a tres horas y media en coche / a dos horas en tren.)**

Glosario

el disquete	floppy disk
el reloj de pulsera	wristwatch
el terreno	pitch

9

FIVE O'CLOCK, 1ST JANUARY
times and dates

 ¿Preparados?

1 Time

¿Qué hora es?	**What's the time?**
¿Tiene hora, por favor?	**Have you got the time** please?
¿A qué hora sale el tren?	**At what time** does the train leave?

Es la una

Son las dos

Son las siete

Son las doce

Son las once menos cuarto
Son las diez cuarenta y cin[co]

Son las nueve menos veinte /
Son las ocho cuarenta

Son las siete y
veinticinco

Son las ocho y media /
Son las ocho treinta

Son las tres y cinco

Son las nueve y cuarto /
Son las nueve quince

■ You can see from the clocks above that, in Spanish, just as in English, there are
two ways of saying the time: 'a quarter to three' or 'two forty-five'.

 **¡Ojo!**

To say the time you use *son las* . . . with every hour except *una*, where you say *es la una*.

When using the 24-hour clock, you don't put an *y* between the hours and minutes.

■ To ask 'at what time' something happens, you say *¿A qué hora . . . ?* and the reply will be *a la una / a las dos*, etc.

> *¿A qué hora llega el vuelo desde Londres? A las trece treinta.*
> **At what time** does the flight from London arrive? **At** 13.30.

■ To distinguish **a.m.** and **p.m.** in timetables, opening times and other official uses, the 24-hour clock is used:

> *El museo abre a las 16.30.*   The museum opens at 4.30 p.m.

In conversation, you say *de la mañana* for a.m., *de la tarde* from about 1 p.m. till dark, and *de la noche* for later times. Spanish life often goes on to *las dos de la madrugada* (the early morning) or later!

> *Son las dos y media de la tarde.*   It's half-past two in the afternoon / 2.30 p.m.

mediodía = noon, midday; *medianoche* = midnight

2 Days and dates
■ The days of the week are:

lunes	Monday	*viernes*	Friday
martes	Tuesday	*sábado*	Saturday
miércoles	Wednesday	*domingo*	Sunday
jueves	Thursday		

■ The months are:

enero	January	*julio*	July
febrero	February	*agosto*	August
marzo	March	*setiembre*	September
abril	April	*octubre*	October
mayo	May	*noviembre*	November
junio	June	*diciembre*	December

¡Viva la gramática!

 **¡Ojo!**

There are a number of small points to remember:

1. All days and months are spelt with a small letter.

2. Except for *el primero*, you use the cardinal numbers (*dos*, *tres*, etc.) in dates.

3. The number always comes first.

4. You put *de* between the date and the month:

primero de abril	1st April / April 1st
dos de mayo	2nd May / May 2nd
doce de octubre	12th October / October 12th
veinticinco de diciembre	25th December

■ There are two ways of asking 'What's the date?' and replying 'It's the . . .':

¿A cuánto estamos? Estamos a tres de febrero.
¿Qué fecha es? Es el tres de febrero.
What's the date? It's 3rd February.

■ 'On' a certain day or date is simply *el*, and '**on** Saturdays' is *los sábados*:

*¿Qué haces **el** sábado?*	What are you doing **on** Saturday (=next Saturday)?
Los *sábados siempre voy a la ciudad con mi madre.*	**On** Saturdays (=all Saturdays) I always go to town with my mother.
*Las clases terminan **el** veinte de diciembre.*	Classes end **on** the 20th December.

■ 'In' a month is simply *en*:

***En setiembre** volvemos al cole*	We go back to school **in September**.

■ Years are said in full, no shortened versions like 'nineteen ninety-nine' (it gets easier in the 21st century!):

1999	*mil novecientos noventa y nueve*
2002	*dos mil dos*

■ You put *de* between the month and the year:

4-8-98   *cuatro de agosto **de** mil novecientos noventa y ocho*

56

3 Seasons

The four seasons are:

la primavera	spring	*el otoño*	autumn
el verano	summer	*el invierno*	winter

■ Just use *en* for 'in spring' etc.

> ***En la primavera*** *vamos a España.* In the spring we're going to Spain.

 ## ¿Listos?

1 ¿A qué hora?

He aquí el día de Martín. Escoge la hora en el recuadro que corresponda con la hora del reloj.

Here is Martin's day. Match the times in the box on the next page to those on his watch. The first one is done for you as an example.

Ejemplo:

1. A las seis y media de la mañana, Martín se despierta

1. `06:30` Martín se despierta. 2. `06:45` Martín se levanta. 3. `07:50` sale de casa.

4. `08:05` llega el autobús. 5. `08:30` empieza el trabajo. 6. `13:00` come el almuerzo

en la cantina. 7. `17:15` va a Correos. 8. `18:50` sale del trabajo.

9. `19:35` llega a casa. 10. `21:10` pone el televisor. 11. `24:00` se duerme.

¡Viva la gramática!

A la una de la tarde
A las ocho menos veinticinco de la tarde
A las ocho menos diez de la mañana
A medianoche
A las seis y media de la mañana
A las ocho y media de la mañana
A las siete menos diez de la tarde
A las nueve y diez de la noche
A las siete menos cuarto de la mañana
A las ocho y cinco de la mañana
A las cinco y cuarto de la tarde

2 ¿Qué hora es?

Di qué hora es en estos relojes. Dilo primero de la manera 'conversacional' y luego de la manera 'digital'.

Say the time according to these clocks, first the 'conversational' way and then the 'digital' way, using the 24 hour clock.

Ejemplo:

– **Son las once y veinte de la noche.**
– **Son las veintitrés veinte.**

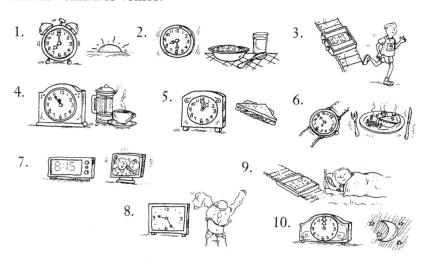

58

3 ¿Qué fecha es?

Escribe las fechas siguientes, o léelas a tu compañero/a de clase, que tiene que escribirlas.

Write out the following dates, or read them aloud to your partner, who has to write them down. Take turns in reading and writing.

1. 08-01-1998
2. 10-02-1999
3. 03-03-2000
4. 14-04-2001
5. 20-05-2005
6. 21-06-1986
7. 18-07-1939
8. 04-08-1914
9. 25-09-1931
10. 12-10-1898
11. 30-11-1492
12. 31-12-1109

 ¡Ya!

4 Días de mi vida

a. Cuenta oralmente a tus compañeros de clase, con la hora, unas diez cosas que hiciste ayer.

Give a spoken account to your classmates about ten things you did yesterday, with the time you did them.

b. Escribe un párrafo, describiendo lo que haces en un día típico de tu vida en el cole. ¡No olvides decir a qué hora haces estas cosas!

Write a paragraph describing what you do in a typical day at school. Don't forget to say at what time you do these things!

5 ¿Qué fecha es tu cumpleaños?

a. Pregunta a tus compañeros de clase la fecha de su cumpleaños.
Ask your classmates the date of their birthday.

Ejemplo:
A.   **¿Qué fecha es tu cumpleaños?**
B.   **Es el nueve de octubre.**

b. Pregunta a tus compañeros su fecha de nacimiento.
Ask your classmates their date of birth.

Ejemplo:
A.   **¿Cuál es tu fecha de nacimiento?**
B.   **Es el nueve de octubre de mil novecientos ochenta y cinco.**

c. Si quieres más práctica, sigue preguntando el cumpleaños o fecha de nacimiento de los hermanos y las hermanas de tus compañeros.

For further practice, continue asking your classmates the birthdays or dates of birth of their brothers and sisters.

6 ¿Qué día?

Con un calendario de este año o del año que viene, escoge unas fechas y pregunta a tu compañero/a de clase en qué día caerán.

With the aid of a calendar for this or next year, ask your partner which day of the week various dates fall on.

Ejemplo:
A.   **El tres de mayo, ¿qué día es?**
B.   **Es miércoles.**

10

THE WEATHER AND HOW YOU FEEL

 ¿Preparados?

1 How to talk about the weather

Spanish uses several types of phrase to talk about the weather. All can be used in a variety of tenses, but the present tense forms are listed here.

a *Hacer* **expressions (mostly used when there is nothing visible)**

¿Qué tiempo hace?	
*Hace buen tiempo**	The weather is good / fine
*Hace mal tiempo**	The weather is bad
Hace calor	It is warm / hot
Hace frío	It is cold
Hace fresco / fresquito	It is cool / chilly
Hace sol	It is sunny
Hace viento	It is windy

The expressions marked * can be qualified by *muy*; the others can be qualified by *mucho* and *poco*, and all by *bastante* and *demasiado*.

*¡Hace **muy** buen tiempo hoy!*	The weather is very good today.
*Hacía **bastante** mal tiempo en Irlanda.*	The weather in Ireland was quite bad.
*Hace **mucho** frío en esta habitación.*	It's very cold in this room.
*Hace **bastante** fresquito hoy.*	It's quite chilly today.
*Hizo **poco** sol en Mallorca.*	It was not very sunny in Majorca.
*¡Hace **demasiado** calor en Sevilla!*	It's too hot in Seville!

¡Viva la gramática!

¡Consejo!

Hacer is an irregular verb: you will often use it for weather expressions in the imperfect (*hacía*) and the preterite (*hizo*) tenses, as in two of these examples: check it in the verb tables.

b *Hay* expressions (mostly used where there is something visible)

Hay lluvia	It is rainy
Hay nieve	It is snowy
Hay niebla	It is foggy
Hay neblina	It is misty
Hay nubes	It is cloudy
Hay hielo	It is icy
Hay escarcha / heladas	It is frosty
Hay tormenta / tempestad	It is stormy
Hay chubascos	It is showery

All of these can be qualified by the appropriate form of *mucho*, *bastante*, *poco* and *demasiado*.

Hay niebla en la carretera de Burgos.	There is fog on the Burgos road.
Hubo mucha lluvia en Galicia.	There was a lot of rain in Galicia.
Hay bastante nieve para esquiar.	There is enough snow to ski.
Había poca lluvia para el cultivo.	There wasn't enough rain to grow things.
Hay demasiadas nubes para tomar el sol.	It's too cloudy to sunbathe.

¡Consejo!

Hay is an irregular present tense part of *haber*: use this verb in other tenses as in two of the examples.

c *Estar* expressions

Está lloviendo / llueve	It is raining / rains
Está nevando / nieva	It is snowing / snows
Está nublado	It is cloudy
Está cubierto	It is overcast
Está despejado	It is clear
Está oscuro	It is dark

The first two are simply verbs used in a normal way (see others below); the others consist of the verb *estar* with an adjective in masculine form.

Las fotos no salen bien si está nublado.	Photos don't come out well if it is cloudy.
Como estaba cubierto cogí el paraguas.	Since it was overcast I took an umbrella.

d Verbs

In addition to *llover* and *nevar* above there are other verbs to describe the weather.

 **¡Ojo!**

The ones with an asterisk have spelling changes! (See Chapter 21.)

brillar (el sol)	to shine (sun)
*llover	to rain
*nevar	to snow
*helar	to freeze
*deshelar	to thaw
granizar	to hail
lloviznar	to drizzle
relampaguear	to flash (lightning)
*tronar	to thunder

¡Llueve tanto aquí en Devon!	It rains so much here in Devon!
Cuando graniza se estropean las uvas.	When it hails the grapes get ruined.
Relampagueaba en las montañas.	There was lightning in the mountains.

2 Weather forecast – el boletín meteorológico

Weather forecasts use a range of expressions, and verbs in various tenses – to describe recent and present conditions as well as future weather. Here are some words and expressions you will come across to add to those above:

Adjectives

bochornoso	muggy, sultry, thundery
cálido	hot (weather, climate)
caliente	hot (substances, liquids)
caluroso	hot (day, climate)
fresco	fresh, cool
frío	cold
lluvioso	rainy

¡Viva la gramática!

nuboso	cloudy
soleado	sunny
templado	moderate
tempestuoso, tormentoso	stormy

Nouns

precipitaciones	precipitation (rain, snow, etc.)
nevadas	snowfalls, snowstorms
nubosidad	cloud(iness)
intervalos nubosos	cloudy spells
cielos despejados	clear skies
claros	clear spells
borrascas	storms, squalls
el frente frío / caliente	cold / warm front
la gota fría	cold front
el ciclón / anticiclón	cyclone / anticyclone
el sistema frontal	frontal system
fuertes marejadas	swell
mares gruesas	heavy seas
olas de 1 m / 2 m etc.	1 m / 2 m waves, etc.
con riesgo de	with the risk of
en aumento	. . . increasing . . .

Temperature

veinticinco grados	25 degrees
las temperaturas . . .	temperatures
se mantendrán altas/bajas	will stay high/low
la temperatura máxima	the maximum temperature
mínima	minimum
en (ligero) ascenso	(slowly) rising
descenso	falling

Wind

. . . soplarán . . .	will blow
. . . predominarán	will predominate
vientos fuertes	strong winds
moderados	moderate winds
flojos	weak winds
de componente Sur	southerly
Norte	northerly
Este	easterly
Oeste	westerly

3 Expressions using *tener*: talking about how you feel

The verb *tener* is used in many expressions which describe how you feel or your attitude or situation. They use *tener* followed by a noun where English uses 'to be' with an adjective. (*Tener* is irregular – see verb tables.)

tener	*calor*	to be hot
	frío	cold
	hambre	hungry
	sed	thirsty
	sueño	tired, sleepy
	miedo	afraid
	cuidado	careful
	éxito	successful
	suerte	lucky
	prisa	in a hurry
	razón	right

Note that if you want to say that you are *very* hot, afraid, etc., you use *mucho/a* not *muy*:

| *Tengo **mucho** frío.* | I'm very cold. |
| *Tenemos **mucha** sed.* | We're very thirsty. |

4 Expressions of time using hacer

Hace is used to express 'ago', and can be used in the present or imperfect:

| *Llegué **hace** diez minutos.* | I arrived ten minutes ago. |
| ***Hacía** dos años que volvimos.* | We had returned two years previously. |

Hace is also used, with or without *desde* to convey the idea of time spent doing something:

Espero desde hace diez minutos / Hace diez minutos que espero.
I have been waiting for ten minutes.
Vivíamos allí desde hacía dos años. / Hacía dos años que vivíamos allí.
We had been living there for two years.

Note also *hacer falta* used to express the idea of needing:

| *Me hace falta mucho dinero.* | I need lots of money. |

¿Listos?

1 El tiempo

Escoge la letra adecuada para indicar el tiempo que corresponde a la frase.
Choose the letter of the weather which fits the sentence.

1. Hace mucho sol.
2. Llueve.
3. Hace viento.

4. Hace frío.
5. Está nevando.
6. Hace muchísimo calor.

A

B

C

D

E

F

2 Haz parejas

Las dos partes de las siguientes frases están un poco confusas: tienes que hacer frases completas.

The two halves of these sentences have got rather jumbled: match the halves to make complete sentences.

1. Es tarde y tengo que . . .	. . . hace dos años.
2. Me parece que va a llover . . .	. . . ponerme el abrigo.
3. Mira, llegas tarde: espero desde . . .	. . . tengo mucha prisa.
4. ¡Madre mía, qué frío hace! Voy a . . .	. . . ¿dónde está el paraguas?
5. La clase de español empieza pronto . . .	. . . hace diez minutos.
6. Vamos a esquiar en Sierra Nevada . . .	. . . hay hielo.
7. Hace mucho sol en Torremolinos y . . .	. . . vamos a quedarnos en casa.
8. Hace muy mal tiempo y . . .	. . . coger un taxi.
9. Ten cuidado en la carretera, porque . . .	. . . vamos a broncearnos.
10. Mi amigo murió en un accidente . . .	. . . allí hay mucha nieve.

3 Anagramas climáticos

Completa estas frases con la palabra (en forma de anagrama) más adecuada de las que se ofrecen al lado.

Complete these sentences by choosing and unscrambling the anagram which fits best.

1. ¡Madre mía – qué tormenta! Mira el **regalompá / loihe / toiven**.

2. Hace tanto **roíf / lorac / piemto** que vamos a ir a la piscina.

3. En Menorca **ache / los / lilovó / mucho**: tuvimos que comprar un paraguas.

4. Aquel día, estaba **etandos / nodevan / chiedano** en los Pirineos.

5. El ruido del **nutreo / trenfe / coral /** me da miedo.

6. Se ven muchas **vallius / vienes / snube** en el cielo.

7. El sol **ballabir / vollia / aslabop**.

8. Las temperaturas **rhaan / vellanor / ajábran** mañana por la mañana.

9. Según el pronóstico va a llegar una **spettedam / ivene / dadiusnob**.

10. Las Islas Canarias serán afectadas por un **tenfre rífo / bachusoc / rolac**.

H 4 ¿Qué tiempo hace?

Describe el tiempo o la sensación que mejor convenga a las siguientes situaciones.
Describe the weather or feeling which best fits the following situations.

1. ¡Madre mía! ¡Voy a quitarme el suéter!

2. Si vas a ir a pie, ponte el impermeable.

3. El guardia que dirigía el tráfico llevaba gafas de sol.

4. Los niños están construyendo un muñeco de nieve.

5. Mamá, ¡quiero un helado!

6. ¿Vamos a la playa?

7. Madre mía, ¡mira ese pastel de chocolate . . . parece delicioso!

8. Oye, es peligroso cobijarte debajo de un árbol.

9. ¡Cuidado! Vas a romper el paraguas.

10. ¿Por qué no quieres hacer paracaidismo?

¡Viva la gramática!

11. ¡Vete a la cama!

12. ¡Qué bien! ¡Has ganado la lotería!

13. ¡Sí, soy muy inteligente!

14. Mi coche es muy viejo y no anda.

15. Déme una limonada, por favor.

 ¡Ya!

5 Explicaciones

Trabaja con un(a) compañero/a. Uno/a inventa una situación y pide una explicación. El otro / la otra da la razón – que siempre será algo mencionado en esta unidad.

Work with a classmate. One invents a situation and asks the other for an explanation, which will always be something mentioned in this unit.

Ejemplo:
A. **Pero chico/a, ¿por qué llevas tanta ropa puesta?**
B. **Porque tengo frío.**
A. **¿Por qué te escondes ahí?**
B. **Porque no he hecho los deberes, ¡y tengo miedo al profesor!**

6 El pronóstico del tiempo

En grupos o en parejas, hablad del tiempo – primero de ayer, luego del tiempo que hace hoy, y por fin del tiempo que va a hacer mañana.

In groups or pairs, talk about the weather – first yesterday's, then about today's weather, and finally about what the weather will be like tomorrow.

Ejemplo:
A. **Ayer hizo mucho frío, ¿verdad?**
B. **Sí, tuve mucho frío camino del cole.**
A. **Hoy hace mejor tiempo, ¿no?**
B. **¡Tienes razón!**
A. **Dicen que mañana va a llover.**
B. **Bueno, no vamos a poder jugar al fútbol.**

H 7 *El meteorólogo*

En un periódico o una revista, escoge un pronóstico del tiempo y cuéntale a tu compañero/a el tiempo que va a hacer. El/ella podría usar un mapa del país en el que apuntar lo que le digas, utilizando los símbolos adecuados.

Pick a weather forecast from a newspaper or magazine and tell your partner what the weather is going to be like. He/she could use a map of the country to note what you say, using appropriate symbols.

Glosario

el abrigo	(over)coat
broncearse	to get a suntan
el impermeable	raincoat
las gafas de sol	sunglasses
cobijarse	to take shelter
el paracaidismo	parachuting

11

'HE', 'SHE', 'HIM', 'HER'
subject and disjunctive pronouns

 **¿Preparados?**

Pronouns are words which replace the names of things and people (nouns).

1 Subject pronouns

Subject pronouns are those mostly used in front of a verb, referring to a person or thing who/which is the subject or 'doer' of the action. Here are all the subject pronouns in Spanish:

		Singular		**Plural**
first person	*yo*	I	*nosotros/as*	we
second person	*tú*	you (familiar)	*vosotros/as*	you (familiar)
third person	*él*	he, it	*ellos*	they
	ella	she, it	*ellas*	they
	usted/Vd.	you (formal)	*ustedes/Vds.*	you (formal)

Note the following points:

■ as you can see, there are three singular 'persons' and three plural.

■ 'he', 'she' and formal 'you' (*usted*) forms go together because they share the same verb forms; the same happens in the plural with 'they' and the formal plural 'you' (*ustedes*).

■ 'we', 'you' (familiar) plural and 'they' have masculine and feminine forms, the others do not.

Uses
■ Subject pronouns are not often used with verbs, as they are in English. Spanish

verb forms, whether spoken or written, are quite clear and different from one another, so the ending tells you clearly who is doing the action with no need for a subject pronoun. Compare the following:

Estoy leyendo un libro.   **I** am reading a book.
Vamos a la playa.   **We** are going to the beach.

■ Subject pronouns **are** sometimes used with verbs for clarity or emphasis.

*¡**Tú** tienes que quedarte en casa y **nosotros** vamos al parque!*
You have to stay at home and **we** are going to the park!
***Ella** habla sólo inglés, pero **yo** hablo español y francés también.*
She only speaks English, but I speak Spanish and French too.

They are also often used by themselves in answer to a question, or with a name.

¿Quién rompió esa ventana? Él.   Who broke that window? **He** did.
¿Quién es? Soy yo. / Yo, Manuel.   Who is it? It's **me**. / It's **me**, Manuel.

 ¡Ojo!

When using the verb *ser* to say who people are, the verb takes the person form of the subject pronoun:

*¿**Eres tú**? Sí, **soy yo**.*   Is that you? Yes, it's me.
*¿**Son ellos**? Sí, **son ellos**.*   Is it them? Yes, it's them.

■ 'You': most of the time in Spain, when talking to someone you know, *tú* is used for singular you (one person) and *vosotros/as* for plural you (more than one person). The polite/formal forms *usted* and *ustedes* are still used when you talk to a stranger/strangers older than you. If in doubt, use the formal form until you are sure you can use *tú/vosotros*.

 ¡Consejo!

In Latin America the use of *tú/vosotros* or *ustedes* depends on which country you are in, so it is a good idea to find out before you visit a country what the custom is.

2 Disjunctive pronouns

In spite of their horrible name, these are actually quite useful! In fact they have another name which shows one of their uses clearly: prepositional pronouns. They are used with prepositions such as *con*, *para*, *al lado de*. Here are some examples of how they are used:

*Fui al cine con **ella**.*	I went to the cinema with **her**.
*¿El café solo? Para **mí**.*	The black coffee? For **me**.
*José se sentó al lado de **nosotros**.*	José sat down next to **us**.

The various disjunctive pronouns are as follows:

	Singular		**Plural**	
first person	*mí*	me	*nosotros/as*	us
second person	*ti*	you (familiar)	*vosotros/as*	you (familiar)
	usted/Vd.	you (formal)	*ustedes/Vds.*	you (formal)
third person	*él*	him, it	*ellos*	them
	ella	her, it	*ellas*	them
	sí	. . . self	*sí*	. . . selves

You will have noticed by now that some of these are the same as the subject pronouns – in fact all but the first two, which is quite handy!

Uses

Disjunctive / prepositional pronouns are used after prepositions:

*Siéntate al lado de **mí**.*	Sit down next to **me**.
*El café para **él** y el coñac para **ellos**, ¿no?*	The coffee for **him** and the cognac for **them**, isn't that right?
*Mi amiga vivía no lejos de **nosotros**.*	My friend lived not far from **us**.

■ Note also the following combined forms:

conmigo	with me
contigo	with you
*Mis amigos no querían salir **conmigo**.*	My friends didn't want to go out **with me**.
*Mira, papá, Juanita quiere ir **contigo**.*	Look, Dad, Juanita wants to go **with you**.

There is another similar one: *consigo* – with him/her/it/you (formal). This can only be used when there is a reflexive idea implied:

*El chico no quería llevar todos sus libros **consigo**.*	The boy didn't want to take all his books **with him**.

¿Listos?

1 Sopa de pronombres
Busca todos los pronombres de sujeto y disyuntivos en esta sopa de pronombres.
Sólo falta uno . . . ¿cuál es?

Look for all of the subject and disjunctive pronouns in this wordsearch. Only one is missing: which is it?

S	U	S	O	R	T	O	S	O	N
I	T	A	U	L	U	G	X	C	O
M	F	R	S	D	E	L	L	O	S
U	S	T	E	D	E	S	L	N	O
V	C	O	N	M	I	G	O	T	T
B	M	S	S	A	L	L	E	I	R
W	Y	O	A	L	L	E	L	G	A
I	P	V	O	S	O	T	R	O	S

2 Pronombres casados
Para completar estas frases, escoge la terminación que mejor convenga.
To complete these sentences, choose the most appropriate endings.

1. La chica nos llamó   llegasteis antes que ellos.
2. Las que llamaron a la puerta son   a mí me enfada?
3. Sois vosotros los que   antes que usted.
4. Pueden llevar a su hijo   ellas.
5. No sé exactamente lo que   cómprame unos caramelos para mí.
6. Mire usted: yo llegué   a nosotros por teléfono.
7. Por favor, ve tú a la tienda y   usted quiere.
8. ¿Sabes lo que   consigo si quieren.

H 3 Exploración espacial
Rellena los espacios en blanco con el pronombre que mejor convenga.
Fill the spaces with the pronoun which fits.

73

¡Viva la gramática!

1. ... vas al cole en bici, ¿no?

2. ... somos más majos que ellos, ¿verdad señor?

3. ... son las más inteligentes de la clase.

4. ¿Tengo que ir ... a ver al director?

5. ... espera encontrar trabajo en esta fábrica.

6. No debes sentarte delante de ..., porque queremos ver la película.

7. Cuando dije que quería ir al cine, mis amigos decidieron ir....

8. ¡Me gusta estar cerca de ..., amor mío!

9. Bueno, ¡sus gafas están detrás de ... en el sofá!

10. Vamos a ver, dices que tienes el pasaporte ..., ¿no?

11. Dice usted que quiere llevar el perro ... en el tren: ¡pues no se permite!

12. La chica le vio a Juan, y fue a sentarse al lado de....

 ¡Ya!

4 Acusaciones

Trabaja con todos los miembros de tu clase. El profesor / La profesora quiere saber quién hizo varias cosas. Tenéis que usar todos los pronombres de sujeto posibles para contestar a sus preguntas, pero sin repetirlos. (Hay 12 posibilidades en total.)

Work with the whole class. Your teacher wants to know who has done several things and asks you a series of questions. You have to use all the possible subject pronouns to answer his/her questions, but without repeating them. (There are 12 possibilities in all.)

Ejemplos:
– **Chicos, ¿quién rompió la ventana?**
– **¡Ellos!**
– **¿Quién escribió en la pizarra?**
– **¡Nosotros!**
– **¿Quién perdió su paciencia?**
– **¡Usted!**

H 5 *Dónde está?*

Tu compañero/a quiere saber dónde están varios objetos. Contesta utilizando preposiciones y pronombres disyuntivos como en los ejemplos.

Your classmate wants to know where various things are. Answer using prepositions and disjunctive pronouns as in the examples.

Ejemplos:
A.　　**¿Dónde está mi bolígrafo?**
B.　　**¡Está delante de ti, idiota!**
A.　　**¿Dónde están las gafas de Pepe?**
B.　　**¡Están al lado de él, imbécil!**

H 6 *El artículo relleno*

Busca un artículo o un anuncio publicitario en un periódico o en una revista: copiándolo, pon todos los pronombres de sujeto delante de los verbos.

Choose an article or advert from a newspaper or magazine. Copy the text and put the subject pronouns in front of the verbs.

Glosario

exploración espacial	space exploration
majo	good, pretty, smart
la fábrica	factory
la película	film
enfadar	to annoy

12

'IT', 'TO ME' object pronouns

 ¿Preparados?

Whatever language we speak, we all take short cuts! For example:

Where is my pen? I left **it** on the table with my book. Now I can't find **them**.

Clearly, 'it' is the pen, and 'them' refers to the pen and the book together. Using these **object pronouns** avoids the need to repeat 'pen' and 'book'.

1 Object pronouns: what use are they?
Object pronouns replace the names of things or people which/who:

■ are the victims of an action (direct object pronouns).

> Where is my pen? Have you seen **it**?
> This is my new friend: I like **him** very much.

■ are on the receiving end of an action (indirect object pronouns).

> They should have given them to **us**.
> She sent a letter to **him**.

2 Direct object pronouns
Here are the direct object pronouns in Spanish, with their meanings:

me	me	*nos*	us
te	you (familiar singular)	*os*	you (familiar plural)
le/lo	him, it	*les/los/las*	them
la	her, it		
le/lo/la	you (formal singular)	*les/los/las*	you (formal plural)

Note: 'him' can be translated by either *lo* or *le*, and 'them' (masc.) by *los* or *les*.

3 Indirect object pronouns

The indirect object pronouns in Spanish are as follows, with meanings:

me	to me	*nos*	to us
te	to you (familiar singular)	*os*	to you (familiar plural)
le	to him, her, it	*les*	to them
le	to you (formal singular)	*les*	to you (formal plural)

4 The position of object pronouns

These object pronouns – direct and indirect – usually come just in front of the verb, but they can also be placed on the end of some parts of the verb: **sometimes** on the end of infinitives and gerunds (the *-ando/-iendo* form); **always** on the end of affirmative commands (telling somebody to do something), but **never** on the end of negative commands (telling somebody NOT to do something).

Lo encuentro muy aburrido.	I find it very boring.
Le dieron una medalla de oro.	They gave him a gold medal.
Tienen que encontrarnos en el bar./ *Nos tienen que encontrar en el bar.*	They have to meet us in the bar.
Tienes que enviarme una carta./ *Me tienes que enviar una carta.*	You must send me a letter.
He perdido mi boli – estoy buscándolo./ *Lo estoy buscando.*	I've lost my biro – I'm looking for it.
Mi padre está pagándole./ *Mi padre le está pagando.*	My father is paying him/her.
Déme su pasaporte, por favor.	Give me your passport, please.
Póngalo en el mostrador.	Put it on the counter.
No lo pierdas, costó mucho dinero.	Don't lose it, it cost a lot of money.
¡No me mandes flores!	Don't send me flowers!

5 Two object pronouns together

■ Sometimes two of these object pronouns can be used together; when this happens, the indirect object pronoun is **always** put first.

*Siempre **me los** dan mis padres.*	My parents always give them to me.

¡Viva la gramática!

Os lo mandarán tus abuelos.	Your grandparents will send it to you.

■ If both are third person – in other words '(to) him/her/it/them/you' (formal) – the indirect object pronoun changes to *se* to avoid having two words beginning with *l-*.

Se las robaron ayer en el cole.	They stole them from him yesterday at school.
No *se lo* mandarán.	They will not send it to them.

How can you tell in the two examples above who is involved? You can't! Sometimes extra words can be added to avoid any chance of confusion.

Se las robaron *a él* ayer.	They stole them from him yesterday.
No se lo mandarán *a ellas*.	They will not send it to them.

 **¡Ojo!**

Sometimes Spanish uses one of these pronouns when we wouldn't bother in English.

¡Ya lo sé!	I know (it).

The same happens in some commonly used expressions:

Ya lo creo.	I should think so.

 ¿Listos?

1 Sustituciones

En cada una de las siguientes frases, sustituye las palabras subrayadas con el pronombre adecuado.

In each of the following sentences, replace the words underlined with the appropriate pronoun.

Ejemplo:
Quiero comer <u>estas manzanas</u>.
Quiero comer*las*.

1. Hoy es el cumpleaños de mi novia: voy a llamar <u>a mi novia</u>.

2. He visto unos caramelos deliciosos: quiero comprar <u>los caramelos</u>.

3. Estas rosas son muy bonitas: voy a comprar <u>estas rosas</u>.

4. Bueno, ¡ya está! He comprado <u>las rosas</u> . . .

5. . . . pero no he comprado <u>los caramelos</u>.

6. Voy a ver <u>a mi novia</u> esta tarde.

7. Daré <u>las rosas a mi novia</u> en seguida.

8. Ella buscará un florero para las rosas, y pondrá <u>el florero</u> en la mesa.

9. La visitará su amiga, y mi novia mostrará <u>a su amiga las rosas</u>.

10. Sus padres han invitado <u>a nosotros</u> a cenar, pues iremos a ver <u>a sus padres</u>.

2 La Lotería

Emparejando las dos partes que corresponden, forma frases completas.
Pairing the two parts which match, make complete sentences.

1. Compraron esta casa porque	acabo de comprarlo.
2. Siempre escuchamos las noticias cuando	no la veo en la calle.
3. Mis abuelos son muy generosos, y	mandarle nuestras señas.
4. No saben dónde está su perro desde que	os la daré mañana.
5. Vamos a escribir a María para	las oímos en la radio.
6. El camarero sabe lo que queremos y	lo perdieron en el parque.
7. Si queréis una foto mía,	nos va a traer café.
8. Ya sé que me amas y	los quiero mucho.
9. Mi amiga salió hace dos minutos y	les gusta mucho.
10. Llevo este pantalón porque	yo te quiero.

H 3 Huevos revueltos

Pon las palabras en el orden correcto para formar frases enteras.
Put the words in the correct order to form whole sentences.

1. le a perro doy un mi caramelo bañar de antes

2. en café: ayer vi la trabaja esta el chica

3. esta deberes voy manzana, hizo ofrecerle los a porque

4. euros regalaré trabajas mucho te veinte si

5. dónde no los sé perdí

6. puerta, la la después cierra por con siempre de salir llave

7. esta parece mira me guapa chica, muy

8. las las mesa, en pero cartas la yo no cogí vi

 ¡Ya!

4 *¡Contéstame!*

Tú tienes que inventar una serie de afirmaciones y preguntas: en cada caso, preséntala o pregúntala a un(a) amigo/a: éste/a tiene que contestar utilizando un pronombre de objeto directo o indirecto.

You have to invent a series of statements and questions: in each case, give them to a friend: he/she has to answer using a direct or indirect object pronoun.

Ejemplos:
A. **Mira a este alumno nuevo. ¡Parece imbécil!**
B. **Sí, sí, ya *lo/le* veo.**
A. **¿Dónde están mis gafas?**
B. **¡Idiota! *Las* tienes en la cabeza.**
A. **Pásame la sal, por favor.**
B. ***Te la* pasé hace un momento.**

H 5 *Acusaciones*

Tu profesor(a) o un(a) compañero(a) de clase te acusa de varios pecados o errores: pero en cada caso lo niegas, como en los ejemplos – sustituyendo los sustantivos con los pronombres objetos apropiados.

Your teacher or a classmate accuses you of various sins or errors; in each case you deny it, as in the examples – replacing the nouns with appropriate object pronouns.

Ejemplos:
A. **Dejaste tus deberes en casa, ¿no?**
B. **¡Pero señor, los tengo aquí!**
A. **Oye, ¿rompiste tú esta ventana?**
B. **¡No señor, no la rompí!**
A. **Robaste mi reloj de oro, ¿verdad?**
B. **¡Sí, lo siento. Se lo devolveré en seguida!**

H *6 ¡Mañana!*

Tus padres quieren que hagas algo para ayudar en casa – pero tú tienes demasiado trabajo, e insistes en que lo vas a hacer . . . mañana.

Your parents want you to do something to help at home but you have too much work to do and insist that you will do it . . . tomorrow.

Ejemplos:

A. **¡Limpia tu dormitorio!**
B. **Sí, voy a hacerlo mañana.**
A. **¡Saca la basura!**
B. **La sacaré mañana.**
A. **¿Quieres preparar la cena?**
B. **No, la voy a preparar mañana.**

Glosario

la medalla de oro	gold medal
el boli (bolígrafo)	biro
el mostrador	counter
huevos revueltos	scrambled eggs
la afirmación	statement
el pecado	sin
negar	to deny
sustituir	to substitute/replace
devolver	to return
la basura	rubbish

13

'THE PERSON WHO ...'
'THE THING WHICH ...'
relative pronouns

 ¿Preparados?

What is a relative pronoun?

A relative pronoun is used to join a clause to a noun in order to give you more information about it:

The teacher **who** gave us this homework
The shop assistant to **whom** I was talking (**who** I was talking to)
The plane **which** leaves at ten o'clock
The purse **that** you found on the bus
The baby **whose** mother was ill

 **¡Ojo!**

Don't confuse these **relative** pronouns with **interrogative** (= question) pronouns in the next chapter. They are often the same words, but used in different ways. **Relative pronouns don't ask questions** (and don't have accents)!

1 Que

Que is the most frequently occurring relative, and is the one you usually use for 'who', 'whom', 'that' and 'which' where no preposition is involved:

*¡La profe **que** nos puso estos deberes está loca!*	The teacher **who/that** gave us this homework is mad!
*El chico **que** viste ayer es el hermano de Montse.*	The boy **who(m)/that** you saw yesterday is Montse's brother.

*El autobús **que** va al aeropuerto sale de la plaza.*	The bus **which/that** goes to the airport leaves from the square.
*El vuelo **que** tomamos sale a las diez.*	The flight **which/that** we are taking leaves at ten.

2 After a preposition

After a preposition (*a*, *de*, *sobre*, *delante de*, etc.), use the following guidelines:

■ Referring to things: use *el que / la que / los que / las que*, agreeing with the thing(s) you are referring back to:

> *Esta es <u>la</u> habitación **en <u>la</u> que** dormimos.*   This is the room **in which** we sleep.
> *He aquí <u>el</u> aparador, **al lado d<u>el</u> que** hemos colocado el televisor.*
> Here's the sideboard, **beside which** we've placed the TV.

■ Referring to a person: use *quien / quienes* or *el que / la que / los que / las que*, agreeing with the person(s) you are referring back to:

> *<u>La</u> profesora **con quien / con <u>la</u> que** fuimos a España también enseña francés.*
> *The teacher **with whom** we went to Spain also teaches French.*
> *Los niños **a quienes / a los que** escribimos viven en Sudamérica.*
> The children **to whom** we are writing / we are writing **to** live in South America.

¡Consejo!

You may also find *el cual / la cual / los cuales / las cuales* used in the some way and meaning the same thing.

¡Ojo!

1. In English we sometimes leave out the 'who', 'which' or 'that', but in Spanish you **must never leave out** *que* or *quien*.

2. In English also we can say 'the children we are writing **to**', with the preposition at the end. Again, you **must never** attempt to do this in Spanish: the preposition always comes **before** the relative pronoun, as in the examples above.

3 Cuyo

Cuyo means 'whose', and must **agree with the thing(s) possessed**:

*Es una confitería **cuy<u>os</u>** <u>pasteles</u> son muy buenos.*	It's a cake shop **whose** cakes are very good.

83

> *Esta es la chica **cuya** madre trabaja en el banco.*
>
> This is the girl **whose** mother works in the bank.

4 El que, la que, los que, las que

These forms are also used in the sense of 'the one who/which', 'those who/which':

> *De todos estos abanicos, **el que** me gusta más es éste.*
>
> Of all these fans, **the one (which)** I like best is this one.
>
> *De las camisas, **las que** me gustan son ésta y ésa.*
>
> Of the shirts, **the ones (which)** I like are this one and that one.

5 Lo que

Lo que means 'what' in the sense of 'that which':

> *Descríbeme **lo que** ves.*
>
> Describe to me **what** you see.
>
> ***Lo que** no me gusta es el color.*
>
> **What** I don't like is the colour.

 ¿Listos?

1 *Este es mi colegio*

Estás enseñando tu colegio a tu amigo/a español(a). Escoge el pronombre relativo correcto en cada caso.

You are showing your Spanish friend around your school. Choose the correct relative pronoun in each case.

1. Esta es la profesora (que / a quien) enseña geografía.

2. Los profesores (al que / que) enseñan idiomas son muy jóvenes.

3. He aquí el patio (en la que / en el que) jugamos durante el recreo.

4. Este es el laboratorio (con el que / al que) vamos para la física.

5. He aquí la cantina. Es la sala (en la que / en los que) comemos.

6. ¿Conoces a Jaime? Es el amigo (con la que / con quien) voy al colegio.

7. Este es mi profesor de español. Es (la que / el que) más me gusta de todos los profesores.

8. (La que / Lo que) no me gusta en el colegio es el uniforme.

H **2** *En el parque zoológico*

Estás visitando un parque zoológico en España, y, al leer los avisos que ponen para describir a los animales, encuentras que se han borrado todas las palabras relativas. Rellena los espacios en blanco con una palabra relativa que convenga. Usa un diccionario para buscar los animales cuyos nombres no conozcas.

At a zoo in Spain, when you read the notices describing the animals you find that all the relative pronouns have been erased. Replace them, using a dictionary to look up any animals or other words you don't know.

1. La girafa es un animal .... tiene el cuello muy largo.

2. El camello es un animal en .... se puede montar.

3. El avestruz es un ave .... huevos son muy grandes.

4. El loro es un pájaro con .... se puede hablar.

5. El león es el animal .... se llama el rey de los animales.

6. El tigre es un animal .... está en peligro de extinción.

7. El oso polar es un animal .... piel es blanca como la nieve.

8. El canguro tiene un bolsillo en .... lleva a sus bebés.

9. Los hombres .... llevan uniforme verde te ayudarán si tienes problemas.

10. El animal .... hace más daño a otros animales es el hombre.

 ¡Ya!

3 ¿Qué es?

Tienes que hacer descripciones o definiciones de varios artículos corrientes, y tus compañeros de clase tienen que adivinar de lo que hablas.

You give descriptions or definitions of a number of common articles, using relatives, of course, and your classmates have to guess what you are talking about. Points are scored for correct definitions and answers, but lost if at least one relative pronoun is not used in the definition.

¡Viva la gramática!

Ejemplo:

A.   **Es un artículo con *el que* escribimos, pero *que* se puede borrar con una goma.**

B.   **Es un lápiz.**

4 *En la cocina*

Trabajo en parejas o grupos. Un(a) amigo/a español(a), que habla poco inglés, te visita, y te pregunta acerca de varios platos muy corrientes en Gran Bretaña. Tienes que explicárselos, utilizando unos pronombres relativos.

Pair of group work. A Spanish friend, who speaks little English, is asking you about various common British dishes. You explain them, using relative pronouns where possible.

Ejemplo:

A.   **¿Qué es el 'fish and chips'?**

B.   **Es un plato *que* consiste en pescado y patatas fritas (y *que* se come tradicionalmente envuelto en un periódico).**

También puedes hablar de:

> roast beef   Yorkshire pudding   gravy   jacket potatoes   custard
> Christmas pudding   y otros platos, quizás de tu región

H 5 *En casa*

Escribe unas ocho frases describiendo tu casa o piso. Cada frase debe contener por lo menos **un** pronombre relativo.

Write about eight sentences describing your house or flat. Each sentence should contain at least **one** relative pronoun.

Ejemplo:

La sala de estar, *que* está al lado de la cocina, es bastante cómoda. Es la habitación en *la que* vivimos y vemos la tele . . .

14

ASKING AND EXCLAIMING
interrogatives and exclamations

 **¿Preparados?**

How to ask questions

Written questions in Spanish always have an upside-down question mark at the beginning as well as a normal one at the end. Some questions also begin with an interrogative (a question word), others do not.

1 Simple questions

These are questions usually answered with a 'yes' or 'no'. In written Spanish an upside-down question mark shows that the next sentence is a question, and in spoken Spanish you raise your voice at the end of a question.

¿Es la chica más alta?	Is she the tallest girl?
Sí, es la chica más alta.	Yes, she is the tallest girl.
José, ¿has comprado chicle?	José, have you bought some chewing-gum?
No, no he comprado chicle.	No, I haven't bought any chewing-gum.

2 Questions with an interrogative

These are questions which begin with a question word – an interrogative. Here are the main interrogatives:

¿Cómo?	How?
¿Cuál? ¿Cuáles?	Which one? Which ones?
¿Cuándo?	When?
¿Cuánto/a/os/as?	How much?/How many?
¿Dónde?	Where?
¿De dónde?/¿Adónde?	Where from?/Where to?
¿Quién? ¿Quiénes?	Who?
¿Qué?	What?
¿Por qué?	Why?

¡Viva la gramática!

Some examples:

¿Cómo se puede salir?	How can we get out?
¿Cuál de los dos prefieres?	Which of the two do you prefer?
¿Cuándo tienes que estar allí?	When do you have to arrive?
¿Cuántas quieres?	How many do you want?
¿Dónde están tus amigos?	Where are your friends?
¿Quién es ese hombre?	Who is that man?
¿Qué quieres?	What do you want?
¿Por qué no hablas?	Why don't you speak?

Note that:

■ all have a written accent.

■ *¿cuál?, ¿quién?* can be singular or plural to match the word they go with, and *¿cuántos?* can be masculine or feminine as well as singular or plural.

■ *¿quién?, ¿qué?* and some others can have prepositions like *a, de, para* in front of them.

■ *¿quién?* can mean 'who' or 'whom'.

3 Exclamations

Some of the above interrogatives can be used in exclamations:

¡Qué . . . !	What a . . . !
¡Qué lástima!	What a pity!
¡Cuánto/a/os/as . . . !	What a lot of . . . !
¡Cuánto dinero!	What a lot of money!
¡Cómo . . . !	Isn't it ....ing! / Doesn't he/she . . . !, etc.
¡Cómo llueve!	Isn't it raining!

■ Note the upside-down exclamation mark which goes at the beginning.

 ## ¿Listos?

1 *¿Cuál?*
Cada frase necesita una interrogación o exclamación, pero ¿cuál?
Each sentence needs an interrogative or exclamation, but which?

1. Llaman a la puerta; ¿............... es?

2. ¡.............. canta esta chica!

3. ¿.............. quieres, éstos o aquéllos?

4. ¿De .... eres?

5. ¿.............. haces esto?

6. ¿.............. llega mamá?

7. ¡.............. bien!

8. Madre mía, ¿............... es esto?

9. ¿.............. se abre esta lata?

10. ¡.............. gente hay en la calle!

H 2 *Inventa*

Inventa una frase nueva para usar cada interrogación.
Invent a new sentence to use each interrogative.

 ¡Ya!

3 *Interrogaciones*

Imagina que eres periodista o detective: tienes que interrogar a un(a) compañero/a usando una por una cada interrogación de la lista de la sección 2.

Imagine you are a reporter or a detective: you have to interrogate a classmate using one by one each interrogative in the list in Section 2.

Ejemplo:
A.   **Bueno, ¿qué hacías a las ocho?**
B.   **Estaba viendo la televisión.**
A.   **¿Dónde?**
B.   **En el salón.**
A.   **¿Con quién?**
B.   **Con mi amigo.**

4 *Reacciones*

Entre los amigos, os contáis cosas para provocar reacciones . . . contestad usando exclamaciones.

¡Viva la gramática!

Among your friends, tell each other things to provoke reactions ... answer using exclamations.

Ejemplo:
A.   Ayer compré este sombrero nuevo.
B.   ¡Qué bien!
C.   ¡Qué sombrero más bonito!
A.   Mi madre bailó en la cocina.
B.   ¡Cómo baila!

15

'NO!', 'NEVER!', 'NOBODY!'
negatives

 **¿Preparados?**

What is a negative?
The basic negative word is 'not', or *no* in Spanish. You use it to say you **don't** do something; it also means 'no', of course. Other negative words are 'never', 'no-one'/'nobody', 'nothing', 'nowhere', 'not . . . any', 'none', 'neither'. In both English and Spanish, many of them begin with the letter *n*.

a Making verbs negative
To say you **don't**, **didn't**, **won't** do something, simply put *no* before the verb:

Fuimos.	*No fuimos.*
We went.	We **didn't go**.
Voy a verle.	*No voy a verle.*
I'm going to see him.	I'm **not** going to see him.
Hablamos francés.	*No hablamos francés.*
We speak French.	We **don't** speak French.

b Other negative words
The most common negative words are:

nada	nothing, not . . . anything
nadie	nobody, no-one, not . . . anybody/anyone
nunca	never, not . . . ever
jamás	never, not . . . ever
ninguno	none, not any
en ninguna parte	nowhere, not . . . anywhere
ni . . . ni . . .	neither . . . nor . . .
tampoco	neither, not . . . either

¡Viva la gramática!

c Using other negative words with a verb

 **¡Ojo!**

When you use these negative words with a verb, you must put *no* before the verb **if the negative word comes after it**. If it comes **before**, you **don't**. Most of these negatives are easy to use:

*¿Qué haces? No hago **nada**.*	What are you doing? I'm **not** doing **anything**.
*¿Con quién hablas? No hablo con **nadie**.*	Who are you talking to? I'm **not** talking to **anybody**.
*¿Quién sabe la respuesta? **Nadie** la sabe.*	Who knows the answer? **Nobody** knows it.
* **Nunca** como carne. No como **nunca** carne.*	I **never** eat meat.
***Ni** mi madre **ni** mi hermana comen carne.*	**Neither** my mother **nor** my sister eats meat.
*No bebemos **ni** café **ni** té.*	We drink **neither** coffee **nor** tea.

 **¡Ojo!**

It's worth watching the following points:

■ *Tampoco* is the negative of *también*:

*Yo como carne **también**.*	I eat meat **too**.
*Yo **no** como carne **tampoco**.*	I **don't** eat meat **either**.

■ Be careful with *ninguno* (the negative of *alguno* 'some/any'), as it needs to agree with the noun it refers to:

*¿Tienes alguna idea? No, **no** tengo **ninguna** idea*
Have you any idea? No, I have **no** idea/I **don't** have **any** idea.

It drops the *-o* and takes an accent before a masculine singular noun:

*No hay **ningún** problema.*	There's **no** problem/There **isn't any** problem.

■ You use *en ninguna parte* for location, *a ninguna parte* where there is motion towards 'nowhere':

*No encuentro mis gafas **<u>en</u> ninguna parte**.*	I **can't** find my glasses **anywhere**.
*Hoy **no** vamos **<u>a</u> ninguna parte**.*	We're **not** going **anywhere** today.

d Using negatives without a verb

All these negatives can be used by themselves, without *no*:

¿Has ido alguna vez a Méjico? No, **nunca**.	Have you ever been to Mexico? No, never!
Yo **tampoco**.	Nor me either./Neither have I.
¿Quién sabe? **Nadie**.	Who knows? Nobody.

e *Ya no*

This means 'not any more/no more/no longer':

Ya no *como carne de vaca.*	I **no longer** eat beef.
Martín **ya no** *viene a este colegio.*	Martin **no longer** comes to this school.

 ## ¿Listos?

1 *¡Soy inocente!*

En el colegio acusan a Tomás de haber robado un monedero a una compañera de clase y su profesor/a le hace algunas preguntas. Claro que él contesta a todas con negativas. Escoge las respuestas de la columna B.

At school Tomás is accused of stealing a purse from a classmate and his teacher is interrogating him. He replies with negatives, of course. Match words from column B to the questions.

A	B
1. ¿Qué hacías en el aula durante el recreo?	a. Ni él ni ella
2. ¿Quién estaba contigo?	b. A ninguna parte
3. ¿Jorge y Miriam te ayudaban?	c. Nada
4. ¿Y Esteban?	d. Ninguno
5. ¿Adónde ibas?	e. Nadie
6. ¿Has robado algo antes?	f. Él tampoco
7. ¿Tienes algún problema en casa?	g. Nunca

2 *¡Y también soy perfecto!*

Tomás está herido por estas acusaciones, y escribe una pequeña carta a sus profesores. Rellena los espacios en blanco con una palabra escogida del recuadro.

¡Viva la gramática!

Tomás is hurt by these accusations, and writes a short letter to his teachers. Fill the gaps with words chosen from the box.

> Queridos profesores:
>
> Soy un alumno perfecto. __(1)__ llego tarde al colegio y durante la clase no charlo con __(2)__. No soy __(3)__ problema para mi colegio. __(4)__ soy problema para mis padres. __(5)__ mi padre __(6)__ mi madre se quejan de mí. Y todas las noches hago mis deberes y no voy __(7)__ con mis amigos. ¡Y __(8)__ robo __(9)__ a __(10)__! Después de este incidente ¡__(11)__ me gusta este colegio!
>
> Cordialmente,
>
> Tomás.

a ninguna parte	nadie	nada	ni	nadie	ni	ningún
	nunca	ya no	nunca	tampoco		

 ¡Ya!

3 ¡Nunca!

a. Haz una lista de las cosas que *nunca* haces (puedes añadir la razón si quieres).
Make a list of things you *never* do (you can give a reason if you like).

Ejemplo:
Nunca bebo café (porque no me gusta).

b. Ahora di quién *no* lo hace *tampoco*.
Now say who *doesn't* do it either.

Ejemplo:
Mi hermana no bebe café tampoco (porque no le gusta tampoco).

c. Ahora di lo que *ya no* haces.
Now say what you *no longer* do.

Ejemplo:
Ya no juego con mis muñeca.

d. Ahora haz una lista de las cosas que *nadie* entre tu familia y tus amigos hace.
Now make a list of the things *nobody* amongst your family and friends does.

Ejemplos:
Nadie fuma.
Nadie come paella.

e. Haz lo mismo diciendo *ninguno de mis amigos / ninguna de mis amigas.*
Now list some of the things that *none of your friends* do. (You can also include brothers, sisters, etc.)

Ejemplos:
Ninguna de mis amigas fuma.
Ninguno de mis hermanos tiene coche.

H *4 ¡Qué negativo eres!*

Trabajando en grupos o en clase, uno tiene que escoger como respuesta *nada*, *nadie*, *nunca*, *jamás*, *a/en ninguna parte* y los otros tienen que sugerir preguntas.

Working in groups or as a class, one pupil chooses *nada*, *nadie*, *nunca*, *jamás*, *a/en ninguna parte*, and the others think up questions to which it could be the answer and then supply the complete answer. The questions could, if desired, be limited to a particular action or subject.

Ejemplos:
A. nadie/lenguas extranjeras
B. ¿Quién habla alemán en esta clase? Nadie (habla alemán).
C. ¿Con quién hablabas en italiano? (No hablaba en italiano con) nadie.
D. ¿Quién tiene un diccionario ruso? Nadie (tiene un diccionario ruso).

A. a/en ninguna parte
B. ¿Adónde fuiste anoche? (No fui) a ninguna parte.
C. ¿Dónde está Antonio? (No está/no le veo) en ninguna parte.

16

'FOR ME', 'WITHOUT YOU'
prepositions

 **¿Preparados?**

What are prepositions?
These are words which tell you the relationship between two nouns or pronouns.
This may be in place (e.g. 'in front of', 'near', 'above'); in time (e.g. 'before', 'after',
'until'); and various other relationships (e.g. 'because of', 'in spite of', 'by means
of').

1 The basic prepositions

a *a*
This preposition basically means 'to':

Mañana vamos a Barcelona.	Tomorrow we're going **to** Barcelona.
Envío una postal a mi tía.	I'm sending a postcard **to** my aunt.

 **¡Ojo!**

'To arrive in' is always *llegar a*:

Llegaremos a Barcelona a las siete.   We'll arrive **in** Barcelona at seven.

You also use *a* to mean 'at a time of day':

Te veré a las ocho.   I'll see you **at** eight.

¡Ojo!

a + el = al

Vamos al cine?   Shall we go to the cinema?

The 'personal' *a* is explained in full in Chapter 18.

b *en*

This preposition means 'in', 'on' or 'at':

Pronto estaremos en Barcelona.	We'll soon be **in** Barcelona.
Ponga las patatas en la cesta, por favor.	Put the potatoes **in** the basket, please.
Y ponga la cesta en la mesa.	And put the basket **on** the table.
¿Encuentras Barcelona en el mapa?	Can you find Barcelona **on** the map?
Jaime está en la escuela.	Jaime is **at** school.

 **¡Ojo!**

Compare:

Voy a casa	I'm going (**to**) home. (motion involved)
Estoy en casa	I'm **at** home. (merely location, no motion)

c *de*

■ This preposition means 'of', and is used to denote possession. Remember there is no *'s* in Spanish (there is more about this in Chapter 6):

He encontrado el bolígrafo de Jaime.	I've found Jaime**'s** pen.
Este es el cuaderno de mi hermana.	This is my sister**'s** exercise book.
Necesito un plano de Barcelona.	I need a plan **of** Barcelona.

■ It is also used in Spanish for such expressions as 'a strawberry ice-cream', 'a football match' and the materials things are made of:

¿Quieres un helado de chocolate?	Do you want a chocolate ice-cream?
¿Viste el partido de tenis en la tele?	Did you see the tennis match on TV?
Mi novio me dio un anillo de oro.	My boyfriend gave me a gold ring.

■ It also means 'from':

Tengo un regalo de mi tío.	I've got a present **from** my uncle.
¿Conoces a mi prima de Sevilla?	Do you know my cousin **from** Seville?

 **¡Ojo!**

de + el = del

El precio del billete.	The price **of the** ticket.
Pili salió del cine.	Pili came out **of the** cinema.

■ *Con* means 'with'

¡Ojo!

Remember the special forms *conmigo* 'with me', *contigo* 'with you', and the reflexive form *consigo* meaning 'with himself/herself/themselves' (see Chapter 11).

*Voy al cine **con** Isabel.*	I'm going to the cinema **with** Isabel.
*Isabel va al cine **conmigo**.*	Isabel is going to the cinema **with me**.

■ For the uses of *para* and *por*, see Chapter 17.

2 Prepositions of place

entre	between, among
sobre	on
encima de	on top of, above
detrás de	behind
delante de	in front of
al lado de	beside, next to
al otro lado de	on the other side of
alrededor de	around
debajo de	under, below
contra	against
desde	from
hasta	as far as
desde ... hasta ...	from ... to ...
dentro de	inside
enfrente de	opposite
junto a	next to
cerca de	near
lejos de	far from, a long way from
a la derecha de	on the right of
a la izquierda de	on the left of
en el centro de	in the centre of
al final de	at the end of

*Vivimos **enfrente del** parque.*	We live **opposite** the park.
*La caja estaba **encima del** armario.*	The box was **on top of** the cupboard.
*El museo está **al otro lado de** la calle, **cerca de** la iglesia.*	The museum is **on the other side of** the street, **near** the church.
*Esta carretera va **desde** Barcelona **hasta** Madrid.*	This road goes **from** Barcelona **to** Madrid.

3 Prepositions of time

Some are also used in a 'space' sense, as you saw in section 2 above.

desde	from
hasta	until
desde ... hasta ...	from ... until ...
después de	after
antes de	before
dentro de	within, inside, in ....'s time
durante	during

*Esta clase dura **desde** las diez **hasta** las once.*	This lesson lasts **from** ten **until** eleven.
***Después de** la clase, hay recreo.*	**After** the lesson there is break.
***Dentro de** dos semanas estaremos en España.*	**In** two weeks' **time** we'll be in Spain.

4 Other prepositions

sin	without
sobre	about, on the subject of
acerca de	on the subject of
a pesar de	in spite of
a causa de	because of

*Nuestra profe nos habla mucho **sobre** España.*	Our teacher talks to us a lot **about** Spain.
***Sin** ella, no sabríamos mucho **acerca de** España.*	**Without** her, we wouldn't know much **about** Spain.

 ¡Consejos!

1. Many prepositions are linked to the next word by *de*. Don't forget that *de = el = del*!

2. *a, de, en, para, sin, antes de, después de* are also used with infinitives. This is explained fully in Chapter 34.

3. *Sin* is usually used without *un/una*:

   *No puedo escribir **sin bolígrafo**.*   I can't write **without a pen**.

¿Listos?

1 El apartamento de vacaciones

Esta es la descripción del apartamento que vas a alquilar en la Costa del Sol en España. El agente te explica, con la ayuda del plano, dónde están las varias habitaciones. Escoge una preposición del recuadro para rellenar los espacios en blanco.

This is a description of the apartment you are going to rent on the Costa del Sol. The agent is explaining to you, with the help of the plan, where the various rooms are. Fill the gap with a preposition from the box.

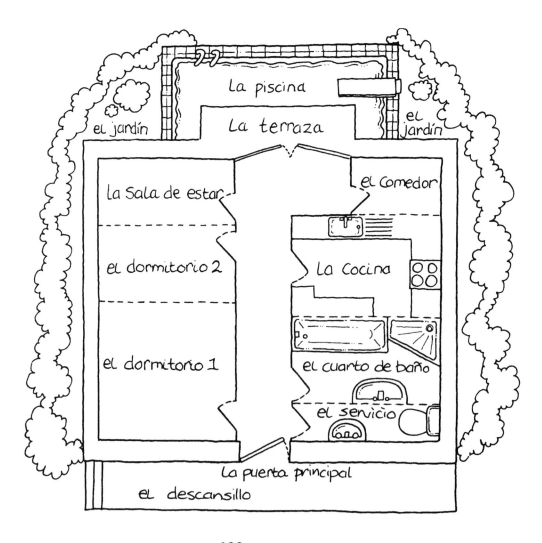

 **¡Ojo!**

de + el = del

1. El apartamento está .... el tercer piso.
2. Hay un descansillo grande .... la puerta principal.
3. El servicio está .... la puerta principal.
4. El cuarto de baño está .... el servicio.
5. El dormitorio grande está .... el cuarto de baño.
6. Los dos dormitorios están .... el pasillo.
7. La sala de estar está .... el pasillo.
8. El pasillo está .... el apartamento.
9. Hay un jardín .... de los apartamentos.
10. La piscina está .... la terraza.

a la izquierda de	a la derecha de	en el centro de	debajo de	en
alrededor de	enfrente de	al final de	delante de	al lado de

2 *El curso escolar*

Escribes a tu amigo/a español(a), describiendo el curso escolar en Gran Bretaña. Rellena los espacios en blanco con preposiciones escogidas del recuadro. Puedes utilizar las preposiciones más de una vez.

You are describing the British school year to your Spanish friend. Fill the gaps with prepositions chosen from the box. You can use the prepositions more than once.

El curso escolar en Inglaterra y Gales dura ....1...... setiembre ....2...... julio. En Escocia empieza ....3...... agosto y termina ....4...... junio. Nuestros profesores dicen que la mayor parte del trabajo se hace ....5...... el largo trimestre de otoño ....6...... Navidad. El segundo trimestre, ...7...... Navidad y Semana Santa es muy corto, y ....8...... Semana Santa siempre hay exámenes. Estamos ahora ....9...... noviembre, y esto significa que ......10..... seis meses hago mis exámenes de GCSE. ......11..... los exámenes hay las vacaciones de verano, y ......12..... las vacaciones, ...13..... setiembre, espero entrar ......14..... el 'Sixth Form'. Entonces, ...15..... mayo, ¡tengo mucho trabajo!

después de	hasta	desde	antes de	dentro de	en	entre	durante

¡Viva la gramática!

3 Un accidente en la calle
Carmen describe un accidente que vio en la calle esta mañana, pero ha mezclado sus preposiciones. ¿Sabes ponerlas en orden?

Carmen is describing an accident she saw in the street this morning, but she has got her prepositions all mixed up. Can you help her to sort them out?

Esta mañana, *con* la calle había un grupo *sin* personas *debajo de* un accidente. Cuando llegué allí vi que un hombre estaba *lejos de* un coche, y *entre* coche estaba su bicicleta. El conductor del coche, un hombre *al lado del* barba, todavía estaba *de* el coche y las tiendas, hablando *al final de* dos policías. Recientemente se cerró el hospital del barrio y ahora estamos *con* hospital. La ambulancia tuvo que llevar al ciclista al otro hospital, que está bastante *alrededor de* aquí.

 ¡Ya!

4 Mi casa o mi piso
Con la ayuda del ejercicio 1 y de las listas de preposiciones en la sección **¿Preparados?**, describe el plano de tu casa a tu compañero/a de clase, que tiene que dibujarlo según lo que tú le describes.

With the help of exercise 1 and the lists of prepositions in the **¿Preparados?** section, describe the layout of your house or flat to your partner, who has to draw what you describe.

5 Un día típico
Describe oralmente o por escrito un día típico de tu vida, utilizando cada una de las preposiciones que aparecen a continuación por lo menos una vez.

Describe orally or in writing a typical day in your life, using the prepositions listed below at least once each. By all means use other prepositions as well.

Ejemplos:
Siempre como mi desayuno *antes de* las ocho.
***Durante* el recreo . . .**

a	desde	hasta	desde . . . hasta	antes de	después de	durante

H *6 Durante las vacaciones*

Escribe unas 150 palabras, describiendo lo que hiciste durante unas vacaciones recientes, y utilizando por lo menos 10 de las preposiciones de todas las que aparecen en este capítulo.

Write about 150 words, describing what you did during a recent holiday, and using at least 10 of any of the prepositions in this chapter. You can talk about one event, or the holiday in general.

Glosario

el apartamento	apartment
el descansillo	landing
el trimestre	term

17

'PARA' OR 'POR'?

 **¿Preparados?**

Para and *por* are also prepositions, but they deserve a chapter to themselves, since people learning Spanish often seem to get them confused, thinking that they both mean 'for'. This may be due to two possible reasons:

■ *por* looks and sounds rather like 'for'.
■ those who have learnt French first often confuse it with the French word *pour*, which does mean 'for'. In fact, in general terms, *para* = French *pour* and *por* = French *par*!

1 *Para*

Para basically means 'for'. You use it in the following cases:

a 'intended for', 'destined for'

*Esta carta es **para** usted.*	This letter is **for** you.
*Voy a comprar un regalo **para** mi madre.*	I'm going to buy a present **for** my mother.
***Para** mí, una coca-cola.*	**For** me, a coca cola.
*¿A qué hora sales **para** casa?*	What time are you leaving **for** home?
*Me entreno **para** el gran partido.*	I'm training **for** the big match.
*Tengo que terminarlo **para** las siete.*	I have to finish it **for** seven o'clock.

b 'in order to', 'to' + infinitive

*Trabajamos mucho **para** aprobar nuestros exámenes.*	We're working hard (**in order**) **to** pass our exams.
***Para** ir a la estación, tome la segunda calle a la derecha.*	(**In order**) **to** get to the station, take the second street on the right.
***Para** comprar eso, tienes que ir al supermercado.*	(**In order**) **to** buy that, you must go to the supermarket.

¡Consejo!

¿Para qué . . . ? means 'What for . . . ?' and usually needs an answer of *para* + **verb in the infinitive**:

*¿**Para qué** necesitas esa llave?*	What do you need that key for?
*¡**Para entrar** en mi casa!*	**(In order) to get into** my house!

¿Para qué sirve . . . ? Sirve para + **infinitive** means 'What's it used for? It's used to . . .'

*¿**Para qué sirve** esto? **Sirve para hacer** café.*	What's this **used for**? It's **used to make** coffee.

2 *Por*

Por basically means 'by' or 'through', and **only occasionally** means 'for'. You use it in the following cases:

a 'through', 'via', 'along', 'throughout'

*¿Este autobús pasa **por** Ávila?*	Does this bus go **through/via** Avila?
*Mari-Carmen andaba **por** la calle.*	Mari-Carmen was walking **along** the street.
*Este cantante ha viajado **por** toda España.*	This singer has travelled **all over/throughout** Spain.

b 'by', 'by means of'

*La comida fue preparada **por** todos.*	The meal was prepared **by** everybody.
*Le hablé **por** teléfono ayer.*	I spoke to him **by** telephone yesterday.
***Por** avión*	**By** plane, **by** airmail.

c 'through', 'by', 'because of'

*La reconocí **por** su pelo.*	I recognised her **by/because of** her hair.

¡Viva la gramática!

¡Consejo!

In this sense *por* is sometimes used with a verb in the infinitive:

***Por tener** el pelo rubio, era muy fácil reconocerla.*	Through having (= because she had) blond hair, it was very easy to recognise her.

d 'per'

*El coche hacía ciento cincuenta kilómetros **por** hora.*	The car was doing 150 kilometres **per/an** hour.
*Hay dos bocadillos **por** persona.*	There are two sandwiches **per** person.

e 'for' (only in the following cases)

■ 'in exchange for' especially with *pagar* + a sum of money and *gracias*:

***Pagué** dieciocho euros **por** esta falda.*	**I paid** 18 euros **for** this skirt.
***Gracias por** el regalo que me mandaste.*	**Thanks for** the gift you sent me.

■ 'for the sake of', 'on behalf of', 'in favour of':

*Lo hago **por** mi familia.*	I'm doing it **for** (**the sake of**) my family.
*Estoy **por** pasar el día en la playa.*	I'm **for/in favour of** spending the day on the beach.

■ *ir por* ('to go for', 'to go and get'):

*Voy a la carnicería **por** unas chuletas.*	I'm going to the butcher's **for** some chops.

■ referring to spans of time:

*Estaremos en Madrid **por** un mes.*	We will be in Madrid **for** a month.

f in the following (and many other) expressions

por la mañana	in the morning
por la tarde	in the afternoon
por la noche	in the evening, at night
por si acaso	just in case
por favor	please
por aquí	this way, over here
*por allí/**por** ahí*	this way, over there

por todas partes	everywhere
por lo tanto	therefore
por Navidad	at Christmas
por Semana Santa	at Easter
por lo general	generally
por desgracia	unfortunately
por fin	at last, finally
por ahora	for now
por el momento	for the moment
por supuesto	of course
por ejemplo	for example

 ¡Ojo!

para siempre	for ever

 ## ¿Listos?

1 La Navidad en casa

Tu amiga española describe cómo pasa las fiestas de Navidad y Año Nuevo en su casa. Rellena los espacios en blanco con *para* o *por*.

Your Spanish penfriend describes the Christmas and New Year festivities in her house. Fill the blanks with *para* or *por*:

Madrid, el 22 de diciembre

¡Hola Emma!

Gracias .... tu carta y tu christmas. Te escribo ahora ....
describirte qué hacemos .... la Navidad aquí en Madrid.

Durante diciembre compro unas figuras .... el Belén. La
Nochebuena, 24 de diciembre, mi hermana casada y su familia
vienen aquí .... tomar la cena preparada .... mis padres. A
medianoche todos salimos a la iglesia .... oír la misa del
gallo.

El día 25 .... la mañana mi hermano y yo nos levantamos
bastante tarde. Luego .... la tarde damos un paseo .... el parque
Ya he comprado unos regalos .... mi familia, pero .... lo general

---

los españoles no nos damos regalos el día 25 de diciembre.

El día 31 de diciembre se llama la Nochevieja, y..... la noche, a eso de las once, mucha gente sale a la Puerta del Sol en el centro de la ciudad. ¡Hay mucha gente..... las calles! Todos llevamos uvas –¡ doce uvas..... persona! Cuando el gran reloj de la Plaza da las doce, tenemos que comer las uvas: ¡una uva..... cada campanada!

El día de Año Nuevo, primero de enero, iremos a la sierra de Guadarrama a hacer el esquí. Necesitas ser millonario..... esquiar. Tuve que pagar mucho dinero..... mis esquís.

El día cinco de enero..... la noche,..... todas partes de España los niños ponen sus zapatos en el balcón. Los tres Reyes Magos vienen a traerles regalos. Los niños también dejan unas patatas en el balcón..... los caballos de los Reyes. ¡Uy! ¡Qué horror! He olvidado comprar un regalo..... mi hermano mayor! ¡Me va a matar! ¡Esto es todo..... ahora! ¡Te llamaré..... teléfono el día de Año Nuevo! Un abrazo..... todos.

Emilia.

¡Ya!

2 En El Corte Inglés

Has ido al gran almacén El Corte Inglés en Madrid y has comprado unos regalos para tu familia y tus amigos. Haz una lista de unas ocho cosas que has comprado. Luego tu compañero/a de clase te pregunta lo que pagaste por cada cosa.

You've been to the El Corte Inglés department store in Madrid and bought some presents for your family and friends. Make a list of about eight things that you bought. Your partner then asks you what you paid for each item.

Ejemplo:

A.   **¿Cuánto pagaste por el cinturón?**

B   **Pagué doce euros por el cinturón.**

3 Vamos a Cádiz

Haces proyectos para un viaje de vacaciones por España. Empiezas en Irún en el norte, y necesitas llegar por fin a Cádiz en el sur. Cada uno describe su ruta.

You are making plans for a trip around Spain. You start at Irún in the north and need to get to Cádiz in the south. Each pupil describes his/her route.

Ejemplos:

A.   **Para ir a Cádiz, yo voy a pasar por Burgos, Valladolid, Mérida y Sevilla.**

B.   **Para viajar a Cádiz, yo iré por Zaragoza, Madrid, Almería y Jerez.**

¡Viva la gramática!

4 ¿Para qué?

a. Tienes que preguntar a tu compañero/a de clase para qué va a varios sitios, y el/ella tiene que explicar para qué.

You ask your partner what he/she is going to various places for, and he/she has to explain what for.

Ejemplo:

A. **¿Para qué vas al supermercado?**

B. **Para comprar cosas de comer.**

Otros sitios posibles: el cine, la playa, la zapatería, la farmacia, la parada de autobús, el quiosco de periódicos, la heladería.

b. Ahora le señalas algo en el aula y preguntas *¿para qué sirve?*
   Now you point to something in the classroom and ask what it is used for.

Ejemplo:

A. (señalas un bolígrafo) **¿Para qué sirve esto?**

B. **Sirve para escribir.**

Glosario

la campanada	chime
el christmas	Christmas card
la figura	figure
el millonario	millionaire
la misa del Gallo	Midnight Mass
los Reyes Magos	the Three Kings

18

WHEN A PERSON IS THE OBJECT
personal 'a'

 ¿Preparados?

What is the 'personal' *a*?

■ When the direct object of a verb is a definite person or persons, you slip in the preposition *a* before it. There is no English equivalent, so there is nothing printed in bold in the English translations.

*¿Ves **a** aquella chica?*	Do you see that girl over there?
*¿Conoces **a** mi amigo español?*	Do you know my Spanish friend?
*Encontré **a** Elena en la cocina.*	I found Elena in the kitchen.

■ You don't use it with objects or things:

¿Ves aquel avión?	Do you see that aeroplane?
Encontré mis gafas en la cocina.	I found my glasses in the kitchen.

■ But it is often used with pet animals:

*Adoro **a** mi gatito.*	I love my pussy-cat.
*Llevo **al** perro al veterinario.*	I'm taking the dog to the vet.

 **¡Ojo!**

$a + el = al$

¡Viva la gramática!

¿Listos?

1 Mudando de casa

Estás mudando de casa, y hay mucho que hacer. Tu mamá te hace muchas preguntas. Rellena los espacios en blanco con *a* donde sea necesario.

You are moving house, and there is a great deal to do. Your mum is asking you lots of questions. Put an *a* in the gaps only where necessary.

1. ¿Has visto . . . tu padre?

2. ¿Has encontrado . . . mis gafas?

3. ¿Dónde has dejado . . . tu hermanito?

4. ¿Has enviado . . . Jorge a las tiendas?

5. ¿Has visto . . . el cartero?

6. ¿Has ayudado . . . tu hermana a limpiar su dormitorio?

7. ¿Has pagado . . . la vecina por la leche?

8. ¿Has limpiado . . . el cuarto de baño?

9. ¿Has puesto . . . el gato en el comedor?

10. ¿Conoces . . . nuestros nuevos vecinos?

¡Ya!

2 En el globo de cristal

En dos equipos, cada uno imagina que tiene un globo de cristal, y tiene que describir a quien ve. El otro equipo tiene que adivinar quién es.

In two teams, each pupil imagines he/she has a crystal ball, and describes who he/she sees in it. The other team has to guess who it is (it can be a pupil, a teacher, or a well-known personality). Don't forget to say *Veo **a** una mujer / un hombre / una persona*, etc., and in reply *Ves **a** . . .*: you lose a point if you don't!

Ejemplo:
A.   **Veo *a* una mujer que tiene el pelo moreno. Lleva sandalias.**
B.   **¡Ves *a* la señorita Dorcan!**

19

MAKING IT SMALLER
diminutives and other suffixes

 **¿Preparados?**

What is a suffix?

A suffix is an ending that you add to a word to modify its meaning, but usually not to change it completely. In English we use the suffix '-let' to make a diminutive, that is, to make something smaller: pig > piglet, book > booklet.

1 Diminutives

Diminutives are very common in Spanish. The most frequent way of making a diminutive is to add the ending *-ito* (m) / *-ita* (f) to the noun. Note that this sometimes involves an adjustment to the spelling, and that sometimes the ending is *-cito/-cita* or *-ecito/-ecita*:

una casa	a house	*una casita*	a little house, a cottage
un chico	a boy	*un chiquito*	a little boy
un pueblo	a village	*un pueblecito*	a little village, hamlet

Sometimes these diminutives are used as a way of expressing fondness, endearment, or 'pet' names:

la abuela	grandmother	*la abuelita*	grannie
Jaime	James	*Jaimecito*	Jim, Jimmie

Other diminutive endings you might come across are: *-illo/-illa*, *-ico/-ica*, although these sometimes suggest insignificance as well as smallness.

113

2 Augmentatives

These, as their name suggests, have the opposite effect, and make the noun bigger.
The most common one is *-ón/-ona*:

una silla	a chair	*un sillón*	an armchair
una casa	a house	*una casona*	a big house

3 Other suffixes

■ *-udo* added to a part of the body makes it a big one!

¡Cabezudo!	Big-head! (as these are adjectives, a big-headed girl would be *cabezuda*).
orejudo	having big ears (from *la oreja* 'ear')

■ *-azo* added to a noun means 'a blow with':

un balazo	a bullet wound (from *una bala* 'a bullet')
un naranjazo	what someone would receive if you threw an orange at them!

 ¿Listos?

1 ¡Hola, Anita!

¿Cuál será la forma diminutiva de los siguientes nombres españoles muy corrientes?
What would be the diminutive form of the following very common Spanish names?

Chicas		**Chicos**	
Ana	Anita	Pedro	Pedrito
Juana		Pablo	
Paca*		Miguel	
Rosa		Rafael	
Carmen*		Juan	
Mercedes*		Carlos*	

*¡Cuidado con éstos!

2 Unos dibujitos . . .

Mira estos dibujos y escoge una de las palabras del recuadro para describir cada uno.
Look at these drawings and choose a word from the box to describe each one.

barbudo	un pelotazo	Martincito	nariguda	un manotazo	una mesita
		un hombrecillo	peludo		

¡Ya!

3 ¿Cómo te llamas, amiguito?

Si vuestra profe os ha dado nombres españoles, decidid entre vosotros cómo os vais a llamar, empleando diminutivos. Si hay lector(a), él/ella podrá ayudaros.

If your teacher has given you Spanish names, decide amongst yourselves what the diminutive of your name would be. If you have a Spanish assistant, get him/her to help you.

20

TALKING ABOUT NOW
the present tense of regular verbs

 ¿Preparados?

What is the present tense?
A tense consists of the set of verb forms used to describe actions within a particular time-scale. We use the present tense to describe an action which **is happening now**, or which **is true at the moment**:

Pablo come una manzana.	Pablo **is eating** an apple.
Pablo come manzanas a menudo.	Pablo often **eats** apples.

The Spanish present tense is used in both instances, though the form 'he is ....ing' can also be used (see Chapter 33).

1 Formation
The present tense of regular verbs (ones which behave in the same way as all other verbs in their 'family') is formed as follows:

	hablar	to speak	**comer**	to eat	**escribir**	to write
yo	hablo	I speak	como	I eat	escribo	I write
tú	hablas	you speak	comes	you eat	escribes	you write
él/ella	habla	he/she speaks	come	he/she eats	escribe	he/she writes
usted	habla	you speak	come	you eat	escribe	you write
nosotros/as	hablamos	we speak	comemos	we eat	escribimos	we write
vosotros/as	habláis	you speak	coméis	you eat	escribís	you write
ellos/ellas	hablan	they speak	comen	they eat	escriben	they write
ustedes	hablan	you speak	comen	you eat	escriben	you write

(See Chapter 11 for an explanation of the difference between *tú, vosotros/as* and *usted(es)*.)

Note the following points:

■ There are three main 'families' of verbs, each known by its infinitive form, e.g. *hablar*, *comer* and *escribir* (see Chapter 34). Once you know the six forms for one verb in each family, you know them for all, as the members of each family all behave in the same way.

■ In each case, the basic part of the verb form is the infinitive without the *-ar*, *-er* or *-ir*; the relevant ending is added to this 'stem'.

■ Each ending is so clearly different from all the others in both spoken and written form that in Spanish the subject pronoun (person word) is not usually used unless for emphasis or to avoid ambiguity. (See Chapter 11 on pronouns.)

2 Patterns

■ To help you to learn the forms in the above verb tables, it is useful to remember the following points which make up the patterns:

the *-a-* in the endings for *-ar* verbs.
the *-e-* in the endings for *-er* verbs.
the *-e-* and the *-i-* in the endings for *-ir* verbs.

■ The endings for each person are similar with each verb:

the *yo* form always ends in *-o* (except for a very small number of verbs). (See Chapter 21 for the present tense of irregular verbs.)
the *tú* form always ends in *-s*.
the *él/ella/usted* form always ends in a vowel: *-a* or *-e*.
the *nosotros/as* form always ends in *-mos*.
the *vosotros/as* form always ends in *-is*.
the *nosotros/as* and *vosotros/as* forms always have the vowel of the infinitive.
the *ellos/as* form always ends in *-n*.

(Many of these features are also largely true of other tenses and of irregular verbs – see Chapter 21.)

3 Uses

The present tense in Spanish, as explained above, can be used:

■ to describe what is going on at the moment:

Pablo come una manzana.   Pablo is eating an apple.

■ to describe what happens constantly or repeatedly, or something which is true or valid at the moment: a general statement covering 'now' but not limited to 'now':

Pablo come manzanas a menudo.   Pablo often eats apples.

The present tense can also be used for the following:

■ an action about to happen (in the immediate future), as in English:

Mamá llega a las cuatro.   Mum arrives at 4 o'clock.

■ actions in the past being described in a dramatic, vivid way (this is known as the historic present):

Anoche, pues, encuentro a mi amigo en la calle, y me invita al bar ...
Last night, then, I meet my friend in the street and he invites me to go to the bar ...

■ to say how long you have been doing something (English uses a past tense for this as you will see in the examples); this can only be used if the action is still going on at the time of speaking.

Espero desde hace cinco minutos./Hace cinco minutos que espero.
I have been waiting for five minutes (and I am still waiting!)

The same idea can also be expressed by using the structure *llevar* + gerund in the present tense:

Llevo tres horas pintando.   I have been painting for three hours.

¿Listos?

1 *¡Arréglatelas!*
Haz frases enteras emparejando estas frases incompletas, luego ponlas en el orden que te parece más lógico.

Make whole sentences by pairing off these half-sentences, then put them in the order which seems most logical.

1. Los sábados por la noche	compro mis discos.
2. Los sábados por la mañana	subimos al autobús cerca de casa.
3. En una tienda del pueblo	bailamos en la discoteca.
4. El sábado a mediodía	llamo un taxi.
5. Para ir al pueblo	siempre como hamburguesas.
6. Si hay un partido de fútbol	me quedo en la cama hasta las diez.
7. Para volver a casa	compro una entrada.

2 ¡Lleno por favor!

Completa estas frases con la forma correcta del verbo que se ofrece en paréntesis.
Complete these sentences with the correct form of the verb given in brackets.

1. Mi profesor .... español, francés y alemán. (hablar)

2. ¡Pero yo sólo .... un poco de español! (hablar)

3. A mediodía yo .... en el comedor del colegio. (comer)

4. Pero no me .... nada la comida del colegio. (gustar)

5. Con la comida .... agua. (beber)

6. Después, nosotros .... un rato en el patio. (charlar)

7. Esta tarde nosotros .... matemáticas. (estudiar)

8. Luego nosotros .... en la piscina del colegio. (bañarse)

9. Camino de casa, yo .... una coca-cola en el supermercado. (comprar)

10. Al llegar a casa, yo .... algo. (comer)

H 3 Sábado

Escribe una carta a un(a) amigo/a español contando lo que haces los sábados. Si quieres, puedes basarlo en las frases del ejercicio 1.

Write a letter to a Spanish friend telling him/her what you do on Saturdays. If you wish, you can base it on the sentences in exercise 1.

¡Viva la gramática!

¡Ya!

4 En este momento

Usando verbos regulares, describe lo que haces tú y lo que hacen tus amigos y
familiares en este momento. Tu profesor y tus compañeros de clase pueden hacerte
preguntas, si quieres.

Using regular verbs, describe what you are doing and what your friends and family
are doing at the moment. Your teacher and your classmates can ask you questions, if
you wish.

Ejemplo:

A. **¿Qué haces en este momento?**
B. **¡Hablo español, claro!**
C. **Y, ¿qué hace tu madre?**
B. **Pues, trabaja en una oficina de turismo.**

5 ... en general

Esta vez habláis de cosas más generales, o sea de la vida en general. Podéis inventar
y contestar preguntas usando verbos regulares. Puedes apuntar todo lo que dices y
oyes.

This time talk about more general things, about life in general. You can make
things up and answer questions using regular verbs. You can note down all you say
and hear.

Ejemplo:

A. **Oye, ¿qué tomas para el desayuno?**
B. **Como cereales.**
C. **¿Y tu hermana?**
B. **Come pan tostado y un pollo asado.**

H 6 ¡Cuéntamelo!

Describe lo que pasa en los pósteres y carteles que se ven en vuestra aula, si los hay.
Si no, puedes mirar por la ventana y describir lo que ves. Al terminar, haz la misma
descripción por escrito.

Describe what is going on in the posters and pictures in your classroom, if there are
any. If not, you can look out of the window and describe what you can see. When
you finish, put the same description into writing.

Ejemplo:

A.   Se ve a varias personas que toman el sol en una playa en España.

B.   Los chicos del año ocho juegan al fútbol, y las chicas juegan al hockey, pero ¡no juegan muy bien!

Glosario

el rato	while
charlar	to chat
contar	to tell a story
apuntar	to note down
el pan tostado	toast
el pollo asado	roast chicken

21

TALKING ABOUT NOW
the present tense of irregular verbs

 **¿Preparados?**

What are irregular verbs?

Irregular verbs are those which do not behave like or belong to one of the three major verb families described in Chapter 20: in other words, they are unpredictable. As well as the main irregular verbs, this chapter introduces some verbs which have spelling changes, some of which are actually quite predictable – once you know the rules!

1 Minor spelling changes and irregular verbs

Some Spanish verbs have spelling changes in certain forms of the present tense:

■ A couple of verbs have a first-person singular (*yo*) form ending in *-oy*, but are otherwise mostly like regular *-ar* verbs:

> *dar*: *doy, das, da, damos, dais, dan* (to give)
> *estar*: *estoy, estás, está, estamos, estáis, están* (to be) (See Chapter 37.)
> (Note the accents on some forms.)

You will see the *-oy* ending in a couple of completely irregular verbs later in this chapter.

■ A few verbs have a **-g-** in the first person singular, but are regular apart from this:

> *caer*: *caigo, caes* . . . (to fall)
> *hacer*: *hago, haces* . . . (to do/make)
> *poner*: *pongo, pones* . . . (to put)
> *salir*: *salgo, sales* . . . (to go out)
> *traer*: *traigo, traes* . . . (to bring)
> *valer*: *valgo, vales* . . . (to be worth)

■ A few verbs have the spelling change shown above as well as being stem-changing verbs. (See the section on stem-changing verbs.)

decir: *digo, dices, dice, decimos, decís, dicen* (to say)
tener: *tengo, tienes, tiene, tenemos, tenéis, tienen* (to have)
venir: *vengo, vienes, viene, venimos, venís, vienen* (to come)

and another has a -*g*- and is also quite irregular:

oir: *oigo, oyes, oye, oímos, oís, oyen* (to hear)

■ A group of verbs ending in -*ecer*, -*ocer*, and -*ucir* have -*zc*- in the first person singular of the present tense and forms based on it, but are otherwise irregular:

conocer: *conozco, conoces . . .* (to know a person/place)
parecer: *parezco, pareces . . .* (to seem, to look)

■ Verbs with infinitives ending in -*uir* take a -*y*- in all singular forms and the 3rd person plural (they/*ustedes*):

construir: *construyo, construyes, construye, construimos, construís, construyen* (to build)

■ Certain verbs need an accent on a weak -*i*- or -*u*- in all singular and the 3rd person plural forms:

criar: *crío, crías, cría, criamos, criáis, crían* (to breed, bring up)
continuar: *continúo, continúas, continúa, continuamos, continuáis, continúan* (to continue)

■ Other verbs with slight spelling changes:

coger: *cojo, coges, coge, cogemos, cogéis, cogen* (to take)
saber: *sé, sabes, sabe, sabemos, sabéis, saben* (to know)
ver: *veo, ves, ve, vemos, veis, ven* (to see)

■ The following verbs are totally irregular:

ir: ***voy, vas, va, vamos, vais, van*** (to go)
ser: ***soy, eres, es, somos, sois, son*** (to be) (See Chapter 37.)

Note the -*oy* ending for the 1st person singular (*yo*), as for *dar* and *estar*.

■ A special form of the verb *haber* is used to mean 'there is/are':

Hay *mucha gente aquí.*   There are a lot of people here.

2 Stem-changing verbs

These verbs have a rather fancy name, and can also be called 'root-changing' or 'radical-changing' verbs. In fact they simply have a spelling change in their 'root' or 'stem' – the basic bit left when you take the *-ar*, *-er* or *-ir* off the infinitive, in other words the part to which the endings are added. These changes are predictable once you know the rules.

There are several types as follows:

Type 1: (only *-ar* and *-er* verbs)
Here are examples of *-ar* and *-er* verbs of this type, and *jugar*, the only one of its type:

-e- > -ie-	-o- > -ue-	-u- > -ue-
pensar	*volver*	*jugar*
to think	to return	to play
pienso	vuelvo	juego
piensas	vuelves	juegas
piensa	vuelve	juega
pensamos	volvemos	jugamos
pensáis	volvéis	jugáis
piensan	vuelven	juegan

 **¡Ojo!**

Note the following points:

1. Apart from the spelling change in the stem, these verbs are regular in having the same endings as regular verbs. Only the present tense is affected, including the subjunctive and some imperative forms. (See Chapters 40 and 36.)

2. The spelling change consists of a 'stretching' of *-e-* to *-ie-* or *-o-* to *-ue-* (*jugar* has *-u-* to *-ue-*, but this is the only verb with this change).

3. The 'stretching' happens in forms 1, 2, 3, and 6 if you give each a number; they are sometimes called '1-2-3-6' verbs'. What they have in common is that in these forms, the stress (the loudest part of the word when you speak) is on the vowel which stretches. If you take the stress off, it goes back to normal; to remember when this change happens, it might help to think of it as an 'elastic vowel'.

Type 2: (only *-ir* verbs)

-e- > -ie-	-o- > -ue-
preferir to prefer	*dormir* to sleep
prefiero	duermo
prefieres	duermes
prefiere	duerme
preferimos	dormimos
preferís	dormís
prefieren	duermen

- The forms affected are exactly as for Type 1, and for the same reasons, and the endings are quite regular.

- Notice also the gerunds (see Chapter 33): *preferir > prefiriendo*; *dormir > durmiendo*. A similar change happens in two forms of the preterite tense (see Chapter 28).

Type 3: (only *-ir* verbs)

-e > -i	
pedir	to ask for
pido	pedimos
pides	pedís
pide	piden

- Once again, the same forms change and the endings are regular.

- This change also affects the preterite tense (see Chapter 28).

- Look again at **pedir**: if you arrange these stem-changing verbs as we have here, you can also call them 'boot verbs' . . . can you see how this will help you remember which parts 'stretch' and which do not? Look again!

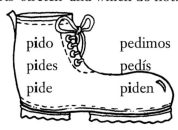

¡Viva la gramática!

N.B. You may spot similar spelling changes affecting words other than verbs if you compare pairs of words with a common base. Here are some examples:

e >< ie: *ventana / viento* – window / wind
o >< ue: *molino / muela* – mill / tooth (the grinders!)
u >< ue: *juguete / juego* – toy / game

The difference is always to do with stress! These changes also explain differences between certain Spanish words and the versions in other languages, such as 'price'>*<precio*, and *vol* (French for 'flight') and *vuelo*.

Common stem-changing verbs

The following is a list of some of the most useful stem-changing verbs. Some dictionaries and wordlists tell you that the verb is stem-changing as follows: *pensar* (*ie*) – *to think*. Note the reflexive verbs (ending in *-se*) – take off the *se* and then work out the form you need.

Type 1 – o > ue   u > ue   e > ie

acordarse	to remember	*jugar*	to play
acostarse	to go to bed	*llover*	to rain
almorzar	to have lunch	*mostrar*	to show
aprobar	to approve, pass (exam)	*mover*	to move
cerrar	to close	*nevar*	to snow
comenzar	to begin	*pensar*	to think
contar	to tell (a story)	*perder*	to lose
costar	to cost	*poder*	to be able to
despertarse	to wake up	*recordar*	to remember
empezar	to begin	*sentarse*	to sit down
encontrar	to find	*soñar*	to dream
entender	to understand	*volar*	to fly
fregar	to scrub, wash (dishes)	*volver*	to return

Type 2 e > ie, i   o > ue, u

divertirse	to enjoy oneself	*preferir*	to prefer
dormir	to sleep	*sentir*	to feel
morir	to die		

Type 3 e > i			
despedirse	to say goodbye	*repetir*	to repeat
freír	to fry	*seguir*	to follow
pedir	to ask for	*sonreír*	to smile
reírse	to laugh	*vestirse*	to dress

 ¿Listos?

1 *Conexiones*

Busca los verbos relacionados con las palabras de la lista A, luego busca otras palabras relacionadas con los verbos de la lista B.

Look for verbs related to the words in list A, then look for words related to the verbs in list B.

A

juguete dicho conocimiento lluvioso vuelta pensamiento poderoso dormitorio cuenta recuerdo

B

volar soñar freír mover nevar despertarse encontrar comenzar salir jugar

2 *Empastes*

Rellena los espacios en blanco con la forma que mejor convenga del verbo que se ofrece en paréntesis . . . y que sea correcta, ¡naturalmente! Algunos son regulares, otros irregulares.

Fill in the blank spaces with the most appropriate form of the verb given in brackets . . . and make it correct, of course! Some are regular, others are irregular.

Hoy ......1...... (ser) domingo: no ......2...... (haber) clases, y no ......3...... (tener) trabajo. ......4...... (hacer) buen tiempo. ¿Por qué no ......5...... (ir) a la playa, tú y yo? Bueno, si tú ......6...... (preparar) los bocadillos, yo ......7...... (sacar) las bicicletas del

¡Viva la gramática!

garaje. Luego ....8....... (comprar) coca-cola en el supermercado camino de la playa. Si ....9....... (querer), ...10..... (poder) comprar helados en la playa. ......11..... (poder) ponernos el traje de baño, y si ......12..... (tener) calor y ......13..... (hacer) sol, nos ......14..... (bañar) en seguida. Mi madre ......15..... (decir) que hoy ......16..... (preparar) la cena para las seis porque esta tarde ......17..... (ir) al cine con mi padre: los dos ......18..... (querer) ver la nueva película de Antonio Banderas. Se ......19..... (llamar) 'Pasos lentos', y se ......20..... (tratar) de un hombre que sólo ......21..... (tener) una pierna. Pues, esta tarde nos ......22..... (quedar) en casa a ver la televisión, ¿vale?

H 3 Londres: ¡capital!

Pon un verbo en la forma correcta en cada espacio, escogiendo entre los que se ofrecen abajo ... pero cuidado, ¡sobran verbos! Otra vez, no todos son irregulares ...

Put a verb in the correct form into each space, choosing from those given below ... but be careful as there are more than you need. Again, not all are irregular ...

Londres ya no ....1....... la ciudad más grande del mundo, pero todavía se ....2....... considerar una de las más famosas. En Londres ....3....... algunos de los monumentos más conocidos del mundo, y ....4....... muchas actividades y diversiones. En Londres se ....5....... las Casas del Parlamento, y se ....6....... visitar el Palacio de Buckingham. Si ....7....... ver un espectáculo, sólo ....8....... que escoger entre los muchos que se ....9....... todos los días. Si ......10..... a Inglaterra en viaje de negocios, ¿por qué no ....11..... un par de días en la capital?

poder	encontrar	estar	tener	comer	hacer	presentar	hacer	poner
	querer	pasar	ir	ofrecer	poder	ser		

¡Ya!

4 Adivinanzas

Inventa explicaciones de lo que haces, usando el presente de un verbo irregular. Puedes hacer este ejercicio por escrito o hablando con tus compañeros.

Invent explanations of what you do, using the present of an irregular verb. You can do this exercise in written form or talking to your classmates.

Ejemplo:

A.   **¿Por qué vas a esta academia?**
B.   **¡Porque mis compañeros van allí!**

1. ¿Por qué vas al restaurante?

2. ¿Por qué vas a la estación en moto?

3. ¿Qué haces cuando tienes frío?

4. Tienes sueño: ¿qué haces?

5. ¿Qué haces si tienes prisa para llegar al aeropuerto?

6. ¿Por qué vas todos los días al campo de fútbol?

7. ¿Por qué vas a ver al médico?

8. ¿Por qué quieres hablar con esa chica?

9. ¿Por qué buscas un diccionario?

10. ¿Cuál de estos dos libros prefieres?

Al terminar puedes/podéis inventar otras preguntas y respuestas.

5 *¿Qué hacemos esta tarde?*

¿Queréis salir esta tarde? Usando el presente para describir actividades en el futuro, hablad de lo que queréis hacer esta tarde. Tratad de usar verbos irregulares.

Do you want to go out this evening? Using the present tense to describe future activities, talk about what you want to do this evening. Try to use irregular verbs.

Ejemplo:

A.   **Esta tarde vamos al café después de las clases, ¿no?**
B.   **Sí, y luego escuchamos discos en casa de Juanita, ¿vale?**
C.   **Si quieres, traigo mis discos compactos también.**

H 6 *Inventa un folleto de información turística*

Escribe el texto de un folleto de información turística sobre tu pueblo o ciudad. Describe también las actividades posibles en la región. Trata de usar verbos irregulares.

Write the text of a tourist information leaflet about your town or city. You should also describe the activities available in the region. Try to use irregular verbs.

¡Viva la gramática!

Ejemplo:

Este pueblo tiene una piscina y un estadio moderno. En la playa cerca de aquí se puede tomar el sol, y mucha gente hace deportes acuáticos.

H 7 *Reacción en cadena*

Describe con tus amigos – en parejas o en grupos – una serie de cosas que haces tú, o que hacen tus amigos. En cada caso, la primera letra del verbo tiene que ser igual que la última letra de verbo anterior. A cada uno le toca inventar una frase . . .

With your friends – in pairs or groups – describe a series of actions which you or your friends do. In each case the first letter of the verb has to be the same as the last letter of the previous verb. Each of you has to take a turn inventing a sentence . . .

Ejemplo:
A.   Hoy tú va*S* al cole . . .
B.   . . . ¡pero yo *SalgO* con mi novia!
C.   ¿Le *OfreceS* un regalo para su cumpleaños?
D.   No *SÉ* qué comprarle . . .
E.   . . . pero *ES* muy simpática.

¡A ver quién consigue la cadena más larga! Luego repite este ejercicio individualmente por escrito.

Glosario

el empaste	filling
camino de	on the way to
el paso	footstep
lento	slow
tratarse de	to be about
la diversión	entertainment
el viaje de negocios	business trip
el par	pair
la cadena	chain

22

REFLEXIVE VERBS

 **¿Preparados?**

¿Cómo te llamas? ¡Me llamo verbo reflexivo!
A reflexive verb was probably one of the first things you learnt in Spanish, though you probably didn't know it at the time! So, what is a reflexive verb?

All verbs have a subject (the 'doer') and most have an object (the recipient or 'sufferer'); with reflexive verbs, subject and object are the same: the action reflects on the 'doer'. Most reflexive verbs describe actions you do to yourself, and are accompanied in English by a 'self' word, 'myself', 'yourself', 'themselves', etc. (the reflexive pronoun). In Spanish the 'self' word is usually put just in front of the verb as seen with this example – the present tense of *lavarse* – 'to wash oneself' (note that *se* is put on the **end** of the infinitive):

me lavo	I wash myself	*nos lavamos*	we wash ourselves
te lavas	you wash yourself	*os laváis*	you wash yourselves
se lava	he washes himself she washes herself it washes itself you wash yourself (*usted*)	*se lavan*	they wash themselves you wash yourselves (*ustedes*)

So, when you put a reflexive verb into a tense you have to take the *'se'* off the infinitive and put the necessary pronoun in front of the verb.

■ Just because a verb is reflexive does not mean it is irregular: most behave the way you would expect, apart from having the reflexive pronoun. Some, of course, are irregular as well as being reflexive.

¡Viva la gramática!

■ Most reflexive verbs can also be used normally, with a slightly different meaning:

me llamo	I am called (I call myself)
llamo	I call
se levanta	he gets (himself) up
levantó el libro	he lifted the book up

■ Here are some of the most useful reflexive verbs:

acostarse	to go to bed
afeitarse	to shave (oneself)
bañarse	to have a bath, bathe, go swimming
despertarse	to wake up
ducharse	to have a shower
irse	to go away
lavarse	to wash (oneself)
levantarse	to get up
pasearse	to go for a walk
peinarse	to comb one's hair
ponerse	to put on, to start to, to become (+emotion)
quitarse	to take off
vestirse	to get dressed
maquillarse	to put on make-up

■ The reflexive is often used for actions which are not really reflexive:

1. to express 'each other' in actions people do to one another:

   Juan y María, os veis todos los días en clase, ¿no?
   Juan and María, you see each other in class every day, don't you?
   Nos saludamos en la calle.
   We said hello to each other in the street.
   Se estaban mirando a través de la habitación.
   They were looking at each other across the room.

2. in 'impersonal expressions' such as the following (see also Chapter 39):

No se habla español en Brasil.	Spanish is not spoken in Brazil.
Se abrió la ventana de la cocina.	The kitchen window opened.

3. where you do something to yourself, when English does not use reflexive but uses a possessive word:

¡Me pongo esta camisa porque voy a una fiesta!
I'm putting this shirt on because I am going to a party.
Se limpió los dientes antes de acostarse.
She cleaned her teeth before going to bed.
¡Si te caes otra vez, te vas a romper una pierna!
If you fall over again, you're going to break your leg!

4. in set expressions such as *irse* – to go away; *caerse* – to fall

   ¡No te vayas!   Don't go (away).

   Some of these have a slightly different meaning compared to the normal meaning of the verb, so it is worth checking them in the dictionary.

5. to express the idea of 'to become' – it just happens that all of the ways of saying this are reflexive! The main ones are:

   volverse, used for unintentional changes:

   Cuando murió su padre, se volvió loco.   When his father died he went mad.

   ponerse, used for temporary change in people, followed by an adjective:

   Si comes demasiado te pondrás gordo.   If you eat too much you'll get fat.
   Cuando llegó Carmen, se puso más   When Carmen arrived, he became
   contento.   happier.

   hacerse, used for ambition and future plans, followed by a noun:

   Quiero hacerme médico.   I want to become a doctor.

■ Reflexive pronouns are normally put just in front of the verb, but they can be put on the end of an infinitive or an *-ing* word (*-ando/-iendo*) and they **must** be put on the end of a **positive** command.

   Te vistes en tu dormitorio.   You get dressed in your bedroom.
   Te vas a vestir / Vas a vestirte en tu   You are going to get dressed in your
   dormitorio.   bedroom.
   Te estás vistiendo en tu dormitorio /   You are getting dressed in your
   Estás vistiéndote en tu dormitorio.   bedroom.
   ¡Vístete en tu dormitorio!   Get dressed in your bedroom!

¡Viva la gramática!

¿Listos?

1 Vamos a escoger ...
Escoge la descripción más adecuada para cada actividad.
Choose the description which fits each activity.

| se viste | se bañan | me peino | nos afeitamos | se ducha | nos paseamos |
| se levanta | te acuestas | te pones el jersey | se lava |

2 ¡Reflexiona bien!
He aquí unas frases que describen lo que hacemos mis amigos y yo todos los días ...
pero se han borrado todos los pronombres reflexivos. Rellena cada espacio con el
pronombre correcto.

Here are some sentences which describe what my friends and I do every day ... but
all of the reflexive pronouns have been deleted. Fill each space with the appropriate
pronoun.

1. Todos los días yo .... levanto a las siete
2. pero Pepe .... levanta a las ocho.
3. Yo .... ducho antes de ir al cole
4. pero Pepe no .... ducha nunca.
5. Antes de entrar en clase, ... reunimos delante del colegio.

6. Los chicos .... saludan dándo.............. la mano, y las chicas ....
   besan.
7. Cuando suena el timbre, ... damos prisa para entrar en el aula.
8. .... siento al lado de María o Fernando
9. y Pepe .... sienta al lado de la ventana
10. ¡pero nadie quiere sentar.............. al lado de él!

H *3 ¿Eres criminal?*

Se ha cometido un atraco cerca de tu casa: tienes que explicar a un detective dónde estábais tú y los miembros de tu familia y qué hacíais cuando se cometió el atraco. Haz frases correctas escogiendo entre los ingredientes ofrecidos, y poniendo los verbos y los pronombres reflexivos en la forma más apropiada.

A crime has been committed near your house: you have to explain to a detective where you and the other members of your family were and what you were all doing. Make up correct sentences choosing from the ingredients offered and putting the verbs and reflexive pronouns into the appropriate form.

Yo	afeitarse	en el jardín.
Mi madre	bañarse	en el cuarto de estar.
Mi padre	vestirse	en la cocina.
Mis hermanos	maquillarse	en el cuarto de baño.
Mi hermana	emborracharse	en el dormitorio.
Mis abuelos	pasearse	delante del espejo.
El perro	broncearse	en el patio.

 ¡Ya!

4 Entrevista

Imagina que tienes que entrevistar a un personaje importante o famoso – un(a) compañero/a de clase – acerca de su rutina diaria. Utiliza verbos reflexivos.

Imagine that you have to interview an important or famous person (your partner) about their daily routine. Use reflexive verbs.

Ejemplo:
Tú: **¿Dónde te preparas antes de un rallye?**
Carlos Sainz: Me preparo practicando en las carreteras de los Pirineos.

¡Viva la gramática!

Tú: ¿Dónde te descansas después de un rallye?
Carlos Sainz: ¡Me descanso en la playa!

5 Comparaciones

Hablas con tus compañeros de clase acerca de vuestros hábitos diarios . . . pero utilizando sólo verbos reflexivos.

With your classmates, talk about your daily routine . . . but only using reflexive verbs.

Ejemplo:
A.   Bueno, siempre me despierto a las seis.
B.   Pues no, ¡nunca me despierto antes de las ocho!
C.   Suelo bañarme todos los días.
D.   ¡Pepe no se baña nunca!

6 ¿Qué hago?

Actúa una acción representada por un verbo reflexivo, y pide a tus amigos que traten de adivinar lo que haces.

Mime an action to represent a reflexive verb and ask your friends to guess what you are doing.

Ejemplo:
A.   ¿Qué estoy haciendo?
B.   Te estás limpiando los dientes.
A.   ¡No! ¡Me estoy pintando los labios!

7 ¿Qué están haciendo?

Describe lo que están haciendo varias personas imaginarias: tu compañero/a tiene que dibujar lo que está haciendo. Puedes decirle si tiene razón o no.

Describe what various imaginary people are doing: your classmate has to draw what he/she is doing. You can tell him/her if he/she is right or not.

Ejemplo:
A.   Una chica se está peinando . . .
B.   ¡No, esta chica parece que se está lavando la cabeza!

H 8 Un día típico

Escribe a un(a) amigo/a describiendo tu rutina diaria, pero utilizando sólo verbos reflexivos.

Write to a Spanish friend describing your daily routine, but only using reflexive verbs.

Glosario

pintarse la cara	to put on make-up
pintarse los labios	to put on lipstick
emborracharse	to get drunk
broncearse	to get a sun-tan
el espejo	mirror
adivinar	to guess

23

LIKING, LOVING AND HURTING
'me gusta', 'me duele'

 ¿Preparados?

 **¡Ojo!**

Pay special attention to these verbs, as they work in a different way from most.

1 Liking things – the verb *gustar*

■ When you say you like something, it is the **thing(s) you like** that tell(s) you what ending to use:

¿Te gusta este cinturón?	Do you like this belt?
No me gusta la paella.	I don't like paella.
¿A tu hermana le gustan estos vaqueros?	Does your sister like these jeans?
Me gustan mucho las películas españolas.	I like Spanish films very much.

■ Have you spotted that the verb ending is the 3rd person singular (= it) or plural (= they)? This is because you are actually using the verb 'back to front', saying that these things **please** the person who likes them. So if you like something **singular**, use *gusta*, and if you like something **plural**, use *gustan*, with the indirect object pronoun of the person who likes. Here is the whole present tense set out so that you can see how it works:

Me gusta(n)	**I** like
Te gusta(n)	**you** (familiar singular) like
Le gusta(n)	**he/she** likes
A usted le gusta(n)	**you** (formal singular) like
Nos gusta(n)	**we** like
Os gusta(n)	**you** (familiar plural) like
Les gusta(n)	**they** like
A ustedes les gusta(n)	**you** (formal plural) like

 **¡Ojo!**

1. Watch how it is done when the 'person who likes' is a noun, e.g. if you want to say 'John likes . . .', 'the children don't like . . .':

   A Juan le gustan las manzanas.   **John** likes apples.
   A los niños no les gusta el colegio.   **The children** don't like school.

2. You **never** say *yo gusto* for 'I like', so don't try!

Other tenses of *gustar*

■ You will meet and use *me gustaría* 'I would like' a great deal. This is the conditional of *gustar*:

    ¿Qué te gustaría hacer?   What **would you like** to do?
    Me gustaría un café.   **I'd like** a coffee.

■ You will also come across it in the preterite, where the two forms are *gustó* if you liked something singular and *gustaron* for something plural:

    ¿Te gustó la película?   **Did you like** the film?
    No me gustaron los actores.   **I didn't like** the actors.

■ and in the future and imperfect:

    No sé si te gustarán.   I don't know if **you'll like them**.
    A mi papá le gustaba jugar al fútbol.   **My dad used to like** to play football.

2 Loving things: *encantar*

This verb works in the same way as *gustar*, but its meaning is stronger:

    Me encantan las fresas.   I love strawberries.
    A mi hermano le encanta el tenis.   My brother loves tennis.
    A mi madre la encantó tu regalo.   My mother loved your present.

3 How much do you like it?

    ¿Te gusta la tortilla española?   Do you like Spanish omelette?
    Sí, me encanta.   Yes, I love it.
    Sí, me gusta mucho.   Yes, I like it very much.
    Sí, me gusta bastante.   Yes, I quite like it.
    No, no me gusta.   No, I don't like it.
    No, no me gusta nada.   No, I don't like it at all.

¡Viva la gramática!

4 Liking doing things

To say what you like or love doing, use *gustar/encantar* (always in the singular) with the infinitive:

*No nos gusta **esperar**.*　　　　　　　　We don't like **waiting**.
*A Raquel le encanta **ver el tenis** en la tele.*　Rachel loves **watching tennis** on TV.

5 'It hurts': aches and pains

Another verb that behaves in this way is *doler*, 'to hurt' or 'to ache'. The most common way to say 'I've got a headache' in Spanish is *me duele la cabeza*. If what hurts is plural, you use *duelen*. Here are some examples.

*¿Dónde **te duele**?*　　　　　　Where **does it hurt**?
*Me **duele** el estómago.*　　　　I've got stomach **ache**./My stomach **hurts**.

*A Pedro le **duelen** las muelas.*　Pedro has tooth**ache**./**Pedro's** teeth **ache**.

 ¿Listos?

1 ¿Qué te gusta?

Estás de intercambio en una familia española. Tu amigo/a te pregunta qué cosas te gustan y no te gustan. Contesta a estas preguntas según la cara.

You are on an exchange staying with a Spanish family. Answer these questions according to the face.

1. **¿Te gusta la paella? Sí, me gusta.**

   ¿Te gusta la paella? No, no me gusta.

2. ¿Te gustan mis amigos y amigas?

3. ¿Te gusta ver la tele?

4. ¿Te gusta jugar al tenis?

5. ¿Te gustan las gambas?

6. ¿Te gusta ir al cine?

7. ¿Te gusta bailar?

140

8. ¿Te gusta nuestro piso?

9. ¿Te gusta ir de compras?

10. ¿Te gusta ir en bicicleta?

2 Tú, el dentista y los caramelos
Escoge la forma correcta del verbo.
Choose the correct form of the verb.

1. Voy al dentista cuando me **duele / duelen** las muelas.

2. No me **gusta / gustan** el dolor de muelas.

3. No me **gusta / gustan** los dentistas.

4. No me **gusta / gustan** ir al dentista.

5. Me **duele / duelen** a menudo las muelas . . .

6. porque me **encanta / encantan** los caramelos.

7. Cuando como muchos caramelos me **duele / duelen** también el estómago.

8. A mi madre le **gusta / gustan** comer caramelos también.

9. A mi madre no le **duele / duelen** las muelas porque tiene las muelas postizas.

10. No me **gustaría / gustarían** tener las muelas postizas.

 ¡Ya!

3 ¿Qué te gusta – de verdad?
a. Haz el ejercicio 1 otra vez, con un(a) compañero/a de clase, esta vez diciendo la verdad.

Do exercise 1 again with a partner, this time answering whatever is true in your case.

b. Sigue trabajando, y piensa en más preguntas que puedes hacer a tu compañero/a.

Carry on working and thinking of further like/dislike questions you and your partner can ask each other.

¡Viva la gramática!

4 Preparativos para el intercambio

Vas a recibir a un(a) chico/a español(a) en tu casa en las próximas vacaciones escolares. Le escribes para saber las cosas que le gustan y lo que le gustaría hacer mientras está en tu casa.

You are soon to have a Spanish boy/girl to stay in your house during the school holidays. You write a letter to him/her asking about the things he/she likes and what he/she would like to do while he/she is there.

Ejemplo:

Querido/a . . .

Te escribo para preguntarte qué cosas te gustan y qué te gustaría hacer aquí en Gran Bretaña. ¿Te gusta(n) . . . ? ¿Te gustaría ir a . . . ?

5 Recibí tu carta . . .

Ahora imagina que has recibido una carta muy similar de tu amigo/a español(a) y escribe tu respuesta, diciendo qué cosas te gustan y qué te gustaría hacer durante tu estancia en España.

Now imagine that you have received a very similar letter from your Spanish friend, and write your reply, saying what things you like and what you would like to do during your stay in Spain.

Ejemplo:

Querido/a . . .

Recibí tu carta, y te escribo para contestar a tus preguntas. Me gusta(n) mucho . . . (No) me gustaría ir a . . .

Glosario

muelas postizas	false teeth

24

WHAT WILL HAPPEN?
the future tense

 ¿Preparados?

What is the future?
The future tense hardly needs any introduction: it is, of course, the tense we use to describe something which hasn't yet happened, i.e. what *will* happen.

1 Formation

In Spanish the 'true' or 'real' future tense (often called the Future simple) is the easiest tense to learn, which is good news! Why? Firstly, all verbs use the same endings, and secondly, almost all verbs add these endings to the whole infinitive, unlike what happens in other tenses; for that reason there is always an *-r-* in the future! Here is the future tense of three regular verbs.

hablar	*comer*	*subir*	
hablar**é**	comer**é**	subir**é**	I will speak / eat / go up
hablar**ás**	comer**ás**	subir**ás**	you will speak / eat / go up
hablar**á**	comer**á**	subir**á**	he/she/it/you will speak / eat / go up
hablar**emos**	comer**emos**	subir**emos**	we will speak / eat / go up
hablar**éis**	comer**éis**	subir**éis**	you will speak / eat / go up
hablar**án**	comer**án**	subir**án**	they/you will speak / eat / go up

■ All forms have stressed endings, and all but the 'nosotros' form have an accent.

2 Irregular stems

 **¡Ojo!**

In the future tense, most verbs which are usually irregular behave themselves for once! A few quite useful verbs have slightly irregular stems for the future; here are the most important ones:

¡Viva la gramática!

haber	ha**bré**	I will have*
saber	sa**bré**	I will know
poder	po**dré**	I will be able to
querer	que**rré**	I will want
poner	pon**dré**	I will put†
tener	ten**dré**	I will have†
venir	ven**dré**	I will come†
salir	sal**dré**	I will go out
decir	di**ré**	I will say
hacer	ha**ré**	I will do/make

*This verb is not used to say who owns something, only being used in tenses containing the verb 'to have' (e.g. the Perfect tense – see Chapter 31).

†These verbs all have 'compounds' – verbs based on them – which behave the same (e.g. *tener – mantener > mantendré* = I will maintain).

¡Consejo!

As you can see, verbs with an irregular future tense stem can usefully be grouped as follows: those which lose an *-e-* (*haber*, etc.); those which gain a *-d-* after *-n-* or *-l-* (*poner*, etc.); and those whose stem is quite different from the infinitive.

3 Uses

- The future tense is used for anything in the future, whether it is about to happen or a long way off:

*Al terminar, **iremos** al café.*	When we're finished, **we'll go** to the café.
*Después de cinco años, **seré** médico.*	After five years **I'll be** a doctor.

- It can also be used when you are not sure about something, as in these examples:

*¿Cuántos años tiene? **Tendrá** unos diez años.*	How old is he? **He'll be** about ten.
*¿Dónde estamos en el mapa? **Estaremos** aquí.*	Where are we on the map? **We're about** here.

4 The future immediate

There is another way in which you can talk about things which are **about** to happen: the so-called **future immediate** is expressed in exactly the same way in Spanish as it is in English, using the verb 'to go' (*ir*) followed by *a* and the infinitive form of the main verb:

| *Vamos a llegar muy pronto.* | **We are going to** arrive very soon. |
| *¿Vas a limpiar tu dormitorio, o no?* | **Are you going to** clean your bedroom or not? |

 ## ¿Listos?

1 *Cambio*

Cambia los verbos de la lista A al futuro, y cambia los de la lista B al futuro inmediato.

Change the verbs in list A into the future tense, and change the verbs in list B into the future immediate.

Ejemplos:

A voy a beber > beberé   **B comeremos > vamos a comer**

A voy a empezar	**B** viajaré en tren
vamos a cantar	¿lo comerás?
van a trabajar	hablarán con papá
vais a venir	lo hará mi amigo
vas a salir	buscaremos sitio
va a saber	¿os pondréis las botas?

2 *Sueños*

Conchita Fantasía cuenta lo que hará cuando gane la lotería nacional. ¡Pero se ha equivocado con los verbos! Para corregir cada frase, escoge el verbo correcto de otra frase.

Conchita Fantasía tells what she will do when she wins the lottery. However, she has got the verbs muddled up! To correct each sentence, choose the correct verb from another sentence.

1. Primero, *aprenderé* todas mis deudas.
2. *Abandonaré* de vacaciones a Florida.
3. *Seré* en una casa enorme.
4. *Compraré* a conducir.
5. *Viviré* un coche fenomenal.
6. *Buscaré* a mi novio, Jorge, ¡que es muy feo!
7. *Pagaré* a un novio más guapo.
8. *Iré* muy feliz.

¡Viva la gramática!

H *3 ¡Una rutina aburrida!*

Mirando los dibujos, cuenta en el orden correcto lo que Mariano va a hacer hoy (usando el futuro inmediato), luego lo que hará mañana (usando el futuro).

Looking at the pictures, write what Mariano is going to do today (using the future immediate), then what he will do tomorrow (using the future tense).

Ejemplo:
Hoy, Mariano va a levantarse a las siete.
Mañana, Mariano se levantará a las siete.

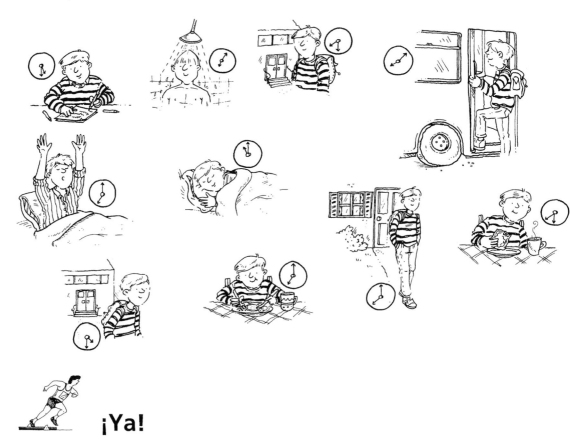

¡Ya!

4 Al recreo

Cada alumno/a tiene que decir lo que va a hacer durante el recreo, y lo que hará esta tarde. Podéis usar el futuro inmediato o el futuro o los dos juntos.

Each member of the class has to say what he/she is going to do at break-time and what he/she will do this evening. You can use the future immediate or the future tense or both.

Ejemplo:
(En el recreo) voy a charlar con mis amigos en el patio.
(Esta tarde) veré mi telenovela favorita.

5 ¡No seas tan entrometido!

Pregunta a tus compañeros/as de clase lo que van a hacer durante el fin de semana, y lo que van a hacer los miembros de su familia.

Ask your classmates what they are going to do during the weekend, and what the members of their family are going to do.

Ejemplo:
A.   **¿Qué vas a hacer este fin de semana?**
B.   **Iré al partido de fútbol, luego iré a visitar a mis amigos.**
A.   **¿Y qué van a hacer tus padres?**
B.   **Como siempre, trabajarán en el jardín.**

H 6 ¿Ambiciones o sueños?

Habla con tus amigos sobre lo que haréis para conseguir el trabajo de vuestros sueños o ambiciones.

Talk to your friends about what you will do to get the job of your dreams or ambitions.

Ejemplo:
A.   **Estudiaré para los exámenes de A Level, luego iré a trabajar en el banco.**
B.   **Voy a salir del cole a los 16 años, y buscaré trabajo como mecánico.**

Glosario

buscar	to look for
el sitio	place, room
equivocarse	to make a mistake
la deuda	debt
charlar	to chat
la telenovela	soap opera
el sueño	dream

25

WHAT WOULD HAPPEN?
the conditional tense

 **¿Preparados?**

What is the conditional?
This tense is used most of the times English uses 'would', and it is so-called because it can also be used to express a condition.

1 Formation
The conditional is formed as a combination of the future and the imperfect: the imperfect -*ía* endings are added to the future tense stem. This is equally true of regular verbs:

hablar	*comer*	*subir*	
hablaría	comería	subiría	I would speak / eat / go up
hablarías	comerías	subirías	you would speak / eat / go up
hablaría	comería	subiría	he/she/it/you would speak / eat / go up
hablaríamos	comeríamos	subiríamos	we would speak / eat / go up
hablaríais	comeríais	subiríais	you would speak / eat / go up
hablarían	comerían	subirían	they / you would speak / eat / go up

. . . and of verbs with irregular stems in the future tense:

haber	habría	I would have
saber	sabría	I would know
poder	podría	I would be able to
querer	querría	I would want

poner	pon**dría**	I would put*
tener	ten**dría**	I would have*
venir	ven**dría**	I would come*
salir	sal**dría**	I would go out
decir	di**ría**	I would say
hacer	ha**ría**	I would do / make

*The 'compound' forms of these verbs behave in the same way (e.g. *poner* – *suponer* > *supondría*, 'I would suppose').

■ Note that although this tense uses the **'-ía'** imperfect endings, it is easy to spot as there is always an **'-r-'** in conditional verb forms: you should never be confused over it!

*com**ía*** (imperfect)	I **used** to eat
*comer**ía*** (conditional)	I **would** eat

2 Uses

You have probably already learnt and used the expression *me gustaría* for 'I would like . . .'. This is an example of the conditional tense – here being used for politeness instead of 'Give me' or 'I want', which are rather abrupt. Some other main uses are as follows:

■ When something depends on a condition (usually after 'if . . .' / *si . . .*):

*Si tuviera mucho dinero, **iría** a España*	If I had lots of money, I **would go** to Spain

Sometimes the actual condition is not expressed, but the conditional is still used:

Sería una idea muy buena.	It would be a very good idea.

■ To talk about the future in the past:

*Ayer me dijo que **estaría** aquí.*	Yesterday she said that she would be here.

¡Viva la gramática!

■ Rather like one of the uses of the future – to express approximations and suppositions – when you are not sure about something:

Entonces, Maruca tendría unos doce años. Then Maruca would have been about 12.

En aquel momento, mamá estaría en el jardín. At that time Mum would have been in the garden.

 **¡Ojo!**

Don't be tempted to use the conditional when English 'would' gives the idea of a repeated action in the past; for this, use the imperfect (see Chapter 26).

Todos los días telefoneaba a su amiga. She would ring her friend every day.

 ¿Listos?

1 Condicionales

Cada una de las frases siguientes contiene un verbo en forma condicional, pero están 'revueltos'. ¿Puedes solucionar los anagramas?

Each of these sentences contains a verb in the conditional, but they are 'scrambled'. Can you 'undo' the anagrams?

1. Desde que tenía once años pensaba que **asíre** divertido tener una moto.

2. Si ganara la lotería, me **procamíra** una moto italiana.

3. Mi amigo Tonio **ferpierarí** una moto japonesa.

4. El otro día mis amigos y yo decidimos que **amísori** a una carrera de motos.

5. Mis amigos dijeron que me **saperíaner** delante del autódromo a las diez.

6. Fue muy espectacular, pero ¡no sabíamos que **rívesamo** un accidente!

7. Momentos antes del accidente, la moto **aravijaí** a unos doscientos por hora.

8. Me gusta ver las carreras de motos, ¡pero no me **staguría** participar!

H 2 *Fantasía*

¿Qué harías si ganaras un millón de libras? He aquí algunas ideas, ¡pero están un poco desordenadas! Pon las palabras en el orden correcto y pon el verbo en la forma del condicional.

What would you do if you won £1 million? Here are some ideas, but they are in a bit of a muddle! Put the words in order and put the verb into the conditional.

1. casa más para padres moderna comprar mis una
2. a mil hermanos cada dar mis libras uno de
3. vacaciones Marbella a familia llevar de a mi
4. me con novio/a el casar mi viene año que
5. pagar bodas magníficas unas
6. amigos familiares y nuestros invitar a todos
7. un hotel banquete de organizar lujo en el
8. luna a secreto un miel para de la ir lugar

H 3 *El excéntrico*

Hablas con un(a) amigo/a acerca de tu padre, que es algo excéntrico. Cambiando al condicional el infinitivo en paréntesis, cuéntale lo que haría tu padre si . . .

You and a friend are talking about your father, who is a bit eccentric. Put the verb in brackets into the conditional, and tell him/her what your father would do if . . .

Ejemplo:
Tu padre, ¿te ayuda con los deberes? No, porque haría errores

1. ¿Se afeita todos los días? No, . . .   (cortarse)
2. ¿Ayuda a tu madre en la cocina? No, . . .   (arruinar la cena)
3. ¿Pone la ropa en la lavadora? No, . . .   (estropear la ropa)
4. ¿Plancha sus pantalones? No, . . .   (quemar los pantalones)
5. ¿Conduce el coche? No, . . .   (tener muchos accidentes)
6. ¿Lleva el perro al parque? No, . . .   (perder el perro)
7. ¿Va de compras a veces? No, . . .   (comprar cosas inútiles)

¡Viva la gramática!

¡Ya!

4 *La invitación irresistible*

Un amigo/a te invita a hacer una serie de cosas. Contesta que te gustaría aceptar. Luego tú le puedes proponer otra cosa.

A friend invites you to do a number of things. Answer that you'd like to accept. Then you can suggest something else.

Ejemplo:

A.   **Oye, ¿te gustaría ir de compras conmigo?**
B.   **Sí, claro que me gustaría. Después, ¿quieres jugar al squash conmigo?**
A.   **De acuerdo; no sé jugar, ¡pero me gustaría mucho!**

5 *¡El novio/la novia de mis sueños!*

Describe a tus compañeros cómo sería tu novio/a ideal, usando el condicional.

Describe to your classmates what your ideal boy/girlfriend would be like, using the conditional.

Ejemplo:

A.   **Mi novio ideal tendría el pelo moreno y llevaría un traje muy elegante.**
B.   **Pues, mi novia ideal sería guapísima, y tendría el pelo rubio.**

6 *Identidad equivocada*

Encuentras por primera vez a un(a) primo/a de Argentina. Los dos estáis un poco sorprendidos. Continuad como en el ejemplo.

You meet an Argentinian cousin for the first time. You are both a bit surprised. Continue as in the example.

Ejemplo:

A.   **¡Creía que tendrías los ojos negros!**
B.   **¡Y yo no sabía que serías tan alto!**

7 ¡Ojalá!

¿Qué pasaría si no tuvieras clase mañana? Imagina lo que harías y no harías, y cuéntaselo a tu amigo/a.

What would happen if you had no lessons tomorrow? Imagine what you would and wouldn't do, and tell your friend.

Ejemplo:

A. **Pues, me levantaría muy tarde, y no me ducharía.**

B. **¡Qué cochino eres! Yo me levantaría temprano, y haría footing en el parque.**

Glosario

la carrera	race
el autódromo	racing circuit
la(a) boda(s)	wedding
de lujo	luxury
la luna de miel	honeymoon
el lugar	place
cortarse	to cut oneself
arruinar	to ruin
la lavadora	washing machine
estropear	to ruin
planchar	to iron
quemar	to burn
conducir	to drive
inútil	useless
el traje	suit
el primo	cousin
sorprendido	surprised
¡ojalá!	if only . . . !
el cochino	pig
temprano	early
el footing	jogging

26

WHAT YOU USED TO DO OR WERE DOING
the imperfect tense

 **¿Preparados?**

What is the imperfect?

This is a past tense, which is used to describe what used to happen or what was going on at some point in the past. It is called 'imperfect' because we are not concerned whether the activity it describes finished or not. If you say 'When I lived in Madrid I used to go to school in the suburbs', we are not interested in when you stopped doing it. 'When you phoned I was having a shower' – we're only concerned with what you were doing at that moment (showering): we're not interested in what happened when you finished! It is worth studying the preterite tense in Chapters 28 and 29 and the contrast between the preterite and the imperfect in Chapter 30.

1 Formation

The imperfect has two sets of endings, one for *-ar* verbs and the other for *-er* and *-ir* verbs. You remove the *-ar*, *-er* or *-ir* to get the stem.

-ar verbs:	*trabajar* (to work)	
yo	trabaj**aba**	I was working / I used to work
tú	trabaj**abas**	you were working / you used to work
él/ella	trabaj**aba**	he/she was working / he/she used to work
usted	trabaj**aba**	you were working / you used to work
nosotros/as	trabaj**ábamos**	we were working / we used to work
vosotros/as	trabaj**abais**	you were working / you used to work
ellos/ellas	trabaj**aban**	they were working / they used to work
ustedes	trabaj**aban**	you were working / you used to work

-er and -ir verbs:	comer (to eat)	vivir (to live)	
yo	comía	vivía	I was eating / I was living I used to eat / I used to live
tú	comías	vivías	you were eating / you were living you used to eat / you used to live
él/ella	comía	vivía	he/she was eating / he/she was living he/she used to eat / he/she used to live
usted	comía	vivía	you were eating / you were living you used to eat / you used to live
nosotros/as	comíamos	vivíamos	we were eating / we were living we used to eat / we used to live
vosotros/as	comíais	vivíais	you were eating / you were living you used to eat / you used to live
ellos/ellas	comían	vivían	they were eating / they were living they used to eat / they used to live
ustedes	comían	vivían	you were eating / you were living you used to eat / you used to live

Only *ser* and *ir* are irregular in the imperfect:

	ser (to be)	
yo	era	I was / I used to be
tú	eras	you were / you used to be
él/ella	era	he/she was / he/she used to be
usted	era	you were / you used to be
nosotros/as	éramos	we were / we used to be
vosotros/as	erais	you were / you used to be
ellos/ellas	eran	they were / they used to be
ustedes	eran	you were / you used to be
	ir (to go)	
yo	iba	I was going / I used to go
tú	ibas	you were going / you used to go
él/ella	iba	he/she was going / he/she used to go
usted	iba	you were going / you used to go
nosotros/as	íbamos	we were going / we used to go
vosotros/as	ibais	you were going / you used to go
ellos/ellas	iban	they were going / they used to go
ustedes	iban	you were going / you used to go

¡Viva la gramática!

Ver (to see) keeps the *-e-* before the ending: *veía, veías*, etc.

 **¡Ojo!**

Remember to write the accent on *-ábamos*, **all the *-ía*-type endings**, and on *éramos* and *íbamos*!

2 Uses

The imperfect has three main uses:

a. To say what **used to happen**, such as habitual or repeated actions:

> *Cuando **íbamos** a la escuela primaria, **salíamos** a las tres de la tarde.*
> When **we went** (= **used to go**) to primary school, **we came out** (= **used to come out**) at 3 p.m.

It is often used together with such time expressions/adverbs as *de vez en cuando* (from time to time), *a menudo* (often), *todos los días* (every day), which help to emphasise the fact that the activity was repeated:

> *A menudo **entrábamos** en la tienda enfrente de la escuela y nos **comprábamos** unos caramelos.*
> Often we **went** into the shop opposite the school and **bought** some sweets.

b. To describe a situation or state of affairs in the past:

> *Anita no **quería** salir con Martín porque no le **gustaba**.*
> Anita **didn't want** to go out with Martin because she **didn't like** him.
> *Según mi abuela la vida **era** más sencilla cuando ella **era** niña hace cincuenta años.*
> According to my grandmother life **was** much simpler when she **was** a girl 50 years ago.

 **¡Ojo!**

The English simple past ('Anita **didn't want**', 'life **was** much simpler') can therefore be the equivalent of the imperfect and not always a 'one-off' event in the preterite.

c To say what **was happening**, what you **were doing** at some time in the past:

> *¿Qué **hacías** cuando te llamé anoche?*
> What **were you doing** when I phoned you last night?

156

¡Tomaba una ducha!
I **was having** a shower!
Veía el fútbol en la tele.
I **was watching** football on TV.

You can also use the imperfect continuous (see page 164) in this way:

*¿Qué **estabas haciendo**? **Estaba tomando** una ducha. **Estaba viendo** el fútbol.*

 # ¿Listos?

1 Cuando estaba en Madrid ...
Escoge la forma correcta del imperfecto.
Choose the correct form of the imperfect.

Cuando estaba en Madrid con mi amiga española, Montse ...

1. De lunes a viernes yo **iban/íbamos/iba** al colegio del barrio con ella.

2. Los sábados ella y yo **acompañaban/acompañaba/acompañábamos** a sus padres a la ciudad.

3. A la hora de comer, todos nosotros **comíamos/comían/comíais** en VIPS.

4. Los domingos generalmente **dábamos/daba/daban** un paseo en el parque del Retiro ...

5. donde **había/habíamos/habían** muchos artistas y músicos ...

6. que **cantaba/cantábamos/cantaban** y **bailabas/bailaban/bailaba**.

7. **Eran/Era/Éramos** muy divertido ...

8. y me **gustaba/gustábamos/gustabais** mucho.

9. Cuando llegó el día de mi vuelta a Inglaterra, ¡yo no **queríamos/querías/quería** volver!

2 Cuando se cortó la electricidad
Ayer se cortó la electricidad. ¿Qué hacía cada persona en aquel momento cuando todo se paró? Escoge la frase que corresponde con cada dibujo.

Yesterday the electricity went off. What was each of these people doing when everything stopped? Choose the phrase which corresponds to each picture.

¡Viva la gramática!

La abuela

Angela

Pedro

Mamá

Papá

Las gemelas

Javier y sus compañeros

Los dos perros

Mercedes

Montse y yo

dormían delante de la estufa	oía música	se afeitaba
veían un partido de fútbol	leíamos una revista	jugaban en el ordenador
cocinaba	pasaba el aspirador	cosía	hacía sus deberes del colegio

3 Cuestionario

Preparas una encuesta sobre cómo era la vida española hace 30 años. Tienes que añadir las terminaciones adecuadas a los verbos.

You are preparing a survey about life in Spain as it was 30 years ago. Add the correct endings to the verb.

a. Primero haces tus preguntas en la calle. ¡Cuidado, porque vas a parar y a preguntar a personas mayores a quienes no conoces, entonces tienes que llamarlas de *usted* o *ustedes*.

First you ask questions in the street. Be careful, as you are going to stop and ask people you don't know, so you must call them *usted* or *ustedes*!

1. ¿Dónde viv.............. usted?

2. ¿Cuántos años ten..............?

3. ¿Cómo er.............. su piso?

4. ¿Ten.............. familia?

5. ¿Usted ib.............. al colegio o trabaj..............?

6. ¿Qué cosas compr.............. en las tiendas?

7. ¿Qué com.............. usted y su familia?

8. ¿Qué periódicos o revistas le..............?

9. ¿Hab.............. televisión en su casa?

b. Ahora, para completar la encuesta, haces las preguntas a la madre o a la abuela de tu corresponsal español(a), que te ha permitido tratarla de *tú*. ¡Las terminaciones son diferentes!

Now, to finish the survey, you are asking your penfriend's grandmother or mother, who has kindly allowed you to call her *tú*. Different endings!

1. ¿Dónde viv..............?

2. ¿Cuántos años ten..............?

3. ¿Cómo er.............. tu piso?

4. ¿Ten.............. familia?

5. ¿Tú ib.............. al colegio o trabaj..............?

6. ¿Qué cosas compr.............. en las tiendas?

7. ¿Qué com.............. tú y tu familia?

8. ¿Qué periódicos o revistas le..............?

9. ¿Hab.............. televisión en tu casa?

4 *Unas impresiones de Inglaterra*
He aquí unas impresiones que Jorge escribió al volver a España después de su intercambio en Inglaterra. Rellena los espacios en blanco con un verbo del recuadro en el imperfecto.

Here are the impressions that Jorge wrote when he went back to Spain after his exchange in Britain. Fill the spaces with one of the verbs in the imperfect from the box.

¡Viva la gramática!

Cuando dejamos el aeropuerto de Madrid __(1)__ muy buen tiempo, pero al volar por encima de Francia las nubes ya __(2)__ a cubrir el cielo, y al aterrizar en Londres __(3)__ a cántaros. ¡El tiempo británico __(4)__ precisamente tal como lo imaginé! Sin embargo, mi amigo inglés y sus padres me __(5)__ en el aeropuerto y me llevaron a casa en su coche. Mientras __(6)__ del aeropuerto hacia la autopista M4, me di cuenta de que __(7)__ por la izquierda y de que la madre de Kevin, mi amigo inglés, que __(8)__ el coche, __(9)__ sentada a la derecha. Kevin y su familia __(10)__ en una calle donde todas las casas __(11)__ en parejas. Me dijo que se __(12)__ «semi-detached» y que __(13)__ muchas casas de este tipo en Inglaterra. A veces Kevin y yo nos __(14)__ con algunos de sus compañeros en la ciudad, pero muchas veces ellos __(15)__ a la casa y __(16)__ o __(17)__ allí. De todas formas nos __(18)__ mucho. Sus amigos __(19)__ unos buenos chavales, y de vez en cuando __(20)__ unos paseos en bici en el campo alrededor de su casa.

charlábamos	conducía	dábamos	divertíamos	empezaban
encontrábamos	era	eran	esperaban	estaba	estaban	había	hacía
íbamos	jugábamos	llamaban	llovía	salíamos	venían	vivían

¡Ya!

5 En mi escuela primaria

Con un(a) compañero/a de clase, haced preguntas unos a otros sobre la vida en su escuela primaria.

With a partner, ask each other questions about life in your primary school.

Ejemplos:

¿Qué asignaturas estudiabas? ¿Qué asignaturas te gustaban más? ¿Quiénes y cómo eran los profesores? ¿A qué hora entrabas y salías? ¿Tomabas el almuerzo en el colegio o volvías a casa? ¿Cómo ibas al colegio? ¿Trabajabas mejor o peor que ahora?

Continuad haciendo más preguntas.

6 *¡A las cinco de la tarde!*

Cada miembro de la clase o del grupo tiene que pensar y decir lo que hacía a las cinco de la tarde el domingo pasado.

Each member of the class or group says what he or she was doing at five o'clock last Sunday afternoon.

Ejemplo:
A.   **Yo daba un paseo en bicicleta.**
B.   **Yo estaba en casa de mi abuela.**
C.   **Yo leía una revista sobre la informática.**

H 7 *Hace cien años*

Imagina que tu ciudad o pueblo está hermanado/a con una ciudad o pueblo en España. De vez en cuando, intercambiáis un boletín de información sobre la ciudad o pueblo. Como sabes escribir el español, te han pedido que escribas una breve descripción (de unas 150 palabras) de cómo era tu ciudad o pueblo hace 100 años.

Imagine that your town or village is twinned with a town or village in Spain. From time to time you exchange an information sheet about the town or village. As you know Spanish, they have asked you to write a brief description (of about 150 words) of what life was like there 100 years ago.

¿Cómo era la gente? ¿Qué hacían, dónde trabajaban? ¿Cómo eran las calles, los edificios?, etc.

Glosario

el chaval	lad, guy
la estufa	fire, stove
imaginarse	to imagine
llover a cántaros	to bucket down with rain
la pareja	pair
el parque del Retiro	large park in the centre of Madrid
VIPS	department store and restaurant in Madrid
la vuelta	return

27

WHAT IS/WAS GOING ON?
continuous tenses

 **¿Preparados?**

What are continuous tenses and what are they used for?
These are the verb forms used when Spanish (and English) wants to describe an
action more vividly, describing what is or was going on (continuing) at the moment.

1 The present continuous

Although the present tense can be used to describe actions which **are happening** at
the moment (see Chapters 20 and 21) you can use the present continuous to give a
much more vivid description: it is often used in a sort of 'eye-witness' situation, to
report what is actually happening at the moment. It is formed by adding the gerund
(see Chapter 33) to the present tense of *estar*. The gerund ends in *-ando* (*-ar* verbs)
or *-iendo* (*-er* and *-ir* verbs).

	hablar	*beber*	*escribir*	
estoy	hablando	bebiendo	escribiendo	I am speaking / drinking / writing
estás	hablando	bebiendo	escribiendo	you are speaking / drinking / writing
está	hablando	bebiendo	escribiendo	he/she/it is speaking / drinking / writing you are speaking / drinking / writing
estamos	hablando	bebiendo	escribiendo	we are speaking / drinking / writing
estáis	hablando	bebiendo	escribiendo	you are speaking / drinking / writing
están	hablando	bebiendo	escribiendo	they are speaking / drinking / writing

In fact, if you think about it, this tense is put together word for word the same as the English present tense form such as in **'he is writing'** = *está escribiendo*!

2 The imperfect continuous

As with the present continuous, although the imperfect is usually enough to describe actions in progress (see Chapter 26) you can use the imperfect continuous to give a more vivid description of what **was happening**. It is formed by adding the gerund (see Chapter 33) to the imperfect tense of *estar*. As with the present continuous, it is used for vivid 'eye-witness' reports.

	hablar	*beber*	*escribir*	
estaba	hablando	bebiendo	escribiendo	I was speaking / drinking / writing
estabas	hablando	bebiendo	escribiendo	you were speaking / drinking / writing
estaba	hablando	bebiendo	escribiendo	he/she/it was speaking / drinking / writing you were speaking / drinking / writing
estábamos	hablando	bebiendo	escribiendo	we were speaking / drinking / writing
estabais	hablando	bebiendo	escribiendo	you were speaking / drinking / writing
estaban	hablando	bebiendo	escribiendo	they/you were speaking / drinking / writing

 ¡Ojo!

For both of these tenses, beware of verbs with irregular gerunds (see Chapter 33).

 ¿Listos?

1 *Conversiones*

Cambia los siguientes verbos A) al presente continuo y B) al imperfecto continuo.

Change the following verbs A) into the present continuous and B) the imperfect continuous.

¡Viva la gramática!

come	hablamos	conducen	dibujas	bebéis
estudio	hacen	miramos	pone	digo

2 Reportaje

He aquí el reportaje de la visita de un personaje importante. Vuelve a escribirlo usando el presente continuo para hacerlo más vivo.

Here is the report on the visit of a celebrity. Re-write it using the present continuous to make it more vivid.

> **Llega** el tren . . . **se para** . . . los pasajeros **bajan** y ¡allí está!* **Sale** de la estación, y allí **espera** un grupo de aficionados. **Se para** y **habla** con ellos. Un chico le **entrega** un cuaderno y le **pide** su autógrafo. Una niña le **regala** un ramo de flores . . . lo **coge** y le **da** un beso. **Sube** a un gran coche negro. **Baja** por la calle y **desaparece**.

[*No hace falta cambiar este verbo.]

3 Descripciones

Describe lo que está pasando en estos dibujos . . . A) en el presente continuo y B) en el imperfecto continuo.

Describe what is happening in the following pictures using . . . A) the present continuous and B) the imperfect continuous.

164

¡Ya!

4 Explicaciones

Trabaja con un(a) amigo/a. Imaginando que sois unos novios que se pelean, uno/a
menciona una situación y pide una explicación. El otro / la otra explica lo que está /
estaba haciendo, usando el presente continuo o el imperfecto continuo.

Work with a friend. Imagining that you are boy and girlfriend having a row, one
mentions a situation and asks for an explanation. The other explains what he/she
is/was doing, using the present continuous or the imperfect continuous.

Ejemplo:
A.   **¿Por qué estás mirando a Maribel?**
B.   **Pues, porque me está sonriendo.**
A.   **¿Por qué estabas en el café anoche con Maribel?**
B.   **Porque estaba tomando un café, y ella estaba trabajando de camarera.**

5 Observaciones

Mira por la ventana. ¿Qué ves? ¿El patio de recreo? ¿Un partido de fútbol? ¿Gente
en la calle? Describe lo que ves, usando el presente continuo. Igualmente, si hay
pósteres en vuestra aula, podrías describir lo que está pasando en uno de los
pósteres.

Look out of the window. What can you see? The school yard? A football match?
People in the street? Describe what you can see using the present continuous.
Alternatively, if there are posters in your classroom, you could describe what is
happening in one of the posters.

Ejemplo:
A.   **Veo a unos chicos que están jugando al fútbol.**
B.   **Y yo, en el póster, veo a gente que está tomando el sol en la playa.**

6 Testimonios

Ha habido un asesinato en el pueblo en que estás pasando las vacaciones. La policía
(el/la profesor(a)) quiere saber dónde estábais y qué hacíais al momento del
asesinato.

There has been a murder in the town in which you are spending your holidays. The
police (your teacher) wants to know where you were and what you were doing at the
time of the murder.

¡Viva la gramática!

Ejemplo:

A. ¿Dónde estaba usted y qué estaba haciendo a las ocho?
B. Estaba en el Café Ideal y estaba tomando un batido de fresa.
C. Y yo estaba en el salón: estaba viendo un programa interesante en la tele.

Glosario

el pasajero	passenger
el aficionado	fan
entregar	to hand over
el cuaderno	exercise book
el autógrafo	autograph
regalar	to give (a present)
el ramo de flores	bunch of flowers
el beso	kiss
desaparecer	disappear
sonreír	to smile
un batido de fresa	strawberry milkshake

28

WHAT HAPPENED?
the preterite tense

 **¿Preparados?**

What is the preterite tense?
The name sounds pretty horrific, but it comes from a Latin expression meaning 'gone before': so, this tense is used for **single**, **completed** one-off actions in the past.

1 Formation

Being a 'simple' tense (consisting of just one word), the preterite of regular verbs consists of a stem – the same as for the present tense (the infinitive minus the *-ar/-er/-ir*) – and a set of endings. Here are the models for regular verbs . . . all you have to do is learn them!

	hablar (to speak)	*comer* (to eat)	*vivir* (to live)	
yo	hablé	comí	viví	I spoke/ate/lived
tú	hablaste	comiste	viviste	you spoke/ate/lived
él/ella/Vd.	habló	comió	vivió	he/she/it/you spoke/ate/lived
nosotros/as	hablamos	comimos	vivimos	we spoke/ate/lived
vosotros/as	hablasteis	comisteis	vivisteis	you spoke/ate/lived
ellos/ellas/Vds.	hablaron	comieron	vivieron	they/you spoke/ate/lived

Some points to note:

■ You will only have to learn one set of endings for *-er* and *-ir* verbs because – as you have already noticed (of course!) – they are both the same.

■ Coincidentally, the *nosotros* (we) form of *-ar* and *-ir* verbs is the same as in the present tense; no problem – there are usually other signs in a sentence to show when the action happened.

¡Viva la gramática!

■ A lot of the usual 'person signs' are here: the *nosotros* (we) form ends in *-mos*, *vosotros* (you familiar plural) ends in *-is*, *ellos* (they) ends in *-n*.

■ The pattern for *-er* and *-ir* verbs is obviously quite close to the one for *-ar* verbs.

■ If you know the rules of stress (see Chapter 43) and can say these patterns aloud, you'll notice that the stress (the loudest part of the word) is **always** the first part of the verb ending; note the accents on **-é/-í** and **-ó/-ió**. (Remember this: it will be useful in the next chapter!)

2 Uses

As you have seen already, this tense is used to describe **single**, **completed** actions in the past. It is useful for talking about what you or someone else **did** on a particular occasion or occasions in the past. Here are some examples:

El autobús **llegó** *a las tres y media.*	The bus arrived at half-past three.
David **bajó** *del autobús.*	David got off the bus.
Volvió *a casa andando.*	He walked home.
Tomó *algo de comer y beber.*	He had something to eat and drink.
Luego **pasó** *una hora jugando al fútbol.*	Then he played football for an hour.
Estudió *desde las seis hasta las ocho.*	He studied from six until eight.

■ As you can see, the preterite describes single events, often a series of them.

■ It is clear that each event happened at a particular moment – in fact the actual time might be given.

■ The action may last for a while, but if we know how long, it is still in the preterite. The last example covers two hours, but it could just as easily be two years or two million – it would still be described in the preterite because the length of time is **defined**!)

There are a few more complications to the preterite tense, though nothing really nasty. We have left them all over to the next chapter: your teacher may feel that this chapter is enough for you anyway. He/she may help you with the few awkward verbs you'll need.

¿Listos?

1 Precisión

Ayer fue un día muy activo para Mariluz. Pero ¿qué hizo precisamente? Escoge el verbo que describe correctamente cada actividad.

Yesterday was a busy day for Mariluz. But what exactly did she do? Choose the verb which describes each activity correctly.

1. se levantó / se despertó / se lavó

2. se bañó / se duchó / se peinó

3. bebió / desayunó / cenó

4. estudió / dibujó / escribió

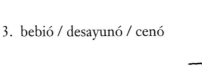

5. bailó / descansó / cantó

¡Viva la gramática!

6. viajó / comió / corrió

7. esperó / trabajó / cocinó

8. tomó el sol / nació / nadó

2 *Conversión*

Los sábados, Paco Ramírez siempre hace las mismas cosas. Aquí nos dice lo que hace los sábados. Imagina que tú eres Paco: ¿qué hiciste el sábado pasado? Usando el pretérito, convierte lo que escribe al pasado, poniendo los verbos en la forma de *yo* o *nosotros*.

On Saturdays, Paco Ramírez always does the same things. Here he tells us what he does every Saturday. Imagine that you are Paco: what did you do last Saturday? Using the preterite, convert what he writes into the past, putting the verbs into the *I* or *we* form.

> Me levanto a las diez, y salgo de casa a las once. Llego a casa de Juan a las diez y media. Vemos la televisión hasta mediodía, luego cogemos nuestras bicicletas para ir al pueblo. Allí tomamos algo de comer en MacDonalds o en la pizzería. Compramos las entradas para ir al partido de fútbol, y entramos en el estadio. Después del partido volvemos a casa. A las siete llamo a Inés . . . nos reunimos a las ocho delante de la discoteca. Bailamos hasta las once, luego la llevo a su casa. Llego a casa a las once y media.

H *3 Un día lluvioso*

Rellena los espacios con el verbo adecuado, poniéndolo en la forma correcta del pretérito.

Fill in the spaces with the appropriate verb, putting it into the preterite.

> El martes pasado, Marta y María ....1...... ir a la playa. Primero,
> ......2...... los trajes de baño y las toallas. Luego ....3...... unos bocadillos.
> Casi ......4...... las gafas de sol: Marta ......5......, y las ......6...... en su
> dormitorio. Por fin ....7...... de casa a las diez: bajando por la calle,
> ......8...... fruta y coca-cola en el supermercado Dani. De repente,
> ......9...... el autobús al final de la calle: las dos chicas ......10...... a correr.
> ......11...... el autobús y, media hora después, ...12...... a la playa. Pero
> cuando Marta y María ......13...... del autobús, ¡......14...... a llover! Las
> chicas ......15...... a casa y ......16...... el resto del día viendo la televisión.

| sacar | llegar | preparar | decidir | salir | comprar | empezar | olvidar |
| bajar | acordarse | buscar | coger | comenzar | volver | pasar |

 ¡Ya!

4 ¡Pero mamá, lo aprendí ayer!
Trabaja con un(a) compañero/a de clase. Es domingo: tu madre / padre te recuerda lo que tienes que hacer para mañana, pero contestas como en el ejemplo.

Work with a classmate. It is Sunday: your mother/father reminds you of what you have to do for tomorrow, but you answer as in the example.

Ejemplo:
Madre: **Oye, tienes que aprender el pretérito.**
Tú: **Sí, mamá, lo aprendí ayer.**

5 ¿Qué hiciste* ayer?
Trabajad en parejas. Tu amigo/a quiere saber qué hiciste ayer y te hace una serie de preguntas. Contéstale como en el ejemplo, luego pregúntale qué hizo* él/ella.

¡Viva la gramática!

Work in pairs. Your friend wants to know what you did yesterday and asks you a series of questions. Answer as in the example, then ask him/her what he/she did.

Ejemplo:

A.   ¿Qué hiciste ayer?
B.   Trabajé todo el día en el supermercado. ¿Y tú?
A.   Pues yo, pasé todo el día viendo vídeos.

Try to use the following verbs: *levantarse, lavarse, desayunar, estudiar, ver la tele, visitar, bañarse, comer, beber, escribir.*

[*For the preterite of *hacer*, see Chapter 30.]

H 6 *Un incidente*

Un(a) alumno/a o el/la profesor(a) representa a un periodista que te entrevista acerca de un incidente o accidente que acabas de ver. Describe lo que ocurrió.

A pupil or the teacher plays the part of a reporter who is interviewing you about an incident or accident you have just seen. Describe what happened.

Ejemplo:

A.   ¿Qué ocurrió exactamente?
B.   El chico abrió la ventana y . . .

Glosario

despertarse	to wake up
peinarse	to comb one's hair
dibujar	to draw
descansar	to rest
cantar	to sing
cocinar	to cook
nacer	to be born
las entradas	tickets (for entry)
de repente	suddenly
olvidar	to forget

29

WHAT HAPPENED?
irregular verbs in the preterite tense

 ¿Preparados?

There are three main groups of verbs which are irregular in the preterite tense, ranging from the very slightly irregular to the very irregular, but they are mostly quite logical and so are not as bad as they sound!

1 Minor spelling changes
A few verbs need spelling changes in the *yo* (I) form just to preserve the normal sound of *c* and *g*, which would otherwise change; here are the most useful:

c > qu:	*buscar* to look for	*busqué, buscaste, buscó, buscamos, buscasteis, buscaron*
also:	*atacar* to attack	*ataqué, atacaste*, etc.
	chocar to crash	*choqué, chocaste*, etc.
	explicar to explain	*expliqué, explicaste*, etc.
	pescar to fish	*pesqué, pescaste*, etc.
	sacar to take out	*saqué, sacaste*, etc.
	tocar to touch, play music	*toqué, tocaste*, etc.

g > gu:	*llegar* to arrive	*llegué, llegaste, llegó, llegamos, llegasteis, llegaron*
also:	*pagar* to pay	*pagué, pagaste*, etc.

The verb *cruzar* changes *z* to *c* in the *yo* (I) form for similar reasons.

z > c:	*cruzar* to cross	*crucé, cruzaste, cruzó, cruzamos, cruzasteis, cruzaron*
also:	*comenzar* to begin	*comencé, comenzaste*, etc.
	empezar to begin	*empecé, empezaste*, etc.

A few verbs change *i* to *y* in the he/she/it, they, *usted* and *ustedes* forms:

i > y:	*leer* to read	*leí, leiste leyó, leímos, leisteis, leyeron*

Other verbs which do this are: *caer, creer, oír* and all verbs ending in *-uir*.

2 Radical-changing verbs

The good news is that most of these behave themselves in the preterite. (Because they only ever change when the stress falls on *e* (>*ie* or >*i*) or *o* (>*ue*), and the stress in the preterite is always on the tense endings, they don't need to change.)

The only ones which are a bit tricky are the radical-changing verbs ending in *-ir*, which have slight changes in the he/she/it, they, *usted* and *ustedes* forms.

Here are some examples:

preferir to prefer	*preferí, preferiste, prefirió, preferimos, preferisteis, prefirieron*
pedir to ask for	*pedí, pediste, pidió, pedimos, pedisteis, pidieron*
dormir to sleep	*dormí, dormiste, durmió, dormimos, dormisteis, durmieron*

3 Pretérito grave

Most 'irregular verbs' fit into this group, whose name simply tells us that the stress in these preterite forms is always on the last-but-one syllable. They all have an irregular stem, but in fact their endings do follow a pattern: see if you can spot where they come from!

First, an example:

	estar (to be)
stem:	**estuv-**
	estuv**e**
	estuv**iste**
	estuv**o**
	estuv**imos**
	estuv**isteis**
	estuv**ieron**

Have you spotted it? You've seen all of the endings before: most are from the preterite of *-er* and *-ir* verbs, and the *-e* and *-o* come from the preterite of *-ar* verbs but with no accent. (That's why this is the *pretérito **grave*** – they don't need an accent as the stress is always on the last but one syllable.)

¡Consejo!

It's a good idea to learn the stems of the other verbs like this, as they are all quite common. Here are the most useful:

	preterite stem	
hacer to do	**hic-**	hic, hiciste, hizo†, hicimos, hicisteis, hicieron
decir to say	**dij-**	dije, dijiste, dijo, dijimos, dijisteis, di**j**eron†
poder to be able	**pud-**	pude, pudiste, etc.
*poner** to put	**pus-**	puse, pusiste, etc.
querer to want	**quis-**	quise, quisiste, etc.

¡Viva la gramática!

	preterite stem	
saber to know	**sup-**	supe, supiste, etc.
tener* to have	**tuv-**	tuve, tuviste, etc.
venir to come	**vin-**	vine, viniste, etc.

 **¡Ojo!**

†Note the special spellings of these forms. The others in this group all follow similar patterns, but it is always worth checking in a verb table if you are not sure.

*The compounds of these verbs behave the same way in the preterite, e.g. *tener > tuve; contener > contuve.*

4 Verbs which are irregular in the preterite

There are just three . . . or is it four?

dar	*ver*	*ir / ser*
to give	to see	to go / to be
di	vi	fui
diste	viste	fuiste
dio	vio	fue
dimos	vimos	fuimos
disteis	visteis	fuisteis
dieron	vieron	fueron

As you can see:

dar – simply behaves like an *-er/-ir* verb, but with no accents; *ver* – isn't really irregular, it just has no accents; but what about *ser* and *ir*? *fui* means 'I was' **and** 'I went'; *fuiste* means 'you were' **and** 'you went', and so on. Yes, they actually **share** their preterite forms! Still, that saves on the amount you need to learn!

5 Uses

Exactly as in Chapter 28

¿Listos?

1 Selección

Elige la forma correcta para traducir los verbos siguientes.
Choose the correct form to translate the following verbs.

1. *dijo* = she said / we said / he says

2. *fuimos* = they went / you were / we went

3. *supisteis* = I know / you knew / he knew

4. *pusieron* = you put / we put / they put

5. *viste* = you saw / she saw / she sees

6. he did = *hizo / hiciste / hicieron*

7. you wanted = *quise / quisisteis / queremos*

8. I paid = *pagó / pagué / pago*

9. she read = *leímos / leyó / leisteis*

10. I began = *empecé / empiezo / empezaron*

2 Producción

Rellena los espacios con la forma adecuada del verbo en paréntesis.

Fill the spaces with the appropriate form of the verb in brackets.

1. Ayer yo .... (ir) al río a pescar.

2. Antes de ir, ... (buscar) mi caña.

3. También .... (tener) que buscar mis botas de goma.

4. Mi hermano menor .... (venir) conmigo.

5. Mis padres me .... (dar) cinco libras.

6. .... (decir) 'adiós' a mis padres.

7. Yo .... (cruzar) la calle, y . . .

8. . . . mi hermano .... (seguir).

9. En el autobús, yo .... (pagar) los billetes.

¡Viva la gramática!

10. Mi hermano y yo .... (estar) media hora en el autobús.

11. Al llegar al río, ¡.............. (ver) un letrero . . .

12. . . . ¡mi hermano .... (leer) 'Prohibido pescar'!

H *3 Invención*

Inventa frases para usar al menos diez de los verbos siguientes.

Invent sentences to use at least ten of the following verbs.

saqué	viste	llegué	fuimos	dio	empecé	leyeron	prefirió
estuve	hiciste	pidió	durmieron	pusisteis	tuviste	vinimos

¡Ya!

4 Quejas

Un(a) amigo/a juega el papel de tu madre / padre que se queja de las cosas que tú tienes que hacer. Contéstale como en el ejemplo.

A friend plays the part of your mother/father, complaining about the things you have to do. Answer as in the example.

Ejemplo:

Madre/padre: Oye, no hiciste los deberes de español.
Tú: **Que sí, mamá/papá. ¡Hice los deberes ayer!**

He aquí unas ideas:

Here are some ideas:

dar de comer al perro/gato　　　　　*pedir el carnet de conducir*
decir adiós a tus tíos　　　　　　　*buscar el balón de tu hermano*
poner tus botas de goma en el garaje　*tocar el piano para la abuelita*
ir a ver al dentista　　　　　　　　*pagar a tu hermana el dinero que le debes*
leer la carta de tu hermano　　　　　*empezar a cortar la hierba*

H *5 Excusas*

Tu novio/a quiere saber por qué no le/la llamaste anoche / el sábado / la semana
pasada, etcétera. Inventa tus excusas, usando el pretérito de los verbos de este
capítulo; también puedes usar la expresión *tener que* como en el ejemplo.

Your boy/girlfriend wants to know why you didn't call him/her last night / on
Saturday / last week, etc. Invent your excuses, using the preterite of the verbs in this
chapter; you can also use the expression *tener que* as in the example.

Ejemplo:
Novio/a: **¿Por qué no me llamaste anoche?**
Tú: **Pues mira, anoche fui a casa de mis tíos. Tuve que ir a la fiesta de
mi prima.**

H *6 Explicaciones*

Un(a) compañero/a, o el/la profesor(a) quiere saber algo de ti y de tu familia.
Cuéntale todo lo que puedas, usando el pretérito de los verbos de este capítulo.
Después, escribe entre 50 y 100 palabras sobre este tema.

A classmate or the teacher wants to know something about you and your family.
Tell him/her all you can, using the preterite of the verbs in this chapter. Then write
between 50 and 100 words on this subject.

Ejemplo:
Profe/compañero: **¿De dónde vino tu familia?**
Tú: **Creo que mis abuelos vinieron de una isla remota. ¡Un día
mi padre me explicó que mis bisabuelos eran piratas! Me
dijeron mis abuelos que mi bisabuelo se llamaba
Barbarroja, y mi madre también lo leyó en un libro que
tiene mi abuela.**

Glosario

la caña de pescar	fishing-rod
las botas de goma	wellington boots
conmigo	with me
el letrero	notice/sign
la queja	complaint
quejarse	to complain
los deberes	homework
ayer	yesterday
dar de comer a	to feed
el carnet de conducir	driving licence
deber	to have to, owe
cortar	to cut
la hierba	grass
la isla	island
remoto	remote
los bisabuelos	great-grandparents
el pirata	pirate

30

WHAT WERE YOU DOING WHEN I SAW YOU?

the preterite and imperfect together

 ¿Preparados?

Which one to use and when? Why worry?

Indeed, why worry? If you have worked through Chapters 26 (the imperfect) and Chapters 28 and 29 (the preterite) you should know these tenses quite well. It is simply because usually only one of these tenses is the right one to use, and it is always best to get things right! So how do you decide?

A reminder

You will remember that:

- The **imperfect** is the past tense used for descriptions, repeated/habitual actions, and 'ongoing' actions.

- The **preterite** is used for single, completed actions in the past, even if they last for a particular period of time.

To sum up: the preterite is used when the **time** or **length of time** is **defined**, and the imperfect is used when the time is **not** defined. That is why a verb in the imperfect often describes the background, or what **was going on when** another action happened, this single action being described in the preterite.

¡Viva la gramática!

These diagrams might help:

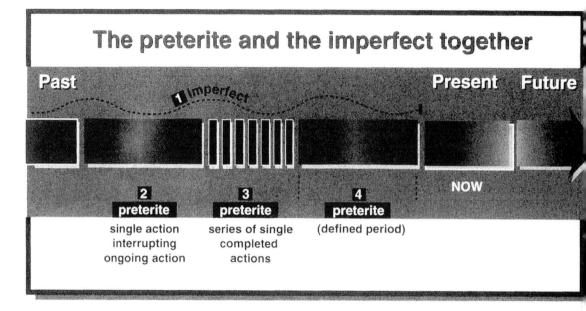

The preterite and the imperfect together

Past   **1** imperfect   Present   Future

NOW

2 preterite	**3** preterite	**4** preterite
single action interrupting ongoing action	series of single completed actions	(defined period)

1. The imperfect describes something which goes **along** the time-line, with no definite beginning or end.

2. The preterite may be an action which happens **while** the imperfect situation is going on . . .

3. . . . or is used for a series/sequence of events . . .

4. . . . or for an action which lasted for a defined length of time.

1. Pepe *was walking* along the road, and *was* not *looking* where he *was going* . . . (imperfect)
2. He *did* not *see* (preterite) what *was* in front of him! (imperfect)
3. He *fell* into a big hole and *broke* his leg! (preterite)

The Spanish version:

1 Pepe *andaba* por la calle, y no *miraba* por dónde *iba*.	**2** No *vio* lo que *había* delante de él.	**3** ¡*Cayó* en un agujero enorme y se *rompió* la pierna!

1. The first picture describes **what the situation was**, and has three verbs in the **imperfect**.

2. The second mentions what Pepe **did not do**, against another bit of **background**.

3. The third says what **happened** as a result, using two verbs in the **preterite**.

Some further points:

■ Try to avoid thinking that 'learnt', 'played', 'did' . . . etc. are always preterite and that 'was/were . . .' are always imperfect: this method will sometimes be right, but it will often let you down.

■ Instead, think **verb** then **which tense**? then **work out the correct form**. This way of doing things is far more reliable!

■ Remember the basic rules at the beginning of this unit.

 ¿Listos?

1 Parejas

He aquí unos verbos en el pretérito y el imperfecto, con sus significados en inglés, pero están revueltos. Busca las parejas adecuadas.

Here are some verbs in the preterite and imperfect tenses, with their meanings in English, but they are muddled. Look for the correct pairs.

miraba	they were buying
leyó	he was reading
estábamos	I looked
viajaron	he read
compraban	they travelled
pusiste	she was travelling
leía	she was looking

¡Viva la gramática!

miré	you were
viajaba	we were
estuvisteis	you put

2 ¡Decisiones!

De estas diez frases, cinco necesitan el pretérito y cinco el imperfecto: ¿pero cuáles? ¡Tú tienes que decidir!

Of these ten sentences, five need the preterite and five the imperfect: but which? You have to decide!

1. ¡Hola, Josefina! ¿Pero, dónde .... (comprar) el sombrero?

2. Cuando entré en la cocina, mi padre .... (preparar) la cena.

3. No me gustaba esa discoteca, porque siempre .... (poner) música aburrida.

4. El año pasado, mis padres .... (ir) de vacaciones a Palma de Mallorca.

5. Antes de subir al tren, Ana se .... (quitar) el abrigo.

6. Nuestro colegio .... (estar) cerca del polideportivo.

7. Durante el viaje a Londres, yo .... (perder) mi cartera.

8. Cuando era niño, mis amigos me .... (llamar) Manolín.

9. El viajero estaba perdido: no .... (saber) qué carretera debía coger.

10. Oye, Rosi, ¿dónde está mi chaqueta? ¿La .... (coger) tú?

H 3 Contrastes

Inventa frases usando las siguientes parejas de verbos. En cada caso, pon uno de los verbos en el pretérito y el otro en el imperfecto, como en el ejemplo.

Invent sentences using the following pairs of verbs. In each case, put one of the verbs into the preterite and the other into the imperfect, as in the example.

Ejemplo:
leer un libro / entrar en el salón
Cuando entré en el salón, mamá leía un libro.

1. tomar un café / entrar en el bar

2. salir de casa / hacer sol

3. ver a su amigo / llevar vaqueros

4. empezar a llover / buscar el paraguas

5. oír las malas noticias / empezar a llorar

6. recibir la carta / hablar con su padre

7. aparcar el coche / llegar a casa

8. estar en Londres / ver a la reina

 ¡Ya!

4 Explicaciones

¡Otra vez el novio celoso / la novia celosa! Quiere saber qué hacías cuando te vio. Trata de usar el pretérito y el imperfecto.

The jealous boy/girlfriend again! He/she wants to know what you were doing when he/she saw you. Try to use the preterite and the imperfect.

Ejemplo:

Novio/a: **¿Qué hacías cuando te vi en la piscina?**
Tú: **Cuando me viste, ¡me bañaba, naturalmente!**
Novio/a: **Pero, ¿por qué estabas con Miguel/Nuria?**
Tú: **Porque vino a la piscina conmigo.**

H 5 Descripciones

Habla con tus amigos de todo lo que hiciste / hicisteis ayer, o el sábado por la tarde, por ejemplo. Usa el pretérito y el imperfecto.

Talk with your friends about all you did yesterday or last Saturday evening, for example. Use the preterite and imperfect.

Ejemplo:
Ayer, cuando me levanté, hacía sol, y decidí dar un paseo por el bosque.

¡Viva la gramática!

Glosario

la pareja	pair
el sombrero	hat
aburrido	boring
quitarse	to take off
el abrigo	coat
perder	to lose
la cartera	wallet
la carretera	road
coger	to take
los vaqueros	jeans
las noticias	news
llorar	to cry
aparcar	to park
el paraguas	umbrella
sacar una foto	to take a photograph
la reina	queen
celoso	jealous
la piscina	swimming pool
el bosque	wood

31

WHAT HAVE YOU DONE?
the perfect tense

 **¿Preparados?**

1 What is the perfect tense?

The perfect tells you what **has happened**, what you **have done** in the recent past.

2 How do you form the perfect?

The perfect tense is made up of the present tense of the *haber* (called the **auxiliary verb**) and the **past participle**. Past participles of *-ar* verbs end in *-ado*, and *-er* and *-ir* verbs end in *-ido*:

-ar verbs:	*trabajar* (to work)	
yo	**he** trabaj**ado**	I have worked
tú	**has** trabaj**ado**	you have worked
él/ella	**ha** trabaj**ado**	he/she has worked
usted	**ha** trabaj**ado**	you have worked
nosotros/as	**hemos** trabaj**ado**	we have worked
vosotros/as	**habéis** trabaj**ado**	you have worked
ellos/ellas	**han** trabaj**ado**	they have worked
ustedes	**han** trabaj**ado**	you have worked

-er and *-ir* verbs:	*comer* (to eat)	*vivir* (to live)	
yo	**he** com**ido**	**he** viv**ido**	I have eaten / lived
tú	**has** com**ido**	**has** viv**ido**	you have eaten / lived
él/ella	**ha** com**ido**	**ha** viv**ido**	he/she has eaten / lived
usted	**ha** com**ido**	**ha** viv**ido**	you have eaten / lived
nosotros/as	**hemos** com**ido**	**hemos** viv**ido**	we have eaten / lived
vosotros/as	**habéis** com**ido**	**habéis** viv**ido**	you have eaten / lived
ellos/ellas	**han** com**ido**	**han** viv**ido**	they have eaten / lived
ustedes	**han** com**ido**	**han** viv**ido**	you have eaten / lived

¡Viva la gramática!

¿Has terminado?		**Have you finished?**	
Hemos comprado una alfombra nueva.		**We've bought** a new carpet.	
Vds no han estado aquí antes, ¿verdad?		**You haven't been** here before, have you?	

 **¡Ojo!**

The bad news first! There are just a few irregular past participles:

abrir	*he abierto*	to open	I have opened
cubrir	*he cubierto*	to cover	I have covered
descubrir	*he descubierto*	to discover	I have discovered
decir	*he dicho*	to say	I have said
volver	*he vuelto*	to return	I have returned
devolver	*he devuelto*	to give back	I have given back
escribir	*he escrito*	to write	I have written
describir	*he descrito*	to describe	I have described
hacer	*he hecho*	to do/make	I have done/made
morir	*ha muerto*	to die	he/she has died
poner	*he puesto*	to put	I have put
romper	*he roto*	to break	I have broken
ver	*he visto*	to see	I have seen
volver	*he vuelto*	to return	I have returned

Todavía **no has visto** *nada.*	**You haven't seen** anything yet.
Me **he roto** *el brazo.*	**I've broken** my arm.

Now for the good news!

■ Unlike French, there is only the one 'auxiliary' verb: *haber*!

■ Also unlike French, in the perfect tense you don't have to make the past participle agree with anything!

 **¡Ojo!**

Make sure you never put anything between *haber* and the past participle:

*¿**Han visto** ustedes esto?*	Have you seen this?
*¿**Ha llegado** el autobús?*	Has the bus arrived?
*¿No te **has lavado**?*	Haven't you washed?

3 Where do you use the perfect?

Easy! You use it to talk about what has happened in the recent past. In fact, you use it in much the same way you would use a perfect in English, to say what you **have done**, what **has happened**:

*¿Dónde **habéis estado** esta mañana?*	Where **have you been** this morning?
*¿**Han visitado ustedes** el castillo?*	**Have you visited** the castle?
*¡Ah! ¡**No he comprado** un regalo para mi madre!*	Oh! **I haven't bought** a present for my mother!

 ¡Ojo!

You **don't** however use the perfect to say **how long you have been doing** something, you use the present:

*Hace tres años que **aprendemos** el español.*   **We've been learning** Spanish for three years.

 ¡Ojo!

To say you have **just** done something, you use the present of *acabar de* + infinitive:

*El tren **acaba de salir**.*	The train **has just left**.
***Acabamos de comprar** unos recuerdos.*	**We've just bought** some souvenirs.

 # ¿Listos?

1 ¿Cómo lo has pasado?

Estás en casa de tu amigo/a español(a). Su abuela te pregunta lo que has hecho y visto mientras has estado allí. Cambia los verbos en tus respuestas al participio pasado para formar el perfecto.

You are staying with your Spanish friend in Spain, and his/her grandmother is asking you what you have seen and done while you have been there. Change the verbs in your answers to the past participle to form the perfect tense. The auxiliary *he* is already done for you.

¡Viva la gramática!

1. He (visitar) el castillo.

2. He (ir) al cine.

3. He (ver*) una nueva película española.

4. He (jugar) al tenis.

5. He (pasar) un día en el colegio.

6. He (comer) una fabada asturiana.

7. He (tomar) el sol en la playa y me he (poner*) muy tostado/a.

8. He (escribir*) varias tarjetas postales.

9. Las he (enviar) a mis amigos y amigas en Gran Bretaña.

10. He (romper*) mis gafas de sol y me he (comprar) otras.

*¡Cuidado con el participio pasado!

2 La semana de actividades

Es la 'semana de actividades' en tu colegio, cuando todos los alumnos salís a hacer alguna actividad fuera de clase. Contáis a vuestros amigos españoles, que acaban de llegar en visita de intercambio, lo que habéis hecho. Pon los verbos en la forma correcta del perfecto.

It's activity week at your school, and you are telling your Spanish exchange partners, who have just arrived, what you have done. Put the verbs into the correct form of the perfect.

1. María y yo (ir = hemos ido) a las montañas de Gales. Lo (pasar) estupendamente.

2. Jorge y Miguel (hacer) camping en la costa. ¡(Preparar) toda su propia comida!

3. Luisa (viajar) hasta Brighton en bicicleta. ¡(Tener) dos pinchazos!

4. Otros dos amigos (pasar) la semana trabajando en un hotel. (Trabajar) de portero y (ayudar) a muchas personas. ¡(Recibir) muchas propinas!

5. Javi (jugar) al baloncesto con un grupo de minusválidos.

6. Merche y Miriam (ser) enfermeras en un hospital.

7. Todos nosotros (aprender) mucho de estas experiencias.

8. Y vosotros, ¿(hacer) un buen viaje? ¿(Instalarse) con vuestras familias? ¿(Probar) la comida inglesa?

3 ¿Lo has hecho?

Trabajas en un supermercado en España, para cobrarte un poco de dinero. El jefe quiere estar seguro de que has hecho todo bien y te hace muchas preguntas. Contesta que sí, utilizando el perfecto.

You are working in a supermarket in Spain to earn a bit of money. The boss wants to make sure that you have done things right, and asks you a lot of questions. Answer 'yes', using the perfect. If you are confident with object pronouns, use them in your answer, if not, simply repeat the boss's whole phrase.

Ejemplo:
¿Has contado las cajas de yogures? Sí, señor, las he contado.
or **Sí, señor, he contado las cajas de yogures.**

1. ¿Has llenado el congelador de pescado?

2. ¿Has puesto las latas de judías en los estantes?

3. ¿Has traído los paquetes de café?

4. ¿Has puesto las etiquetas con los precios?

5. ¿Has contado las botellas de leche?

6. ¿Has lavado el mostrador de tabacos?

7. ¿Has arreglado las carretillas?

8. ¿Has barrido el suelo?

9. ¿Has limpiado los asientos de los cajeros?

10. ¿Has terminado tu trabajo?

4 ¿Qué acaba de pasar?

Rellena el espacio en blanco con una frase que describa el dibujo, utilizando *acabar de* . . .

Fill in the gaps with a phrase describing the drawing, using *acabar de* . . .

Ejemplo: El vuelo No. IB3456 acaba de salir/despegar.

¡Viva la gramática!

1. Enrique ....

2. El camarero .... las bebidas.

3. Antonio y yo ....

4. Los Domínguez .... a su hotel.

5. Yo .... una novela muy larga.

¡Ya!

5 ¿Qué has hecho hoy?

Haz preguntas a tu compañero/a sobre lo que ha hecho hoy.

Ask your partner questions about what he/she has done today. Some of your questions could be a little 'way out' if you like: *¿Has tomado whisky para el desayuno?*!

Ejemplo:
A.   **¿Has tomado café para el desayuno?**
B.   **No, he tomado té.**

Estos verbos serán útiles:

despertarse   levantarse   lavarse   ducharse   salir de casa   venir al colegio
jugar   tener clase de . . .   sacar buenas/malas notas   comer   beber

6 En el consultorio del médico

Trabaja con tu compañero/a. Uno/a es médico, el otro / la otra es paciente, que no está bien. El médico hace preguntas y el paciente contesta, ambos utilizando el perfecto lo más posible.

Work with your partner. One is a doctor, the other a patient, who is not well. The doctor asks questions and the patient answers, both using the perfect whenever possible.

Ejemplo:
Médico: **¿Qué has comido?**
Paciente: **He comido unos mejillones.**

Utilizad estos verbos y frases:

beber	tragar	tener fiebre	vomitar	tener diarrea	cortarse el dedo
tomar aspirinas/pastillas	estar	visitar	romperse el brazo		
tener dolor de cabeza/estómago/garganta					

H 7 *Lo hemos pasado estupendamente*

Escribe una carta a un(a) amigo/a en España, diciéndole lo que has hecho recientemente. Puede ser una semana de actividades, como en el ejercicio 2, o unas vacaciones, o puedes describir lo que has hecho durante las fiestas de Navidad. Tu profesor te ayudará a decidir.

Write a letter to a friend in Spain, telling him/her what you have done recently. It could be an activity week, as in exercise 2, a holiday, or you could describe what you have done during the Christmas festivities. Your teacher will help you decide and ensure you have the necessary vocabulary.

Glosario

barrer	to sweep
el/la cajero/a	cashier, checkout operator
la carretilla	trolley
la diarrea	diarrhoea
la etiqueta	label
la experiencia	experience
la fabada asturiana	bean stew from Northern Spain
Gales	Wales
instalarse	to settle in
minusválido	disabled
el mostrador	counter
pasarlo estupendamente	to have a great time
el pinchazo	puncture

32

WHAT HAD ALREADY HAPPENED? the pluperfect and other compound tenses

 ¿Preparados?

What is a compound tense?
'Compound' tenses are so called because they consist of more than one word. All the tenses in this chapter are formed with *haber* **and the past participle**, and all the rules set out for the **perfect** in the previous chapter apply.

1 The pluperfect

■ The pluperfect tells you what **had happened** before some other event:

> *Ya **había terminado** mi desayuno cuando mi hermano se levantó.*
> I **had** already **finished** my breakfast when my brother got up.

> *Cuando llegamos al puerto el ferry ya **había salido**.*
> When we arrived at the port, the ferry **had** already **left**.

> ***Habíamos leído** el libro antes de ver la película.*
> We **had read** the book before seeing the film.

> *Alberto estaba enfermo porque **había comido** unos mejillones malos.*
> Alberto was ill because he **had eaten** some bad mussels.

■ You form it with the **imperfect** of *haber* and the **past participle**:

		trabajar (to work)	*comer* (to eat)	*vivir* (to live)	
yo	**había**	trabajado	comido	vivido	I had worked / eaten / lived
tú	**habías**	trabajado	comido	vivido	you had worked / eaten / lived
él/ella	**había**	trabajado	comido	vivido	he / she had worked / eaten / lived
usted	**había**	trabajado	comido	vivido	you had worked / eaten / lived
nosotros/as	**habíamos**	trabajado	comido	vivido	we had worked / eaten / lived
vosotros/as	**habíais**	trabajado	comido	vivido	you had worked / eaten / lived
ellos/ellas	**habían**	trabajado	comido	vivido	they had worked / eaten / lived
ustedes	**habían**	trabajado	comido	vivido	you had worked / eaten / lived

 ¡Ojo!

To say you **had just** done something, you use the imperfect of *acabar de* + infinitive: (compare *have just* in Chapter 31, Section 3)

*El tren **acababa de salir**.*　　　The train **had just** left.

2 Other compound tenses

You may also come across:

a. the **future perfect**, which tells you what **will have happened**. You form this with the **future** of *haber* and the **past participle**:

*A esta hora mañana ya **habré terminado** mis exámenes.*
By this time tomorrow, I shall have finished my exams.

*Los estudiantes españoles ya **habrán llegado** a Madrid.*
The Spanish students **will have arrived** in Madrid by now.

b. the **conditional perfect**, which tells you what **would have happened**. You form it with the **conditional** of *haber* and the **past participle**:

*¿Qué **habrías hecho** tú?*　　　What **would you have done?**
*Yo **habría vuelto** a casa.*　　　I **would have returned** home.

This tense is often used in conjunction with *si* (if), and you will find more information about it and practice on it in Chapter 26.

¡Viva la gramática!

 ## ¿Listos?

1 Un catálogo de desastres

Un amigo tuyo te cuenta una lista de desastres que les habían ocurrido a sus amigos recientemente. Escoge la frase de la columna B que corresponda con las de la columna A.

A friend of yours relates a list of disasters which had happened to himself and his friends recently. Match up the phrases in columns A and B.

A	**B**
1. Cuando fui a ver a mis amigos en la cafetería,	a. porque no nos habían dicho que venían.
2. Cuando llegamos a la estación,	b. porque no se había puesto el cinturón.
3. Cuando llegó Fede al cine,	c. porque el chófer no había visto el semáforo rojo.
4. Cuando Anita fue a comprar una falda,	d. ya se habían ido a otro sitio.
5. Ramón me dio un libro para mi cumpleaños,	e. ya la habían vendido.
6. No esperábamos la visita de mis tíos,	f. el tren ya había salido.
7. El coche chocó con el nuestro,	g. porque había comido demasiado.
8. A Felipe se le cayeron los pantalones en la calle,	h. pero ya lo había leído.
9. El pastel que hice salió mal,	i. la película ya había empezado.
10. Rosita tenía dolor de estómago,	j. porque no le había puesto huevos.

H 2 Para el año que viene . . .

Nieves habla de lo que habrán hecho ella, su familia y sus amigos para esta época del año que viene. Rellena los espacios en blanco.

Nieves is talking about what she, her family and her friends will have done by this time next year. Fill the gaps, using the future perfect.

Para esta época del año que viene . . .

1. Yo .... (aprobar) mi bachillerato.

2. Mi hermano Enrique .... (visitar) a nuestros primos en Méjico.

3. Mi madre .... (cambiar) de trabajo.

4. Mi hermanita, Rosita, ... (crecer) unos centímetros más.

5. Mis padres y yo .... (ir) a Inglaterra a ver a nuestros amigos ingleses.

6. Mis tíos .... (venir) a vernos desde Argentina.

7. Y vosotros, ¿qué .... (hacer)?

¡Ya!

H 3 ¿Qué habías hecho ya?

En parejas o en grupos, haced preguntas unos a otros, preguntando ¿Qué ya habías hecho antes de . . . ? o Cuando (hiciste algo), ¿qué habías hecho ya?

In pairs or groups, ask each other questions such as those in the example.

Ejemplo:
A.   ¿Qué ya *habías hecho* antes de salir de casa esta mañana?
B.   Ya *había tomado* mi desayuno, también había . . .
A.   Cuando te despertaste esta mañana, ¿qué *habías hecho* ya?
B.   ¡Ya *había dormido* toda la noche!

H 4 La semana que viene

Piensa en esta hora de la semana que viene. Escribe diez cosas que tú, tu familia y/o tus amigos habréis hecho para entonces.

Think of this time next week and write down 10 things that you and/or your friends and family will have done by then.

Ejemplo:
Para esta hora de la semana que viene mi amiga Julia y yo *habremos jugado* al tenis ¡y yo *habré ganado*!

33

'DOING' AND 'DONE'
gerunds and past participles

 ¿Preparados?

1 Gerunds
a What is a gerund?

A gerund is a special part of the verb used to refer to an action going on at the moment: in other words, it is like the English '..............ing' part of the verb.

Here are the gerund forms of the three regular verb groups:

-ar > *-ando*	*-er* > *-iendo*	*-ir* > *-iendo*

hablar > *hablando*
    = speaking
	comer > *comiendo*
	    = eating
		vivir > *viviendo*
		    = living

As you can see, *-er* and *-ir* verbs share the same gerund form, and there is a logical formula to help you to remember them:

$$\mathbf{a} = \mathbf{a}$$
$$\mathbf{i} + \mathbf{e} = \mathbf{ie}$$

There are a few slightly irregular gerunds:

■ verbs like:
leer	> *leyendo*	= reading
oír	> *oyendo*	= hearing
construir >	*construyendo*	= building

■ radical-changing *-ir* verbs have gerunds as follows:
e > ie/i verbs:	*sentir*	> *sintiendo*	= feeling
	pedir	> *pidiendo*	= asking for
o > ue verbs:	*dormir*	> *durmiendo*	= sleeping

198

b Uses

■ Gerunds are used with *estar* to form the continuous tenses (see Chapter 28).

> *La policía está buscando al ladrón.*
> The police are looking for the thief.

■ They can also be used by themselves for 'while ... ing' and 'by ... ing':

> *Viviendo en España, aprendió el español.*
> While living in Spain, she learnt Spanish.
> *Llamando este número, puedes pedir este fabuloso regalo.*
> By calling this number, you can claim this fabulous gift.

■ You **cannot** use a gerund after verbs like *gustar*, *preferir*, and *encantar*. Instead, use the infinitive:

> *Me encanta jugar al baloncesto.*
> I love playing basketball.

 **¡Ojo!**

Beware also of expressions like: 'running water' – in Spanish this is *agua corriente*. *Corriente* is a verbal adjective, and it is best to check this sort of word in a dictionary.

2 Past participles

a What is a past participle?

This is a part of the verb used to refer to the past, formed as follows:

-ar > *-ado*	*er* > *-ido*	*-ir* > *-ido*
hablar > *hablado* = spoken	*comer* > *comido* = eaten	*vivir* > *vivido* = lived

Once again, *-er* and *-ir* verbs share the same past participle ending. There are a number of irregular past participles, the most useful of which are given in Chapter 35.

b Uses

■ The main use of past participles is in compound tenses such as the perfect (see Chapter 31) and the passive (see Chapter 38):

¡Viva la gramática!

> *Marisa ha encontrado trabajo en el supermercado.*
> Marisa has found a job in the supermarket.

■ Past participles are often used as adjectives, in which case they agree with the noun described, like other adjectives:

Al llegar, vi la ventana rota.	When I arrived, I saw the broken window.
Oficina de objetos perdidos	Lost property office

■ You will recognise past participles in many nouns: the feminine form of a past participle is often used as a noun. Here are a few – try to find others!

entrada	entrance
salida	exit
llegadas	arrivals
un billete ida y vuelta	return ticket (= a going and coming back ticket!)

There are some other more unexpected ones:

un helado	ice-cream
un batido de leche	a milk-shake

 ¿Listos?

1 Sopa de gerundios y participios

He aquí varios gerundios y participios con sus traducciones en inglés. Tienes que buscar parejas correctas.

Here are various gerunds and participles, with their translations in English. You have to find the correct pairs.

volviendo	suffered	*oyendo*	selling
vuelto	returning	*sufrido*	hearing
vendido	heard	*estudiando*	returned
sorprendido	put	*encontrado*	putting
vendiendo	studying	*poniendo*	sold
puesto	found	*oído*	surprised

2 ¿Cómo se hace?

Se hace una tortilla rompiendo huevos . . . Usando un gerundio adecuado, explica cómo se hacen las siguientes cosas.

You make an omelette by breaking eggs . . . Using an appropriate gerund, explain how the following things are done.

1. ¿Cómo se gana la lotería nacional?

2. ¿Cómo se gana un partido de fútbol?

3. ¿Cómo se hace un sandwich?

4. ¿Cómo se habla fácilmente con un(a) español(a)?

5. ¿Cómo se puede ir a ver una película?

6. ¿Cómo haces feliz a tu madre?

7. ¿Cómo pones contento a tu padre?

8. ¿Cómo se llega a Nueva York?

H 3 ¿De dónde viene?

A. La lista A contiene varios adjetivos y sustantivos que tienen verbos como base. Indica el infinitivo del verbo base; ¡se permite usar un diccionario!

B. Busca un adjetivo o un sustantivo basado en los verbos de la lista B.

A. List A contains various adjectives and nouns based on verbs. Give the infinitive of the base verb; you are allowed to use a dictionary!

B. Look for an adjective or a noun based on the verbs in list B.

A (patatas) fritas	B entrar
(el cielo) cubierto	parecer
abierto/cerrado	ir
satisfecho	ver
el permiso	caer
la puesta (del sol)	variar

¡Viva la gramática!

 ¡Ya!

4 *Explicaciones*

Inventa unas preguntas para tu amigo/a o compañero/a de clase como las del ejercicio 2; él/ella tiene que contestarlas usando un gerundio.

Invent some questions for your friend or classmate like those in exercise 2; he/she has to answer using a gerund.

5 *¿Qué has hecho y qué estás haciendo?*

Con tus amigos, haz preguntas y contéstalas usando el perfecto y el presente continuo como las del ejemplo.

Ask and answer questions using the perfect and the present continuous like those in the example.

Ejemplo:

A. **Oye, ¿qué has hecho esta mañana?**

B. **He hecho mis deberes de español, ¡y todavía los estoy haciendo!**

Glosario

el partido	match
la película	film
feliz	happy (all the time)
contento	happy, pleased (for now)
el cielo	sky
cubierto	overcast (sky)
satisfecho	satisfied
la puesta del sol	sunset
caer	to fall
variar	to vary

34

INFINITIVES

 **¿Preparados?**

■ A verb form usually answers three questions:

What?   What action is being carried out?
Who?   Who is doing it?
When? When is it happening / did / will it happen?

For example, 'he writes' tells us: WHAT? = writing; WHO? = he is;
WHEN? = now. In Spanish, 'he writes' is *escribe*: the *escrib-* part tells us WHAT
is being done, and the ending *-e* tells us WHO and WHEN; the ending is
clearly very important . . .

■ But does every verb form do this? No! The **infinitive** only tells us WHAT is
happening, not WHO is doing it or WHEN it is happening. So, why is it called
the **infinitive**? Because the idea contained in such verbs is not defined – it is a
sort of verb 'in neutral'. In Spanish it has no person/tense ending, so really is
infinite or **infinitive**.

■ There are three main types of infinitive in Spanish, one for each family of
'regular' verbs: those ending in *-ar*, those ending in *-er*, and those ending in *-ir*.
These infinitive endings act as a sort of 'surname', telling you which verb family
a verb belongs to. The members of each family behave in a particular way and
have certain features in common, like any other family; the basic part gives the
'stem' to which the verb endings are added. Each verb family shares patterns of
verb forms. So, for example, if you come across a new *-ar* verb such as *cocinar*
and you know the pattern for the regular *-ar* verb *hablar*, you can easily work out
the pattern for *cocinar*. Know the infinitive and know the verb!

¡Viva la gramática!

Uses

1. The infinitive is the part of the verb you find in the dictionary: to look up any verb form in a dictionary it is useful to know its infinitive or how to 'work back' to the infinitive. This is easy to do, as most verb forms make it obvious, e.g. *-a*, *-aba*, *-aron*, *-ar* can only be from an *-ar* verb. Similarly, *-e*, *-en*, *-ían* will be from an *-er* or an *-ir* verb, *-emos* can only be from an *-er* verb, and *-amos* from an *-ar* verb.

2. Infinitives are often used after another verb. In English such expressions sometimes use an infinitive with or without 'to', and sometimes a verb form ending in *-ing*. Spanish always uses an infinitive for these; in some cases the infinitive follows the verb directly, but some verbs have *a* or *de* or, less commonly, *en* or *por* between the main verb and the infinitive.

*¿Te gusta **viajar** en tren?*	Do you like **travelling** by train?
*No, prefiero **ir** en coche.*	No, I prefer **to go** by car.
*¿Que sueles **hacer** los sábados?*	What do you usually **do** on Saturdays?
*Empezaron a **comer**.*	They began **to eat**.
*¡Estoy aprendiendo a **volar**!*	I'm learning **to fly**!
*¡Deja de **jugar** con la pelota!*	Stop **playing** with the ball!
*Trata de **hacer** este ejercicio.*	Try **to do** this exercise.

3. As in English, you can use an infinitive after an adjective.

*Prohibido **fijar** carteles.*	It is forbidden **to put up** posters.
*Fue horrible **ver** a José así.*	It was horrible **to see** José like that.
*Es peligroso **cruzar** la carretera.*	It is dangerous **to cross** the road.

4. Infinitives are used after certain prepositions, especially with the idea of time:

*Es peligroso cruzar la carretera sin **mirar**.*	It is dangerous to cross the road without **looking**.
*Antes de **girar** a la izquierda, mira el retrovisor.*	Before **turning** left, look in the mirror.
*Después de **mirar**, pon el intermitente.*	After **looking**, use the indicator.
*Para **hacer** una tortilla . . .*	In order **to make** an omelette . . .

al plus an infinitive has the same meaning as *cuando* plus a verb in a tense:

*Al **entrar** en la clase, vimos al profesor.*	When **we went** into the classroom, we saw the teacher.

5. There are two verb expressions using *que* with an infinitive – *hay que* and *tener que*:

> . . . *hay que **romper** huevos* . . .   . . . it is necessary **to break** eggs . . .
> . . . *y tienes que **usar** una sartén.*   . . . and you have **to use** a frying-pan.

6. Two other expressions using infinitives are almost like separate tenses – *acabar de* (to have just . . .) (see Chapter 31) and *ir a* (to be going to . . .) (see Chapter 24).

> *Mis amigos acaban de **llegar** . . .*   My friends have just **arrived** . . .
> . . . *y vamos a **ir** todos a la discoteca.*   . . . and we are all going **to go** to the disco.

7. Infinitives are often used by themselves in instructions or warnings:

> ***Batir*** *bien los huevos.*   **Beat** the eggs well.
> ***Abrir*** *el paquete con cuidado.*   **Open** the packet carefully.
> *No **hablar** con el conductor.*   Do not **talk** to the driver.

 ## ¿Listos?

1 Intercambios

Has encontrado estos verbos; ¿qué forma buscarías en el diccionario? Escribe la forma del infinitivo.

You have found these verbs; what form would you look up in the dictionary? Write the infinitive forms.

1. escribe	9. has considerado
2. ponemos	10. he subido
3. vivieron	11. acababas
4. dibujó	12. saldré
5. escuchaba	13. suele
6. volvía	14. pongan
7. pagaremos	15. mintieron
8. comprarán	

¡Viva la gramática!

2 Tortilla española

Cambia las siguientes instrucciones a la forma del infinitivo.
Change the following instructions into the infinitive form.

1. Coge seis huevos y dos kilos de patatas.

2. Pela las patatas y córtalas en trozos.

3. Pon cuatro cucharadas de aceite en una sartén.

4. Calienta el aceite y fríe las patatas.

5. Bate los huevos en una fuente, y añade las patatas: mézclalos bien.

6. Pon los huevos y las patatas en la sartén, y fríelos bien.

7. Usando un plato, da vuelta a la tortilla para freír el otro lado.

8. Termina de freír la tortilla.

9. Saca la tortilla de la sartén, y déjala enfriar.

10. Sirve en forma de pinchos con un vasito de vino.

3 Infinitivo definido

Rellena los espacios en blanco con el infinitivo más adecuado de los que se ofrecen abajo.

Fill in the gaps with the most appropriate infinitive offered below:

Hoy tengo que ....1....... al cole, y vamos a ....2....... clases de matemáticas y geografía. Esta tarde tenemos deporte, y nos obligan a ....3....... a un partido de rugby, aunque prefiero ....4....... al fútbol. Después de las clases espero ....5....... ir a casa de mi amiga. Allí, me gusta ....6....... sus discos compactos, pues tiene un estéreo muy bueno.

Mañana, sábado, quiero ....7....... de compras con mis padres, pues necesito ....8....... unas camisas nuevas; también me hace falta ....9....... un regalo para mi novia, pues el domingo es su cumpleaños. Como le gusta mucho ....10..... la televisión, creo que voy a ....11..... un vídeo; le encanta ....12..... la tarde en casa viendo una buena película en vídeo.

participar	tener	salir	encontrar	buscar	comprar	escuchar
	ir	poder	ver	jugar	pasar	

¡Ya!

4 Aficiones

Dile a un compañero las cosas que te gusta hacer en tus ratos libres.

Tell a classmate what you like doing in your free time.

Ejemplo:
A. **¿Qué te gusta hacer en tus ratos libres?**
B. **Jugar con los videojuegos, ver la tele, escuchar música rock . . . ¿y tú?**
A. **Pues, prefiero salir, ir al cine, visitar a mis amigotes . . .**

5 Obligaciones

Discute con los amigos lo que tenéis que hacer para ayudar a vuestros padres.

Discuss with your friends what you have to do to help your parents.

Ejemplo:
A. **¿Qué tenéis que hacer para ayudar a vuestros padres?**
B. **Lavar el coche, limpiar los zapatos, arreglar mi dormitorio . . .**
C. **Y yo, planchar las camisas, preparar la cena . . .**

H 6 Aspiraciones

Hablad de vuestras esperanzas y aspiraciones, usando un infinitivo cuando podáis.

Talk about your hopes and aspirations, using an infinitive when you can.

Ejemplo:
A. **De mayor, quiero hacerme profesor, pues tienen vacaciones largas.**
B. **Yo voy a hacerme abogado, ¡porque ganan mucho más que los profesores!**
C. **¡Y yo quiero ganar la lotería porque no me gusta trabajar!**

¡Viva la gramática!

Glosario

pelar	to peel
cortar	to cut
la cucharada	spoonful
la sartén	frying-pan
calentar	to heat
freír	to fry
batir	to beat
la fuente	bowl
añadir	to add
mezclar	to mix
darle vuelta	to turn over
enfriar	to cool
el pincho	portion (on a cocktail stick)
el deporte	sport
el partido	match
aunque	although
el estéreo	stereo
me hace falta	I need
la película	film
los ratos libres	free time
el videojuego	video-game
arreglar	to tidy up
planchar	to iron
el abogado	lawyer

35

'CAN', 'MUST' AND 'OUGHT'

 ¿Preparados?

1 'can/could', 'to be able'

a *poder*

Poder is used in most cases for 'can' or 'to be able'. (It's rather irregular, and you will find all its parts in the verb tables in Chapter 44.)

No **puedo** salir esta noche.	**I can't** go out this evening.
Rosa **no puede** comer carne.	Rosa **can't** eat meat.
¿**Puede Vd.** decirme por dónde se llega a la estación?	**Can you** tell me how to get to the station?
Ahora **podrán** comprar un piso nuevo.	Now **they will be able** to buy a new flat.

 ¡Consejo!

If you are uncertain about which tense of *poder* to use for 'could', think of it in terms of 'to be able':

*No **podía** abrir la puerta sin llave.*
I couldn't (= **wasn't able to**) open the door without a key (I didn't have it with me): use imperfect

*No **podría** abrir la puerta sin llave.*
I couldn't (= **wouldn't be able to**) open the door without a key (if I didn't have one): use conditional

¡Viva la gramática!

¡Consejo!

Se puede is a very useful little phrase, meaning 'one/you/we can', 'one/you/we may', and, of course, *no se puede* 'one/you/we can't', 'one/you/we may not':

*Aquí **se puede** comprar todo.*	**One/you can** buy everything here.
*¿**Se puede** pasar? ¡No, **no se puede**!*	**May we** come in? No, **you may not**!

It is often used with a gesture, without actually saying what it is you want to do – it might be 'come in?', 'open the window?', 'take an item of food?', 'smoke?', etc: *¿**Se puede?*** **May I/may we?**

b *saber*

When 'can' refers to a skill that you have learnt, use *saber*, which means 'to know how to':

*¿**Sabes** tocar la guitarra?*	**Can you** play the guitar?
*Quico sólo tiene tres años y **sabe** escribir.*	Quico is only three years old and he **can/knows how to** write.

2 'must', 'have to', 'ought'

a *tener que*, *deber* and *hay que*

These all mean 'must' or 'have to' and are followed by the **infinitive** of what you've got to do:

***Tienes que** volver a casa antes de las doce.*	**You must** be home before twelve.
***Tuvimos que** cambiar una rueda.*	**We had to** change a wheel.
*Vd. **debe** quedarse en la cama.*	**You must** stay in bed.
***Hay que** tomar dos pastillas cada cuatro horas.*	**You must** take two tablets every four hours.

 **¡Ojo!**

1. There is not a great deal of difference between *tener que* and *deber*, but be careful in the negative:

*No **debes** llevar vaqueros.*	You **mustn't** wear jeans (= not allowed!)

*No **tienes que** llevar vaqueros.*	You **don't have to** wear jeans (= no obligation)

2. *(No) hay que* means literally 'it is (not) necessary to'. It never changes its form and can't have a subject – in other words you can't say *Mi padre hay que . . .* It is often used when the action is more important than the person(s) doing it.

¡Consejo!

Se debe and *no se debe* are also used in the sense of 'one must' and 'one mustn't':

No se debe charlar en clase.	One mustn't chatter in class.

b *(no) debería*

'Ought (not) to' is usually expressed by using the conditional of *deber*:

*Carmen, **deberías** acostarte.*	Carmen, **you ought to** go to bed.
*Mi padre **no debería** fumar.*	My father **ought not to/shouldn't** smoke.

¡Consejo!

If you want to say what someone **ought (not) to have done** or **should (not) have done**, use *(no) debería haber* + past participle:

*¡No **deberías** haber copiado tus deberes!*	**You ought not to have copied** your homework.
Deberíamos haber ido ayer.	**We ought to/should have gone** yesterday.

¿Listos?

1 ¡El pobre Carlitos no puede hacer nada!

La mamá de Carlitos es muy estricta y no le permite hacer como los otros chicos de su edad. He aquí a Carlitos que se queja de su vida. Escoge un verbo de los que aparecen en el recuadro.

¡Viva la gramática!

Carlitos' mum is very strict and doesn't let him do as other children of his age do. Here Carlitos is moaning about his restricted life. Fill the gaps with a verb chosen from the box.

No ....1....... salir con mis amigos porque no ....2...... jugar en la calle. ....3...... que quedarme en casa con mi madre. Mi hermana y yo ....4...... ayudar a nuestra madre en la casa. Yo ....5...... leer y escribir pero no ......6...... montar en bicicleta. Todos mis amigos ....7...... nadar, pero yo no. Mi padre no está de acuerdo pero ....8...... que callarse. Los niños ....9...... aprender cómo es la vida. ....10..... permitir a los niños salir a la calle.

debemos	deberían	debo	hay que	puedo	saben	sé	sé	tengo	tiene

2 ¡Hay remedio!

Si hay problema, siempre hay remedio. Escoge una frase de la columna B que dice lo que podrías o deberías hacer para solucionar el problema de la columna A.

Where there's a problem, there's always a solution. Match a phrase from column B saying what you could or should do to solve the problem in column A.

A	B
1. Tienes frío.	a. Podrías invitar a tus amigos.
2. Tienes gripe.	b. Deberías repararla.
3. Estás cansado/a.	c. Podrías tomar el avión.
4. Has perdido tu monedero.	d. Deberías quedarte en la cama.
5. Quieres comprar fruta.	e. Podrías ir a la oficina de turismo.
6. Mañana es tu cumpleaños.	f. Deberías ponerte un jersey.
7. Necesitas cambiar dinero.	g. Deberías acostarte.
8. Quieres ir a España.	h. Podrías ir al banco.
9. Buscas un hotel.	i. Podrías ir al supermercado.
10. Tu bicicleta no funciona.	j. Podrías ir a la policía.

¡Ya!

3 Las reglas del colegio

Habla con tus compañeros de clase sobre las reglas de tu colegio, utilizando *no se puede*, *se debe*, *no se debe*, *hay que*, *no hay que*. Podrías hacer una lista de las 'buenas' y las 'malas'. Luego podrías escribir una explicación para tu amigo/a español.

Discuss your school's rules with your classmates, using the above phrases. You could make a list of those which in your opinion are 'good' and those which you don't like. Then write an explanation of them to a Spanish friend.

Ejemplo:
No se debe **correr en los pasillos.**
Hay que **llevar uniforme.**

4 ¡Más problemas, más remedios!

Mira otra vez el ejercicio 2, y piensa en más problemas. Cada alumno tiene que pensar en un problema. Los otros tienen que pensar en los remedios.

Look again at exercise 2, and think up more problems. Each pupil has to think of a problem, and the others offer solutions, using *podrías* or *deberías*.

Ejemplo:
A.   **Tengo mucho calor.**
B.   **¡Podrías abrir la ventana!**
C.   **¡Podrías quitarte el anorak!**
D.   **¡No deberías correr tanto!**

36

DO'S AND DON'TS | the imperative

 **¿Preparados?**

What is the imperative?
This is simply the 'command' part of the verb – the part we use to tell someone to do something, to give someone an order. You will remember that there are four ways of saying 'you' in Spanish: as a result there are also four command forms! As usual though, there are logical patterns to help you.

a _tú_ and _vosotros_ commands
For _tú_ command forms, take the _tú_ form of the present tense and take off the -s: for _vosotros_ commands, just replace the -r of the infinitive with a -d, apart from a few irregular verbs.

	-*ar* verbs	-*er* verbs	-*ir* verbs
tú	*hablas* → **habla**	*comes* → **come**	*subes* → **sube**
vosotros	*hablar* → **hablad**	*comer* → **comed**	*subir* → **subid**

A few common irregular *tú* forms are as follows:

decir	→	*di*	say	*salir*	→	*sal*	go out
hacer	→	*haz*	do	*ser*	→	*sé*	be
ir	→	*ve*	go	*tener*	→	*ten*	have
poner	→	*pon*	put	*venir*	>	*ven*	come

■ Note that the 'vosotros' forms are all in fact regular.

214

b *usted* and *ustedes* **forms**

These also follow a pattern: for *usted*, take the *yo* (I) form of the verb, remove the -*o* and add -*e* with -*ar* verbs, -*a* with -*er* and -*ir* verbs. For *ustedes* just add -*n* to the *usted* form. Some verbs need spelling changes to preserve the sound of consonants like -*g*- and -*c*-: check them in the verb tables.

	-*ar* verbs	-*er* verbs	-*ir* verbs
usted	hablo → **hable**	como → **coma**	subo → **suba**
ustedes	hable → **hablen**	coma → **coman**	suba → **suban**

c Negative commands

▪ These are no problem for *usted/ustedes*: simply put *no* in front of the positive commands!

▪ For *tú*, add -*s* to the *usted* form; for *vosotros*, add -*is* to the *usted* form as follows:

	-*ar* verbs	-*er* verbs	-*ir* verbs
tú	**no hables**	**no comas**	**no subas**
vosotros	**no habléis**	**no comáis**	**no subáis**
usted	**no hable**	**no coma**	**no suba**
ustedes	**no hablen**	**no coman**	**no suban**

d Adding pronouns to imperatives

When using object pronouns (e.g. 'me', 'us', 'it', 'them', 'to you', 'to them', etc.) with imperatives, put them in front of the verb when negative, but add them to the end of the verb in the case of positive commands. The new, longer word may need an accent to keep the stress in the right place, such as in these examples:

tú	*vosotros*	*usted*	*ustedes*	
cómpralos	*compradlos*	*cómprelos*	*cómprenlos*	buy them
véndela	*vendedla*	*véndala*	*véndanla*	sell it
escríbeme	*escribidme*	*escríbame*	*escríbanme*	write to me
no los compres	*no los compréis*	*no los compre*	*no los compren*	don't buy them
no la vendas	*no la vendáis*	*no la venda*	*no la vendan*	don't sell it
no me escribas	*no me escribáis*	*no me escriba*	*no me escriban*	don't write to me

e Other ways of telling people to do something

■ **Infinitives** can be used to give commands or instructions, particularly in warning notices and sets of instructions such as recipes; you also find them on packets of food and instruction leaflets for tools and equipment.

Abrir el paquete con cuidado.	Open the packet with care.
Cortar en trozos y servir frío.	Cut into pieces and serve cold.
Fijar en la pared con los tornillos provistos.	Fix to the wall with the screws provided.

Of course, there are also instructions using the infinitive after certain common expressions such as:

Prohibido cruzar.	Do not cross.
Se prohíbe aparcar.	No parking.
No se permite pescar.	Fishing not permitted.

■ The *tú* or *usted* form of the present tense is often used to give instructions:

Coge/Coges la primera calle a la derecha.	Take the first street on the right.

■ The *nosotros* form of the present tense expresses 'let's . . .'.

Tomamos un café, ¿vale?	Let's have a coffee, O.K.?

 ## ¿Listos?

1 *Autoservicio*

He aquí varias situaciones, y una serie de órdenes, cada una de las cuales podría ser una reacción lógica a una de las situaciones: tienes que elegir la más adecuada.

Here are various situations and a series of orders, each of which would be a logical reaction to one of the situations: you have to choose the most appropriate one.

1. Tu hermanito va a cruzar la calle.	Abre la puerta.
2. Quieres comprar unos caramelos.	Coge un taxi.
3. Es el cumpleaños de tu novio/a.	Dame un panecillo.
4. Tienes prisa para llegar a una cita importante.	¡Ten cuidado!
5. Manuel tiene mucha hambre.	Vete a buscar la aspiradora.

6. Tu padre quiere el pan.

7. El gato quiere salir.

8. La casa está muy sucia.

Deme un paquete de éstos.

Cómete un bocadillo.

Cómprale un regalo.

H *2 Conversión*

Convierte estas instrucciones en órdenes, utilizando el imperativo de *tú* (1–5), luego la forma de *usted* (6–10). Luego ponlas al plural (*vosotros / ustedes*).

Convert these instructions into commands, using the *tú* imperative form, (1–5), then the *usted* form (6–10). Then put them into the plural (*vosotros / ustedes*).

1. Cerrar la ventana.

2. Enchufar el aparato con cuidado.

3. Lavar y abrir los mejillones.

4. No tirar basura a la calle.

5. No tocar los modelos.

6. Llevar la derecha.

7. En casos de urgencia llamar a la policía.

8. Abrocharse el cinturón.

9. No dejar artículos de valor en las habitaciones.

10. No se permite llevar las sillas al jardín.

 ¡Ya!

3 ¡A sus órdenes!

Tienes varias quejas acerca del estado en que está tu casa. Tu madre/padre (un amigo) te contesta con una orden, como en el ejemplo.

You have various complaints about the state your house is in. Your mother/father answers you with an order, as in this example.

¡Viva la gramática!

Ejemplo:
A.   **Mi cama está sin hacer.**
B.   **¡Pues hazla tú!**
A.   **La hierba ha crecido mucho.**
B.   **Pues, córtala.**

H 4 *¡Sí señor!*

Dile a tu compañero todo lo necesario para hacer algo importante. Luego hazlo otra vez imaginando que no conoces a tu compañero, y utilizando el *usted*.

Tell your classmate all that is necessary to do something important. Then do the same again imagining that you don't know him and using *usted*.

Ejemplos:
Tú: **Lava el coche: coge un cubo, llénalo de agua caliente, y busca la esponja.**
Usted: **Lave el coche: coja un cubo, llénelo de agua caliente, y busque la esponja.**

H 5 *Publicidad*

Trabajando con tus amigos, inventad una serie de anuncios de televisión, usando el imperativo. Algunos serán dirigidos a los jóvenes (*tú / vosotros*) otros a los mayores (*usted / ustedes*).

Working with a friend, invent a series of television advertisements, using the imperative. Some will be aimed at young people (*tu / vosotros*), others at adults (*usted / ustedes*).

Ejemplo:
A.   **Pide estos caramelos a tu mamá. ¡Son deliciosos!**
B.   **Vayan a la Agencia de Viajes Meliá para reservar sus vacaciones.**

Glosario

tener prisa	to be in a hurry
la cita	appointment
tener hambre	to be hungry
sucio	dirty
el panecillo	bread roll
tener cuidado	to be careful
la aspiradora	vacuum cleaner
el bocadillo	sandwich
el regalo	present
la ventana	window
enchufar	to plug in
el aparato	apparatus
con cuidado	carefully
los mejillones	mussels
la basura	rubbish
abrocharse	to fasten
el cinturón	seat belt
sin hacer	untidy (in this context)
el cubo	bucket
la esponja	sponge

37

TO BE OR NOT TO BE?
¿'ser' o 'estar'?

 ¿Preparados?

Two verbs for 'to be'?
Spanish has the luxury of having two verbs to express the idea of 'being'. This is no problem, because they do different jobs: it is simply a question of knowing which one to use and when, and as usual there are a couple of easy rules to learn and remember.

Firstly, here are the two verbs side by side in the present tense. You will find the other tenses in the verb tables.

ser	to be	*estar*
soy	I am	*estoy*
eres	you are (*tú*)	*estás*
es	he/she/it is	*está*
	you are (*usted*)	
somos	we are	*estamos*
sois	you are (*vosotros*)	*estáis*
son	they are	*están*
	you are (*ustedes*)	

You can see that, while *ser* is very irregular, *estar* is almost a regular *-ar* verb! Even so, both mostly have the endings you would expect.

What is the difference between the two? To explain this, it is useful to look at the Latin origins of these two words.

■ *Ser* comes straight from the Latin verb *esse*, which also gives us English words like 'essence': not surprisingly, it is used to refer to 'existence' and 'essence', i.e. **what** things are, **who** people are and **what** they are **like**.

■ *Estar*, on the other hand, is the modern Spanish form of the Latin *stare*, 'to stand' or 'to be' in the sense of place. It also has the sense of 'state' or 'status', so often answers the questions **where** and **how** something is.

Uses

a *ser*

■ *ser* is used to describe who or what something/somebody is – type of person or job, type of animal or object and so on:

*Éste **es** mi amigo.*	This is my friend.
*Mi padre **era** profesor.*	My father was a teacher.
***Es** un perro de aguas.*	He/it is a cocker spaniel.
*Este libro **es** un diccionario español.*	This book is a Spanish dictionary.

■ *ser* is used to describe what somebody/something is like (permanently), where they come from, or what something is made of:

*Rosita **es** una chica muy inteligente.*	Rose is a very intelligent girl.
*El puente **era** muy largo.*	The bridge was very long.
***Somos** de Madrid.*	We are from Madrid.
*Estos zapatos no **son** de cuero.*	These shoes are not (made of) leather.

■ *ser* is used to tell the time:

***Es** la una / mediodía / medianoche.*	It is one o'clock / midday / midnight.
***Son** las once y media.*	It is half-past eleven.

■ *ser* is used to express possession, to say whose something is:

***Es** de José.*	It is José's.
*No **son** tuyos.*	They are not yours.

b *estar*

■ *estar* is used to say where something is:

*Pepe y Manolo no **están** aquí.*	Pepe and Manolo are not here.
*El cine **estaba** al lado del café.*	The cinema was next to the café.

¡Viva la gramática!

■ *estar* expresses what state somebody/something is in:

Está muy contenta de estar aquí.	She is very pleased to be here.
La ventana está rota.	The window is broken.

See also the use of *estar* in continuous tenses (see Chapter 27), with the past participle (Chapter 33) and with the passive (Chapter 38).

¡Consejo!

So, *ser* is generally used for **permanent** things such as identification and permanent characteristics and *estar* is generally used for **position** and changeable **states of being**.

Generally speaking, if there is not a good reason to use *estar*, use *ser*; this is a useful rule, but is not foolproof. In fact, there are also times when the verb used is not the one you would expect, or when either would do, so watch out for such occasions too!

¿Listos?

1 Parejas

He aquí unas parejas de frases: en cada caso, una necesita el verbo *ser* y la otra el verbo *estar*. Escoge el verbo más adecuado para cada frase.

Here are some pairs of sentences: in each case, one needs the verb *ser* and the other the verb *estar*. Choose the most appropriate verb for each sentence.

1. Mi amigo Raúl no .... en el colegio.
   En efecto, Raúl .... un chico muy perezoso.   *es / está*

2. Raúl y su hermana Maruca .... gemelos.
   Los dos .... jugando con su CD Rom en casa.   *son / están*

3. Raúl dice que .... enfermo.
   En realidad, ... un chico muy mentiroso.   *era / estaba*

4. Por eso, ... muy enfadado con Raúl.
   Yo no .... tan imbécil como él.   *soy / estoy*

5. Maruca y yo .... novios.
   ¡Pero no .... haciendo novillos como Raúl!   *somos / estamos*

6. Hoy, sus padres .... muy tolerantes con Raúl.
   ¡Pero un día de éstos .... al tanto de lo que hace!   *serán / estarán*

H *2 ¡Te toca a ti!*

Ahora te toca a ti decidir cuál de los verbos es el mejor, y en qué persona.

Now it is your turn to decide which of the verbs fits better, and in what form.

Galerías Preciosas

___1___ buscando un chico o una chica para trabajar los sábados.

Si tú ___2___ cortés, trabajador e inteligente, te necesitamos

en la nueva sección de música que ___3___ construyendo en el sótano.

El salario ___4___ bueno, y el trabajo ___5___ muy interesante:

el horario ___6___ de nueve a seis, y el supermercado ___7___ abierto

de diez a cinco. Si tú ___8___ buscando trabajo, y esta oferta ___9___

de interés,

¡ven a vernos en seguida, te ___10___ esperando!

 ¡Ya!

3 Adivinanza

Piensas en (una) cosa(s) que no puedes ver, diciendo las primeras letras de la cosa.
Tus amigos tienen que adivinar qué es / son y dónde está(n).

Think of an object you can't see, telling your friends the letters it/they begin(s)
with. Your friends have to guess what it is/they are and where it is/they are.

Ejemplo:

A.   **Estoy pensando en una cosa con dos palabras: la primera empieza con**
         b y la segunda con r.
B.   **¿Es una bicicleta roja?**
A.   **No, es un bolígrafo rojo. ¿Dónde está?**
B.   **¿Está en tu bolsillo?**
A.   **Sí.**

¡Viva la gramática!

H *4 ¿Quién es y dónde está?*

Piensas en una persona importante. Tus compañeros tratan de adivinar quién es, y luego dónde está, y qué está haciendo.

Think of a famous person. Your classmates try to guess who it is and where he/she is, and what he/she is doing.

Ejemplo:
A. **¿Quién es?**
B. **¿Es Carlos Sainz?**
A. **Sí, pero ¿dónde está?**
B. **¿Está en un rallye?**
A. **No, está en casa. Y, ¿qué está haciendo?**
B. **¿Está jugando al ping-pong?**
A. **¡Sí!**

H *5 ¿Qué hora es . . . ?*

Describe una situación a tus amigos: ellos tienen que adivinar qué hora es y qué estás haciendo.

Describe a situation to your friends: they have to guess what time it is and what you are doing.

Ejemplo:
A. **Estoy sentado/a a la mesa con un cuchillo en la mano.**
B. **Son las ocho y estás desayunando, ¿verdad?**
A. **No, son las seis de la tarde, ¡y estoy pelando patatas para la cena!**

6 ¿Cómo es?

Cada miembro de tu grupo tiene que describir a otro, usando el verbo *ser*: a ver si lo podéis hacer sin pelearos!

Each member of your group has to describe another, using the verb ser: see if you can do it without fighting!

Ejemplo:
A. **José es bajo, feo y gordo . . .**
B. **No, es alto, feo y estúpido . . .**
C. **¡Que va! ¡Soy alto, delgado, guapo e inteligente!**

H 7 *¿Cómo estás?*

Describe lo que le ha pasado a alguien: tus compañeros tienen que adivinar cómo se siente esta persona.

Describe what has happened to somebody: your classmates have to guess how this person feels.

Ejemplos:

A.　　**Mis padres han comprado un coche nuevo y van a ir de vacaciones.**

B.　　**¿Están contentos?**

A.　　**Sí, claro.**

Glosario

perezoso	lazy
el gemelo	twin
enfermo	ill
mentiroso	lying
enfadado	angry
imbécil	stupid
hacer novillos	to play truant
estar al tanto	to be aware
te toca a ti	it's your turn
cortés	polite
trabajador	hard-working
construir	to build
el sótano	basement
la oferta	offer
el bolsillo	pocket
el cuchillo	knife
pelar	to peel

38

WHAT WAS DONE?

the passive

 ¿Preparados?

1 What is the passive?

■ Most sentences tell you that 'somebody does/did something', i.e. the order is subject – verb – object: 'Robert bought the computer' *Roberto compró el ordenador*. In this case the verb is **active**.

subject	verb	object
Roberto	*compró*	*el ordenador.*
Robert	bought	the computer.

■ Quite often however, especially in English, you can turn this round and say 'The computer was bought by Robert'. In this case, the object becomes the subject and the person who the action was done by becomes the 'agent'. In this case the verb is **passive**:

subject	verb	agent
El ordenador	*fue comprado*	*por Roberto.*
The computer	was bought	by Robert.

2 How do you form the passive?

■ As in English, you make up a passive verb with the relevant tense of 'to be' *ser* + the **past participle**, which in this case agrees with the subject:

> *Los regalos **fueron escogidos** por Emi.*
> The presents **were chosen** by Emi.

> *Las ensaladas **serán preparadas** por la clase.*
> The salads **will be prepared** by the class.

*Este aparato **es fabricado** por una compañía española.*
This machinery **is manufactured** by a Spanish firm.

 ¡Ojo!

Don't forget to make the past participle agree with what is now the subject!

 **¡Consejo!**

You don't necessarily have to have an agent (i.e. someone who the action was done **by**):

*Nuestra casa **fue construida** en 1986.*
Our house **was built** in 1986.

*Este aparato **es fabricado** en España.*
This machinery **is manufactured** in Spain.

 **¡Ojo!**

Be careful, however, as this structure is used considerably less in Spanish than in English, and you will find alternative ways of expressing it in the next chapter (39).

■ As you see, *ser* is the Spanish verb 'to be' which is used to form the passive. However, you will also find *estar* used with the past participle, and the difference is important:

*La puerta **fue cerrada** por el portero.*
The door **was closed** by the doorman. (i.e. he closed it)

*No podíamos entrar porque la puerta **estaba cerrada**.*
We couldn't get in because the door was closed. (i.e. that was how the door was when we were trying to get in)

*La casa **es pintada** cada año.*
The house is painted every year. (i.e. somebody paints it)

*La casa **está pintada** de verde.*
The house **is painted** green. (i.e. that's how it is)

¡Viva la gramática!

In other words, you use *ser* + **past participle** to describe the action and say what is/was/will be **done**, and *estar* + **past participle** to describe the resultant **state**.

 ¿Listos?

H 1 *¡Orden!*

Cristina escribe una corta historia de su ciudad, pero tiene un problema con su ordenador, y las palabras no salen en el orden correcto. ¿Sabes ponerlas en orden?

Cristina is writing a short history of her town, but she's got a problem with her computer and the words are coming out in the wrong order. Can you put them in order for her?

Ejemplo:
1248: rey fue el el por construido castillo
1248: el castillo fue construido por el rey

1252: rey fueron las el por construidas murallas
1540: construido sobre el fue río puente el
1864: fundada lana de fábrica fue la
1937: fue por Ayuntamiento bomba el destruido una
1953: Ayuntamiento reina fue nuevo abierto la por el
1966: trenes cerrada la de estación fue
1993: alcalde abierto polideportivo el fue el por
1995: peatonalizadas el las por fueron calles Ayuntamiento
1995: en fueron coches el prohibidos centro los
El año que viene: nueva abierta piscina una será

H 2 *El viejo molino*

Lee este párrafo sobre la restauración de un viejo molino, y rellena los espacios en blanco con *ser* o *estar*.

Read this paragraph about the restoration of an old mill, and fill the gaps with the relevant part of *ser* or *estar*.

Este viejo edificio ....1....... construido en el siglo XVIII como molino de agua. La mayor parte ....2....... construida de piedra. ....3....... utilizado para hacer harina pero más tarde ....4....... abandonado. ....5....... comprado hace unos años por unos

amigos míos. Entonces, todas las ventanas ....6...... rotas y las puertas ....7......
podridas. Durante cinco años mis amigos trabajaron cada día. Todas las ventanas y
puertas ....8...... reparadas y una gran rueda ....9...... fabricada y puesta en el
agua. Ahora el molino funciona muy bien. ......10..... completamente restaurada y
muchos sacos de harina ......11..... producidos cada día.

 ¡Ya!

H *3 Una breve historia de mi ciudad o pueblo*

Utilizando las frases del ejercicio 1 como modelo, habla de o escribe un párrafo
sobre la historia de tu propia ciudad o pueblo.

Using the sentences in exercise 1 as a model, talk or write a paragraph about the
history of your town or village. Say when things were built, founded, opened,
closed, etc., and possibly include a couple of things that will be done soon.

Ejemplo:
1370: la ciudad fue fundada

Glosario

fundar	to found
la harina	flour
el molino	mill
las murallas	(town) walls
peatonalizar	to pedestrianise
podrido	rotten
producir	to produce
restaurar	to restore
la rueda	wheel
el saco	sack, bag

39

WHAT WAS DONE?
avoiding the passive

 ¿Preparados?

We said in the last chapter (38) that the passive, although it exists in Spanish, is not used nearly as much as it is in English. This chapter explains what Spanish-speakers tend to do instead, especially when there is no agent (i.e. you are not told who the action is done by).

a Use a reflexive verb
A very common way of getting over the same meaning as the passive is to make the verb reflexive:

*Las ensaladas **se prepararon** en la cocina.*
The salads **were prepared** in the kitchen.

*Este aparato **se fabrica** en España.*
This machinery **is manufactured** in Spain.

*La piscina **se terminará** el año que viene.*
The new swimming pool **will be** finished next year.

*Aquí **se habla** español.*
Spanish **is spoken** here.

***Se prohíbe** fumar en los cines españoles.*
Smoking **is prohibited** in Spanish cinemas.

***Se dice** que hay un fantasma en este castillo.*
It is said that there's a ghost in this castle.

 **¡Ojo!**

Don't forget to make your verb plural if the subject is plural! But don't use this form with people and animals if it makes sense literally: *se mató el turista* could well mean that the tourist killed himself!

 ¡Consejo!

See also Chapter 35 for how to use *(no) se puede* 'you can/can't' and *(no) se debe* 'you must/mustn't'.

b Use the 3rd person plural (*ellos* form), putting the object first with a 'personal *a*' (see Chapter 18)

> *A Carmen la vieron* ayer en la ciudad.
> **Carmen was seen** yesterday in town.

> *A Antonio le mandaron* a Sevilla.
> **Antonio was sent** to Seville.

This construction is particularly handy when you want to say 'he was given something', 'we were sent something', 'I was told something', etc.:

Le dieron un reloj.	**He was given** a watch.
Nos mandaron el paquete.	**We were sent** the packet.
Me dijeron que Vd. no venía.	**I was told** that you weren't coming.

 ¡Consejo!

Learn the following as set phrases, as they are very useful:

Me dijeron	I was told	*Nos dijeron*	We were told
Me dieron	I was given	*Nos dieron*	We were given

c Use an active verb

Where there is an agent (who the action is done **by**), you can always turn the sentence round and revert to an active verb (see the beginning of Chapter 38):

*Los regalos **fueron escogidos** por Emi.*	The presents **were chosen by** Emi.
*Emi **escogió** los regalos.*	Emi **chose** the presents.

¡Viva la gramática!

 ## ¿Listos?

H 1 *¡Más historia!*

He aquí una versión un poco diferente de la historia de una ciudad del ejercicio 1 del capítulo 38. Cambia los verbos al pretérito, utilizando la forma pronominal.

Here is a slightly different version of the history of a town in exercise 1 of the previous chapter. Put the verbs into the preterite, using the reflexive form. Remember: singular subject, singular verb; plural subject, plural verb!

Ejemplo:
Las murallas (construir) en 1252.
Las murallas se construyeron en 1252.

1. El puente (construir) en 1540.

2. La fábrica de lana (fundar) en 1864.

3. El antiguo Ayuntamiento (destruir) en 1937.

4. El nuevo Ayuntamiento (abrir) en 1953.

5. La estación de trenes (cerrar) en 1966.

6. El nuevo polideportivo (abrir) en 1993.

7. Las calles del centro (peatonalizar) en 1995.

8. Los coches (prohibir) en el centro también en 1995.

9. La nueva piscina (terminar) el año que viene.

H 2 *¿A quién . . . ?*

Tienes que decir qué ocurrió a quién, según los dibujos.

Say what happened to whom, according to the sketches, choosing a verb from box A and the remainder of the sentence from box B.

Ejemplo:
A Paqui le enviaron un paquete

Paqui   1 Montse

2 Javier   3 Ana   4 Ramón

5 Rosario   6 Gerardo   7 Pili

A

dar   decir   escribir   mandar   oír   prohibir   ver   enviar

---

B

carta   en la discoteca   entrar   llegar   una postal   un reloj   la verdad
un paquete

 ¡Ya!

H *3 Mi ciudad o pueblo, otra vez*

Haz el ejercicio 3 del capítulo 38, pero esta vez, usa verbos reflexivos.

Do exercise 3 from the last chapter (38) again, but this time use reflexive verbs instead of the passive.

Ejemplo:
*La ciudad **se fundó** en 1370.*

¡Viva la gramática!

H *4 Chismes, o susurros chinos*

a. Os ponéis en un círculo y uno empieza susurrando al oído de su vecino 'Me dijeron que . . .' y tiene que decir algo interesante ¡o quizás escandaloso! sobre un miembro de la clase. Luego el próximo repite el mensaje hasta que se cumpla el círculo. Luego hay que decirlo en voz alta.

Sit in a circle. One begins by whispering a piece of gossip (Me dijeron que . . .) about a member of the class in the ear of his/her neighbour. This pupil passes it on until it has been round the whole circle, when it is said aloud to the whole class or group.

Ejemplo:
Me dijeron que Ramón tiene una nueva novia . . .

b. Se juega igual, pero cada alumno/a tiene que añadir un chisme.

Play in the same way, but each pupil has to add another piece of gossip:

Ejemplo:
Me dijeron que Ramón tiene una nueva novia. ¡Es muy alta!
Me dijeron que Ramón tiene una nueva novia. ¡Es muy alta y delgada!, etc.

40

I WANT YOU TO DO THAT!
the present subjunctive

 ¿Preparados?

What is the subjunctive?
The **subjunctive** is a special form of the verb that you use in certain special circumstances instead of the 'normal' forms of the verb, which, incidentally, are called the **indicative**.

You will, in fact, already be familiar with some subjunctive forms, for example:

¡dígame! – when you answer the phone
¡traiga una coca cola! – in a café
¡tuerza a la izquierda y tome la segunda calle a la derecha! – when asking/giving directions in the street.

These 'imperatives', or commands, already dealt with in Chapter 36, are in fact forms of the present subjunctive, and are used for **all** *usted* and *ustedes* **commands** and **all negative commands** (don't!) as well (see page 215).

1 How to form the present subjunctive
a Regular verbs (compare the 'normal'/indicative present tense on page 116)
This is easy: you just swap over *-a* and *-e/-i* endings, remembering to make the 1st person (*yo*) form end in *-e* or *-a* as well:

trabajar to work	*comer* to eat	*vivir* to live
trabaje	coma	viva
trabajes	comas	vivas
trabaje	coma	viva
trabajemos	comamos	vivamos
trabajéis	comáis	viváis
trabajen	coman	vivan

¡Viva la gramática!

b **'Stem-changing' verbs** (compare the 'normal' present on page 116)

■ These verbs swap endings just like the regular ones, and *-ar* and *-er* (Type 1) verbs have the stem-change in the same place:

-ar: e > ie *pensar* to think	*-ar*: u > ue *jugar* to play	*-er*: e > ie *entender* to understand	*-er*: o > ue *volver* to return
piense	juegue	entienda	vuelva
pienses	juegues	entiendas	vuelvas
piense	juegue	entienda	vuelva
pensemos	juguemos	entendamos	volvamos
penséis	juguéis	entendáis	volváis
piensen	jueguen	entiendan	vuelvan

 ¡Ojo!

Because you have changed the vowel you **may** need a spelling change to the stem, as in *jugar* > *juegue*. This is dealt with in full in Chapter 21.

■ Type 2 *-ir* verbs have the same changes plus an additional change *-o-* > *-u-*, *-e-* > *-i-* in the 1st and 2nd person plural (*nosotros/vosotros*):

sentir to feel	*dormir* to sleep
sienta	duerma
sientas	duermas
sienta	duerma
sintamos	durmamos
sintáis	durmáis
sientan	duerman

 **¡Ojo!**

In Type 3 *-ir* verbs *-e-* becomes *-i-* all through the present subjunctive:

pedir to ask for	pida, pidas, pida, pidamos, pidáis, pidan

¡Consejo!

For a complete list of the verbs you are likely to meet in these groups, see Chapter 21.

c -g- and -zc verbs

There are a number of verbs whose 1st person singular (*yo*) form ends in *-go* or *-zco*. These keep the *-g-* and *-zc-* right through the present subjunctive. You will be familiar with those that you have been using in commands:

-g-
decir to say (**digo**): **diga, digas, diga, digamos, digáis, digan**
caer to fall (**caigo**): **caiga, caigas**, etc.
hacer to do/make (**hago**): **haga, hagas**, etc.
oír to hear (**oigo**): **oiga, oigas**, etc.
salir to go out, leave (**salgo**): **salga, salgas**, etc.
tener to have (**tengo**): **tenga, tengas**, etc.
traer to bring (**traigo**): **traiga, traigas**, etc.
venir to come (**vengo**): **venga, vengas**, etc.

-zc-
conocer to know (**conozco**): **conozca, conozcas**, etc.
reconocer to recognise (**reconozco**): **reconozca, reconozcas**, etc.
parecer to seem, appear (**parezco**): **parezca, parezcas**, etc
traducir to translate (**traduzco**): **traduzca, traduzcas**, etc.

¡Consejo!

This happens to **all** verbs ending in *-ecer, -ocer* and *-ucir*.

d Irregular verbs

The following verbs have an irregular 'stem', but the endings are normal:

ir to go: **vaya, vayas, vaya, vayamos, vayáis, vayan**
ser to be: **sea, seas, sea, seamos, seáis, sean**
saber to know: **sepa, sepas, sepa, sepamos, sepáis, sepan**
haber to have (auxiliary verb): **haya, hayas, haya, hayamos, hayáis, hayan**

¡Viva la gramática!

¡Consejo!

Therefore the present subjunctive of *hay* = 'there is' is *haya*.

¡Ojo!

Dar and *estar* are not really irregular, but watch out for the accents:

> *dar* to give: **dé, des, dé, demos, deis, den**
> *estar* to be: **esté, estés, esté, estemos, estéis, estén**

2 Uses of the present subjunctive

The subjunctive has a range of uses, but we will concentrate here on the ones you are most likely to need to use for GCSE or Scottish 'O' grade.

a Wanting, liking, preferring or telling someone to do something

You use the subjunctive when you want (or don't want) someone **else** to do something. Compare:

• *Yo **quiero** ver el tenis.*	**I want** to watch tennis (**I** both want and watch).
*Yo **quiero** que **tú veas** el tenis.*	I want **you to watch** the tennis (**I** want, **you** watch).
• *¿**Quieres** cerrar la puerta?*	Do **you** want to shut the door? (**you** both want and shut)
*¿**Quieres** que **yo cierre** la puerta?*	Do **you** want **me to shut** the door? (**You** want, **I** shut)
• *¿**Te** gusta bailar?*	Do **you** like dancing? (**You** both like and dance)
*No **te** gusta que **yo baile** con aquel chico, ¿verdad?*	**You** don't like **me** dancing with that boy, do you? (**You** don't like, **I** dance)
• ***Prefiero** ir al cine.*	**I prefer to go** to the cinema (**I** both prefer and go).
***Prefiero** que **vengas** al cine.*	I prefer **you to come** to the cinema (**I** prefer, **you** come).

238

- *Dile a Marcela que venga a verme.*   **Tell** Marcela **to come** and see me (**You** tell, **Marcela** comes).

b You use the subjunctive after time expressions such as *cuando* 'when', *así que* or *en cuanto* 'as soon as', *hasta que* 'until' if the action **has not yet taken place**:

Cuando veas a Marcela, dale esto, por favor.

When you see Marcela, please give her this (you haven't seen her yet).

Compra tu billete en cuanto llegues a la estación.

Buy your ticket **as soon as you arrive** at the station (you haven't arrived yet.)

No continúo hasta que haya silencio.

I won't continue **until there is** silence (there isn't silence yet).

c You use the subjunctive after such 'impersonal' expressions as:

es posible que	it's possible that
es necesario que	it's necessary that
es probable que	it's probable that

Es posible que lleguen temprano.

It's possible that they may arrive early.

Es necesario que lo termines para mañana.

It's necessary that you finish it by tomorrow.

 ¿Listos?

H *1 ¡Qué madre tan mandona!*

La mamá de María es muy estricta y mandona, y la pobre María tiene que hacer lo que su madre le manda. He aquí algunas de las cosas que tiene que hacer. Escoge uno de los verbos en subjuntivo del recuadro para rellenar el espacio en blanco.

María's mum is very strict and bossy, and poor María has to do what her mother tells her. Choose a verb in the subjunctive to fill the gap in each sentence.

1. María, ¡quiero que .... al supermercado en seguida!

2. María, ¡quiero que .... tu cama!

3. María, ¡dile a tu hermana que .... su desayuno!

4. María, ¡dile a tu padre que .... mis zapatos!

¡Viva la gramática!

5. María, ¡no me gusta que .... la radio!

6. María, ¡no me gusta que .... con Pepe!

7. María, ¡prefiero que .... en casa conmigo!

8. María, ¡no me gusta que me .... la lengua!

9. María, ¡no quiero que me .... así!

10. María, niña, ¡sólo quiero que .... contenta!

coma	estés	hables	hagas	limpie	oigas	salgas
	te quedes		vayas	saques		

H 2 ¡Todo es posible!

He aquí unas cosas que pueden ocurrir dentro del próximo año. Pon el verbo en presente del subjuntivo.

Here are some things that may happen in the next year. Put the verbs into the present subjunctive.

1. Es posible que mi clase y yo (ir) a España de intercambio.

2. Es posible que yo (trabajar) en el supermercado Tesco para cobrar dinero.

3. En el verano es posible que yo (jugar) al tenis para el equipo del colegio.

4. Es posible que nuestros amigos españoles nos (visitar) en julio.

5. Es probable que mi hermano (terminar) sus estudios en la universidad.

6. Es muy probable que Miguel (tener) una nueva novia . . .

7. . . . pero ¡es muy posible que ella no (querer) salir con él!

8. Es necesario que todos nosotros (aprobar) nuestros exámenes,

9. . . . pero, Alfonso y Elena, es muy posible que vosotros (suspender), ¿no?

10. También es posible que (haber) una nueva profesora de español en el otoño.

H 3 Proyectos de intercambio

Rachel habla de los proyectos de una visita de intercambio a España, pero una versión habla de lo que pasó el año pasado, y la otra de los proyectos para este año. Tienes que escoger el verbo correcto en cada caso.

Rachel is talking about plans for an exchange visit to Spain, but one sentence of each pair refers to last year's plans, and the other to this year's visit, which has yet to take place. Choose the right verb each time, remembering that you use the subjunctive **if the action has not yet happened**!

1a. En cuanto mi profesor de español *tuvo / tenga* los detalles del intercambio, nos los dio.

1b. En cuanto mi profesor de español *tiene / tenga* los detalles del intercambio, nos los dará.

2a. En cuanto *recibo / reciba* la dirección de mi nueva amiga española, le escribiré.

2b. En cuanto *recibí / reciba* la dirección de mi nueva amiga española, le escribí.

3a. Cuando mi amiga española *contestó / conteste* a mi carta, la llamé por teléfono.

3b. Cuando mi amiga española *conteste / contesta* a mi carta, la llamaré por teléfono.

4a. Cuando *llegamos / lleguemos* al aeropuerto de Madrid, ella estará esperándonos.

4b. Cuando *llegamos / lleguemos* al aeropuerto de Madrid, ella estaba esperándonos.

 ¡Ya!

H *4 ¡Quiero que lo hagas!*

Se puede jugar en parejas, grupos o en la clase completa. Un(a) alumno/a dice a otro/a: *Quiero que* . . . seguido de la acción en subjuntivo. Éste/a lo hace, y si lo hace correctamente, dice a otro/a alumno/a lo que quiere que haga, y el juego sigue así.

To be played in pairs, groups or as a whole class. One pupil tells another what he/she wants them to do. If he/she does it correctly, he/she then tells another pupil what to do, and so on.

Ejemplo:
A. **Roberto, *quiero que dibujes* un gato en la pizarra / en tu cuaderno.**
    (*If Roberto draws a cat, as told, he tells another pupil what to do.*)
B **Pili, *quiero que saques* un bolígrafo de tu lapicero**, etc.

Verbos útiles

escribir leer dibujar sacar poner decir enseñar mostrar tocar ir

¡Viva la gramática!

H *5 Más posibilidades*

Habla del sábado que viene, y di lo que *es posible / probable / necesario que* ocurra.

Talk about next Saturday and the things that may or must happen, using *es posible que, es probable que, es necesario que.*

Ejemplos:
Es posible que vaya al cine con mi novio/a.
Es probable que me compre unos vaqueros nuevos.
Es necesario que lleve el perro al veterinario.

Glosario

el lapicero	pencil case
ocurrir	to happen
la pizarra	black/whiteboard
la posibilidad	possibility
el/la veterinario/a	vet

41

I WANTED YOU TO DO THAT!
the imperfect subjunctive

 **¿Preparados?**

1 What is the imperfect subjunctive?

Almost since you first began learning Spanish, you've been using an imperfect subjunctive: *Quisiera un café con leche* 'I'd like a white coffee' – although admittedly this is a special use of this form. If you've also learnt expressions like *si tuviera mucho dinero* 'if I had a lot of money', or *si fuera rico/a* 'if I were rich', these are also forms of the imperfect subjunctive.

The imperfect subjunctive is used in much the same way as the present subjunctive (Chapter 40), except that the verbs in the sentence are in one or more of the past tenses. This is explained in section 3 below.

2 How do you form it?

There are two forms, one ending in *-ra* and the other in *-se*. Normally it doesn't matter which form you use.

a Regular verbs

-ar verbs end in *-ara* or *-ase*, etc., and *-er* and *-ir* verbs end in *-iera* or *-iese*, etc.:

trabajar to work		*comer* to eat		*vivir* to live	
trabajara	trabajase	comiera	comiese	viviera	viviese
trabajaras	trabajases	comieras	comieses	vivieras	vivieses
trabajara	trabajase	comiera	comiese	viviera	viviese
trabajáramos	trabajásemos	comiéramos	comiésemos	viviéramos	viviésemos
trabajarais	trabajaseis	comierais	comieseis	vivierais	vivieseis
trabajaran	trabajasen	comieran	comiesen	vivieran	viviesen

¡Viva la gramática!

b Irregular verbs

 **¡Ojo!**

Because the stem for the imperfect subjunctive is the **3rd person plural** (*ellos*) of the **preterite**, it will have the same irregularities as the preterite.

The main groups are:

■ Verbs with a 'pretérito grave' (see Chapter 29):

Infinitive	Preterite	Imperfect Subjunctive	
andar	**andu**vieron	andu**viera**	andu**viese**
conducir	**conduj**eron*	conduj**era**	conduj**ese**
decir	**dij**eron*	dij**era**	dij**ese**
estar	**estu**vieron	estu**viera**	estu**viese**
hacer	**hic**ieron	hic**iera**	hic**iese**
ir / ser	**fu**eron	fu**era**	fu**ese**
poder	**pud**ieron	pud**iera**	pud**iese**
poner	**pus**ieron	pus**iera**	pus**iese**
querer	**quis**ieron	quis**iera**	quis**iese**
saber	**sup**ieron	sup**iera**	sup**iese**
tener	**tuv**ieron	tuv**iera**	tuv**iese**
traer	**traj**eron*	traj**era**	traj**ese**
venir	**vin**ieron	vin**iera**	vin**iese**

*Verbs ending in *-eron* in the preterite have no *-i-*: they end in *-era / -ese*.

■ Verbs whose preterite ends in *-yeron* have *-yera* or *-yese*:

oír	**o**yeron	**o**yera	**o**yese
caer	**ca**yeron	**ca**yera	**ca**yese
leer	**le**yeron	**le**yera	**le**yese
creer	**cre**yeron	**cre**yera	**cre**yese

■ Stem-changing verbs with *-e- > -i-* and *-o- > -u-* in the preterite:

pedir	**pid**ieron	**pid**iera	pid**iese**
preferir	**prefir**ieron	prefir**iera**	prefir**iese**
seguir	**sigu**ieron	sigu**iera**	sigu**iese**
dormir	**durm**ieron	durm**iera**	durm**iese**
morir	**mur**ieron	mur**iera**	mur**iese**

3 How do you use the imperfect subjunctive?

In the same way as the present subjunctive, but you use it mainly when the other verbs in the sentence are in the imperfect, preterite or conditional. The following examples are almost the same as those illustrating the present subjunctive on pages 238–239, but they use past tenses with the imperfect subjunctive.

*Yo **quería** que tú **vieras** el tenis.*	**I wanted** you to watch the tennis.
*¿**Querías** que yo **cerrara** la puerta?*	**Did you want** me to shut the door?
*No te **gustó** que yo **bailase** con aquel chico, ¿verdad?*	**You didn't like** me dancing with that boy, did you?
Preferiría que vinieras al cine.	**I'd prefer** you to come to the cinema.
*Era posible que **llegasen** temprano.*	**It was** possible that they might arrive early.
*Era necesario que lo **terminaras** pronto.*	**It was** necessary that you finish it soon.

The imperfect subjunctive is also used after *si* together with the conditional in sentences such as:

*Si **tuviera/tuviese** bastante dinero **compraría** una bici.*	If I **had** enough money I **would** buy a bike.

¿Listos?

Los ejercicios 1 a 4 son casi iguales a los ejercicios del Capítulo 40 sobre el presente del subjuntivo, pero los hemos cambiado para que necesiten el uso del **imperfecto del subjuntivo**. ¿Sabes explicar por qué?

Exercises 1 to 4 are basically the same as some of those in Chapter 40 on the present subjunctive, except that they have been slightly changed so that you need to use

¡Viva la gramática!

imperfect subjunctives. Can you explain why you need to use the imperfect subjunctive?

H 1 *¡Qué madre tan mandona!*

La mamá de María es muy estricta y mandona, y la pobre María tiene que hacer lo que su madre le manda. He aquí algunas de las cosas que tiene que hacer. Escoge uno de los verbos en subjuntivo del recuadro para rellenar el espacio en blanco. Esta vez, la amiga de María cuenta lo que vio al visitar la casa de María.

María's mum is very strict and bossy, and poor María has to do what her mother tells her. Choose a verb in the subjunctive to fill the gap in each sentence. This time, María's friend is recounting what she witnessed when she visited María's house.

1. ¡La madre de María quería que María .... al supermercado en seguida!

2. ¡Quería que María .... su cama!

3. ¡Quería que la hermana de María .... su desayuno!

4. ¡Quería que el padre de María .... sus zapatos!

5. No le gustaba que María .... la radio.

6. No le gustaba que María .... con Pepe.

7. Preferiría que .... en casa con ella.

8. No le gustaba que María le .... la lengua.

9. No quería que María le .... así.

10. ¡Dijo que sólo quería que la pobre María .... contenta!

comiera	estuviera	hablara	hiciera	limpiara	oyera
se quedara	fuera	sacara	saliera		

H 2 *¡Todo era posible!*

He aquí unas cosas que podían haber ocurrido durante el año pasado. Pon el verbo en imperfecto del subjuntivo.

Here are some things that may have happened during the past year. Put the verbs into the imperfect subjunctive.

246

1. Era posible que mi clase y yo (ir) a España de intercambio.

2. Era posible que yo (trabajar) en el supermercado Tesco para cobrar dinero.

3. En el verano era posible que yo (jugar) al tenis para el equipo del colegio.

4. Era posible que nuestros amigos españoles nos (visitar) en julio.

5. Era probable que mi hermano (terminar) sus estudios en la universidad.

6. Era muy probable que Miguel (tener) una nueva novia . . .

7. . . . pero ¡era muy posible que ella no (querer) salir con él!

8. Era necesario que todos nosotros (aprobar) nuestros exámenes,

9. . . . pero, Alfonso y Elena, era muy posible que vosotros (suspender), ¿no?

10. También era posible que (haber) una nueva profesora de español en el otoño.

 ¡Ya!

H *3 ¡No quería que hiciera eso!*

Se puede jugar en parejas, grupos o en la clase completa. Un(a) alumno/a dice a otro/a lo que quisiera que hiciera. Éste/a **no** lo hace, sino que hace **otra cosa**. El primer alumno / la primera alumna tiene que decir: *¡No quería que . . . ! ¡Quería que . . . !*, utilizando el imperfecto del subjuntivo.

To be played in pairs, groups or as a whole class. One pupil tells another what he/she wants them to do. This pupil does **something else**, and the first pupil has to complain *I didn't want him/her to do that! I wanted him/her to do this!*

Ejemplo:
A. **Roberto,** *dibuja* un gato en la pizarra / en tu cuaderno. (*Roberto draws a dog.*)
B. *¡No **quería que dibujaras** un perro! ¡**Quería que dibujaras** un gato!*

Verbos útiles

escribir	leer	dibujar	sacar	poner	decir	enseñar	mostrar	tocar	ir

¡Viva la gramática!

4 Más posibilidades

Habla del sábado pasado, y di lo que *era posible / probable / necesario que* ocurriera.

Talk about last Saturday and the things that may or should have happened, using *era posible que, era probable que, era necesario que*.

Ejemplo:

Era posible que fuera al cine con mi novio/a.

Era probable que me comprara unos vaqueros nuevos.

Era necesario que llevara el perro al veterinario.

42

THE SPANISH ALPHABET

 **¿Preparados?**

The alphabet

a	ah	ñ	eñe
b	be	o	oh
c	ce	p	pe
d	de	q	cu
e	eh	r	ere
f	efe	s	ese
g	ge	t	te
h	ache	u	u
i	i	v	uve
j	jota	w	uve doble
k	ka	x	equis
l	ele	y	i griega
m	eme	z	ceda *or* ceta
n	ene		

You can see that Spanish uses the same letters as most other European languages, but there are some important points about pronunciation of certain letters. You can't learn exact pronunciation from a silent book, so please use these notes together with the help of your teacher or Spanish 'assistant(e)' and practise the examples we give you below.

a Consonants

■ *b* and *v*

b and *v* are pronounced the same as each other. At the beginning of a word they are like 'b': <u>B</u>ien, <u>V</u>erónica, ¡<u>v</u>amos al <u>b</u>anco!

In the middle of a word or between two vowels, you just let your lips come together without giving the letter its full force: *Aca<u>b</u>a<u>b</u>a de <u>b</u>e<u>b</u>er una <u>b</u>otella de jugo de u<u>v</u>a.*

■ ***c, z, qu, cu***

c is pronounced like ***k*** before *a, o, u* and **all consonants**: *<u>C</u>arlos <u>c</u>ompró un <u>c</u>ruasán <u>c</u>rujiente en la <u>c</u>afetería* (a crunchy croissant).

c before *e* and *i*, and *z* always are pronounced like the 'th' in 'thin' in European Spanish. However, in most of Spanish-speaking America, and in the south of Spain, they are pronounced the same as *s*. You should get used to recognising both pronunciations: *Hay <u>c</u>inco <u>c</u>ines en el <u>c</u>entro de <u>Z</u>arago<u>z</u>a.*

qu is only used before *e* and *i*, and is always pronounced as 'k', never 'kw': *¿<u>Qu</u>ién <u>qu</u>iere <u>qu</u>eso?*

cu gives the 'kw' sound in the combinations *cua, cue, cui*: *¡<u>Cu</u>ida tu <u>cu</u>erpo en el <u>cu</u>arto de baño!*

■ *d* has two sounds: at the beginning of a word or before a consonant it is similar to English, though you should put your tongue against the back of your top teeth: *¿<u>D</u>ónde están los <u>d</u>os <u>d</u>ibujos <u>d</u>e <u>D</u>rácula?*
When it occurs between two vowels, or on the end of a word, it is sounded like the 'th' in 'then', although in some parts of Spain it is hardly sounded at all: *Valla<u>d</u>oli<u>d</u> es una ciu<u>d</u>a<u>d</u> más diverti<u>d</u>a que Calatayu<u>d</u>, ¿ver<u>d</u>a<u>d</u>?*

■ *ch* is pronounced as in 'church'; it was a separate letter until 1994, and you may find it listed separately in some older dictionaries: *o<u>ch</u>o mu<u>ch</u>a<u>ch</u>os <u>ch</u>arlan con o<u>ch</u>o mu<u>ch</u>a<u>ch</u>as en la <u>ch</u>urrería.*

■ *f* sounds the same as in English and always replaces 'ph': *<u>F</u>elipe habla <u>f</u>iloso<u>f</u>ía por telé<u>f</u>ono.*

■ ***g, gu*** and ***gü***

g before *a, o, u* or a consonant is sounded rather like 'g' in English, but a bit further down in the throat: *Trái<u>g</u>a un <u>g</u>azpacho y una <u>g</u>aseosa <u>g</u>rande. <u>G</u>racias.*

gu is pronounced 'g' in the combinations *gue/gui*: *El <u>gu</u>ía tocaba la <u>gu</u>itarra en la <u>gu</u>erra*, but it is pronounced 'gw' before *a* and *o*.

To get 'gw' before *e*, you must use ***güe***: *¡Señor <u>gu</u>ardia! ¿Dónde está el anti<u>gu</u>o castillo de Si<u>gü</u>enza?* (The sign is called a 'diaeresis', or *diéresis* in Spanish.)

■ ***ge, gi*** and ***j*** are pronounced rather like the 'ch' in the Scottish word 'loch'. They must not be pronounced like a 'k'! *Mis hi<u>j</u>os, <u>J</u>orge, <u>J</u>aime y <u>J</u>uan, reco<u>g</u>ían a<u>j</u>os en la <u>g</u>ranja.*

■ *h* is never pronounced, wherever it occurs: *¡Pro**h**ibidos los **h**ombres en este **h**ospital!*

■ *l* similar to English but listen carefully to your teacher: *Lo**l**a **l**ee un **l**ibro españo**l**, **l**uego sa**l**e a**l** hospita**l**.*

■ *ll* was treated a separate letter until 1994, and you may still find it listed separately in older dictionaries. It is 'officially' pronounced like the 'll' in 'million', but many Spanish-speakers pronounce it like a strong 'y' or even like an English 'j': so be prepared to recognise these differing pronunciations: *Gui**ll**ermo ha**ll**ó una bote**ll**a **ll**ena de pasti**ll**as en el pasi**ll**o.*

■ *p* is much the same as in English, but without the puff of air: *Pa**p**á **p**rometió una **p**ro**p**ina a **P**aquita, **p**ero no la **p**agó.*

■ *r* is rolled, and *rr* is rolled even more: *Yo que**rr**ía un pe**rr**o, pe**r**o mi pad**r**e no quie**r**e comp**r**á**r**melo.*
Practise the difference between: *pe**r**o – pe**rr**o, que**r**ía – que**rr**ía, ca**r**o – ca**rr**o, pa**r**a – pa**rr**a, co**r**o – Co**rr**eos.*

¡Consejo!

If, as many British people do, you find it difficult to roll an 'r', try sounding a correct Spanish *t* by putting your tongue against your top teeth. Then try to say *tres trenes*, flicking the tip of your tongue off your teeth. Does this help? If so, gradually try other words beginning with *r* . . .

■ *s* is pronounced roughly the same as in English 'bus', though some speakers give it a slight 'sh' sound: *Se**s**enta y **s**ei**s** **s**alchicha**s** **s**obre**s**alientes **s**e venden en e**s**as **s**alchicherías.*

It is only pronounced as in 'as' in words like *de**s**de mi**s**mo, cicli**s**mo, ci**s**ne* before *-d*, *-m*, or *-n*, etc.

■ *t* is pronounced with your tongue against the back of your top teeth. Say 'top teeth' like that in English, to help see the difference.
Now practise: *T**r**ae **t**res **t**ipos de **t**oma**t**es para **t**u **t**ía.*

■ *w* only occurs in imported words, and is usually replaced by *v*.

■ *x* is usually pronounced like *s* before a consonant: *Fue una e**x**cursión e**x**celente y e**x**traordinaria* and usually as 'ks' between vowels: *Te deseamos é**x**ito en tus e**x**ámenes.*

¡Viva la gramática!

 **¡Ojo!**

Have you noticed how few **double consonants** there are in Spanish? You have met *ll* and *rr*, which have different sounds from *l* and *r*. You will meet *cc*, in words like *lección*, *acción*, where the first *c* = 'k' and the second = 'th', and very occasionally *nn* in words like ***innumerable***. Otherwise, any other double consonant will be in imported words like *cassette* (which can also be spelled *casete*).

b Vowels

There are five vowels in Spanish: *a*, *e*, *i*, *o*, *u*, and they only have one sound each.

- *a* pronounced 'ah': make sure you give it its full value, wherever it occurs: *A͟cab͟ab͟a de ll͟am͟ar a͟ l͟a a͟z͟af͟at͟a a͟rgentin͟a.*

- *e* pronounced as in 'pet'. Be careful not to put a 'y' on the end, as in 'they': *M͟erc͟ed͟es, e͟n e͟sta m͟esa qu͟er͟emos tr͟es caf͟és con l͟ec͟he.*

- *i* pronounced like 'ee' in 'feet', as is *y* in the word *y* = 'and': *M͟is h͟ijos y͟ yo viv͟imos aqu͟í en V͟igo con m͟is t͟íos – dijo P͟il͟i.*

- *o* pronounced as in 'not', wherever it comes (never as in English 'no'): *¡H͟ombre! En C͟órd͟oba Man͟ol͟o pesc͟ó o͟ch͟o h͟oras y s͟ól͟o cogi͟ó una b͟ota r͟ota.*

- *u* pronounced like a rounded 'oo' in 'boot' (be careful not to say 'ew'!): *As͟ún b͟uscaba u͟nas u͟vas y u͟n champ͟ú en u͟n s͟upermercado de Ir͟ún.*

c Diphthongs

A diphthong is when two vowels merge to make one sound, although each vowel retains its pronunciation. These are the most common ones. Practise them with your teacher or Spanish assistant:

- *ai/ay*: *¿H͟ay a͟ire acondicionado en Buenos A͟ires? preguntaron M͟aite y J͟aime.*

- *au*: *A͟urelio está a͟usente a c͟ausa de la a͟usencia de a͟utobuses en la a͟utovía.*

- *ei/ey*: *A las s͟eis, el R͟ey se af͟eita, se p͟eina y se pone el jers͟ey.*

- *eu*: *¡E͟uropa y la Unión e͟uropea nos ponen ne͟uróticos!*

- *ia*: *Son necesar͟ias: med͟ia docena de zanahor͟ias ital͟ianas, unas sandal͟ias y var͟ias fotocop͟ias del mapa de Franc͟ia.*

- *ie*: *Las t͟iendas se c͟ierran a las s͟iete los m͟iércoles en el inv͟ierno.*

- *io*: *Se anunci͟ó en la rad͟io que ocurri͟ó un incend͟io en la estaci͟ón del barr͟io.*

- *iu*: *Los v͟iudos y las v͟iudas de la c͟iudad.*

- *oi/oy*: *<u>Oi</u>ga: h<u>oy</u> no v<u>oy</u>. No est<u>oy</u> bien.*

- *ua*: *¿C<u>uá</u>nta ag<u>ua</u>, J<u>ua</u>n?*

- *ue*: *L<u>ue</u>go v<u>ue</u>lvo por el n<u>ue</u>vo p<u>ue</u>nte, ¿de ac<u>ue</u>rdo?*

- *ui/uy*: *F<u>ui</u> a S<u>ui</u>za a c<u>ui</u>dar a un niño m<u>uy</u> r<u>ui</u>doso.*

 **¡Ojo!**

1. In any other combinations the vowels are pronounced separately:
   L<u>eo</u> que la autopista al <u>ae</u>ropuerto de Bilb<u>ao</u> es muy <u>fea</u>.

2. An accent ´ is used to separate vowels which would otherwise form a
   diphthong. This is particularly common in the combinations – *ía*
   (which is one of the imperfect tense endings) and *ío*: *Cada d<u>ía</u> ve<u>ía</u> a
   mi t<u>ío</u> en la pastel<u>ería</u>.*

43

STRESS, ACCENTS AND PUNCTUATION

 ¿Preparados?

1 Stress

What is stress?

It isn't what you suffer from when you study GCSE Spanish! 'Stress' is the emphasis you put on one particular syllable of a word, and it is as important in Spanish as in English to get it right: a m<u>i</u>nute is a min<u>u</u>te unit of time! – and in Spanish *trab<u>a</u>jo* means '**I work**' (present) and *trabaj<u>ó</u>* means **he/she** worked (past).

There are three rules which tell you how to stress a word:

1. Words ending in a vowel, *-n* or *-s* are stressed on the **next to last syllable**:

    c<u>a</u>sa, c<u>a</u>sas, elef<u>a</u>nte, elef<u>a</u>ntes, esp<u>e</u>jo, esp<u>e</u>jos, trab<u>a</u>jo, trab<u>a</u>jas, trab<u>a</u>ja, trabaj<u>a</u>mos, trab<u>a</u>jan

2. Words ending in a consonant other than *-n* or *-s* are stressed on the **last syllable**:

    ciud<u>a</u>d, rel<u>oj</u>, civ<u>il</u>, trabaj<u>ar</u>, com<u>er</u>, sub<u>ir</u> (and all verb infinitives), *est<u>oy</u>, arr<u>oz</u>*

3. If the word does not behave according to Rules 1 and 2, you put an acute accent ´ on the syllable which is stressed. This occurs most often in the following types of word:

a. words ending in a stressed vowel: *ojal<u>á</u>, caf<u>é</u>, champ<u>ú</u>* and preterite and future verb endings: *trabaj<u>é</u>, trabaj<u>ó</u>, beb<u>í</u>, beb<u>ió</u>, ir<u>é</u>, ir<u>á</u>*.

b. words ending in *-n* or *-s* stressed on the last syllable. These include:

■ many ending in *-ión, -ón, -án, -én, -és*: *ración, ratón, andén, capitán, francés* (which lose the accent in the plural or feminine because they then obey rule 1: *raciones, ratones, capitanes andenes, franceses, francesa*), and

■ future endings *irás, iréis, irán* and present endings *trabajáis, bebéis, subís*.

c. words ending in a consonant other than *-n* or *-s* stressed on the next to last syllable: *lápiz, fácil, difícil, árbol*.

d. words stressed on the second from last syllable: *espectáculo, época, teléfono, pájaro*; amongst these are verbs with object pronouns on the end: *dámelo, dígame, voy a dárselo, ¿estás llamándome?*

e. words where an *i* needs to be separated from another vowel and stressed: *día, panadería, país*, and the imperfect **endings** *bebía, bebías*, etc.

 ¡Ojo!

The accent is also used on:

1. interrogative (= question) words (see Chapter 14): *¿qué? ¿quién? ¿cuándo? ¿dónde? ¿cuánto(s)? ¿cómo?*

2. the 'demonstratives' (see Chapter 5) when they stand by themselves as pronouns: *éste/ésta/éstos/éstas, ése/ésa/ésos/ésas, aquél/aquélla/aquéllos/ aquéllas*.

3. where pairs of words are spelt the same, to distinguish one from the other:

si	if	*sí*	yes
mi	my	*mí*	me
tu	your	*tú*	you
te	you	*té*	tea
de	of	*dé*	give
solo	alone	*sólo*	only (= *solamente*)

---

2 Accents

The accent most used in Spanish is the acute. It can be used on any vowel: *á, é, í, ó, ú*, and it only indicates stress: it does not change the sound of a vowel.

¡Viva la gramática!

 **¡Ojo!**

There is no grave ` or circumflex ^ accent in Spanish!

The only other two accents you will meet from time to time are:

the tilde ˜ which distinguishes *ñ* from *n*: *señor, año*.

the diaeresis ¨, which indicates that a *-u* is pronounced between *g* and *e*: *vergüenza*, where otherwise it would be silent.

3 Punctuation

Spanish punctuation marks are the same as in English with the following exceptions:

a. Questions and exclamations begin with an inverted question or exclamation mark (punto de interrogación/admiración):

¿Por qué haces eso?	Why are you doing that?
¡Porque quiero!	Because I want to!

b. The long dash (*la raya*) is used around speech, rather than inverted commas as in English:

Vamos – dijo Ramón – son las doce ya.	'Come on,' said Ramón, 'It's already twelve o'clock.'

Comillas « » are usually used for titles: *«El País»*.

44

VERB TABLE

1 Regular verbs

 ¡Consejo!

The ending for *usted* (*Vd*) is always the same as for *él/ella*, and for *ustedes* (*Vds*), the same as for *ellos/ellas*, so only six endings are shown in the following tables.

	Present	Imperfect	Preterite	Perfect	Future
hablar *to speak, talk*					
yo	hablo	hablaba	hablé	he hablado	hablaré
tú	hablas	hablabas	hablaste	has hablado	hablarás
él/ella/Vd.	habla	hablaba	habló	ha hablado	hablará
nosotros/as	hablamos	hablábamos	hablamos	hemos hablado	hablaremos
vosotros/as	habláis	hablabais	hablasteis	habéis hablado	hablaréis
ellos/ellas/Vds.	hablan	hablaban	hablaron	han hablado	hablarán
comer *to eat*					
yo	como	comía	comí	he comido	comeré
tú	comes	comías	comiste	has comido	comerás
él/ella/Vd.	come	comía	comió	ha comido	comerá
nosotros/as	com**emos***	comíamos	comimos	hemos comido	comeremos
vosotros/as	com**éis***	comíais	comisteis	habéis comido	comeréis
ellos/ellas/Vds.	comen	comían	comieron	han comido	comerán
subir *to go up*					
yo	subo	subía	subí	he subido	subiré
tú	subes	subías	subiste	has subido	subirás
él/ella/Vd.	sube	subía	subió	ha subido	subirá
nosotros/as	sub**imos***	subíamos	subimos	hemos subido	subiremos
vosotros/as	sub**ís***	subíais	subisteis	habéis subido	subiréis
ellos/ellas/Vds.	suben	subían	subieron	han subido	subirán

* These are the only places where *-er* and *-ir* verbs have different endings.

Conditional	Present subjunctive	Imperative (do/don't)	Imperfect subjunctive	Gerund
hablaría	hable		hablara/hablase	hablando
hablarías	hables	habla/no hables	hablaras/hablases	
hablaría	hable	hable/no hable	hablara/hablase	
hablaríamos	hablemos	hablemos	habláramos/ hablásemos	
hablaríais	habléis	hablad/no habléis	hablarais/hablaseis	
hablarían	hablen	hablen/no hablen	hablaran/hablasen	
comería	coma		comiera/comiesen	comiendo
comerías	comas	come/no comas	comieras/comieses	
comería	coma	coma/no coma	comiera/comiese	
comeríamos	comamos	comamos	comiéramos/ comiésemos	
comeríais	comáis	com**ed***/no comáis	comierais/comieseis	
comerían	coman	coman/no coman	comieran/comiesen	
subiría	suba		subiera/subiese	subiendo
subirías	subas	sube/no subas	subieras/subieses	
subiría	suba	suba/no suba	subiera/subiese	
subiríamos	subamos	subamos	subiéramos/ subiésemos	
subiríais	subáis	sub**id***/no subáis	subierais/subieseis	
subirían	suban	suban/no suban	subieran/subiesen	

¡Viva la gramática!

	Present	Imperfect	Preterite	Perfect	Future
abrir *to open*					
Regular except for				he **abierto** etc.	
andar *to walk*					
yo	ando	andaba	**anduve**	he andado	andaré
tú	andas	andabas	**anduviste**	has andado	andarás
él/ella/Vd.	anda	andaba	**anduvo**	ha andado	andará
nosotros/as	andamos	andábamos	**anduvimos**	hemos andado	andaremos
vosotros/as	andáis	andabais	**anduvisteis**	habéis andado	andaréis
ellos/ellas/Vds.	andan	andaban	**anduvieron**	han andado	andarán
caer *to fall*					
yo	**caigo**	caía	caí	he caído	caeré
tú	caes	caías	caíste	has caído	caerás
él/ella/Vd.	cae	caía	**cayó**	ha caído	caerá
nosotros/as	caemos	caíamos	caímos	hemos caído	caeremos
vosotros/as	caéis	caíais	caísteis	habéis caído	caeréis
ellos/ellas/Vds.	caen	caían	**cayeron**	han caído	caerán
conducir *to drive*					
yo	conduzco	conducía	conduje	he conducido	conduciré
tú	conduces	conducías	condu**jiste**	has conducido	conducirás
él/ella/Vd.	conduce	conducía	condujo	ha conducido	conducirá
nosotros/as	conducimos	conducíamos	condu**jimos**	hemos conducido	conduciremos
vosotros/as	conducís	conducíais	condu**jisteis**	habéis conducido	conduciréis
ellos/ellas/Vds.	conducen	conducían	condu**jeron**	han conducido	conducirán
cubrir *to cover*, ***descubrir*** *to discover*					
Regular except for				he **cubierto**	
				he **descubierto**	
dar *to give*					
yo	**doy**	daba	**di**	he dado	daré
tú	das	dabas	**diste**	has dado	darás
él/ella/Vd.	da	daba	**dio**	ha dado	dará
nosotros/as	damos	dábamos	**dimos**	hemos dado	daremos
vosotros/as	dais	dabais	**disteis**	habéis dado	daréis
ellos/ellas/Vds.	dan	daban	**dieron**	han dado	darán

Conditional	Present subjunctive	Imperative (do/don't)	Imperfect subjunctive	Gerund
andaría	ande		**anduviera/**	andando
andarías	andes	anda/no andes	**anduviese**	
andaría	ande	ande/no ande	etc.	
andaríamos	andemos	andemos		
andaríais	andéis	andad/no andéis		
andarían	anden	anden/no anden		
caería	**caiga**		**cayera/cayese**	**cayendo**
caerías	**caigas**	cae/**no caigas**		
caería	**caiga**	**caiga/no caiga**		
caeríamos	**caigamos**	**caigamos**		
caeríais	**caigáis**	caed/**no caigáis**		
caerían	**caigan**	**caigan/no caigan**		
conduciría	**conduzca**		**condujera/**	conduciendo
conducirías	**conduzcas**	conduce/	**condujese**	
		no conduzcas		
conduciría	**conduzca**	**conduzca/**		
		no conduzca		
conduciríamos	**conduzcamos**	**conduzcamos**		
conduciríais	**conduzcáis**	conducid/		
		no conduzcáis		
conducirían	**conduzcan**	**conduzcan/**		
		no conduzcan		
daría	**dé**		**diera/diese**	dando
darías	**des**	da/**no des**		
daría	**dé**	**dé/no dé**		
daríamos	**demos**	**demos**		
darías	**deis**	dad/**no deis**		
darían	**den**	**den/no den**		

¡Viva la gramática!

	Present	Imperfect	Preterite	Perfect	Future
decir *to say, tell*					
yo	**digo**	decía	**dije**	he **dicho**	**diré**
tú	**dices**	decías	**dijiste**	has **dicho**	**dirás**
él/ella/Vd.	**dice**	decía	**dijo**	ha **dicho**	**dirá**
nosotros/as	decimos	decíamos	**dijimos**	hemos **dicho**	**diremos**
vosotros/as	decís	decíais	**dijisteis**	habéis **dicho**	**diréis**
ellos/ellas/Vds.	**dicen**	decían	**dijeron**	han **dicho**	**dirán**
escribir *to write*					
Regular except for				he **escrito** etc.	
estar *to be*					
yo	**estoy**	estaba	**estuve**	he estado	estaré
tú	**estás**	estabas	**estuviste**	has estado	estarás
él/ella/Vd.	**está**	estaba	**estuvo**	ha estado	estará
nosotros/as	estamos	estábamos	**estuvimos**	hemos estado	estaremos
vosotros/as	**estáis**	estabais	**estuvisteis**	habéis estado	estaréis
ellos/ellas/Vds.	**están**	estaban	**estuvieron**	han estado	estarán
haber *to have* (as auxiliary verb only); **hay** *there is, there are*					
yo	**he**	había	**hube**		**habré**
tú	**has**	habías	**hubiste**		**habrás**
él/ella/Vd.	**ha**	había	**hubo**	ha habido	**habrá**
nosotros/as	**hemos**	habíamos	**hubimos**		**habremos**
vosotros/as	**habéis**	habíais	**hubisteis**		**habréis**
ellos/ellas/Vds.	**han**	habían	**hubieron**		**habrán**
there is/are	**hay**	había	**hubo**	ha habido	**habrá**
hacer *to do, to make*					
yo	**hago**	hacía	**hice**	he **hecho**	**haré**
tú	haces	hacías	**hiciste**	has **hecho**	**harás**
él/ella/Vd.	hace	hacía	**hizo**	ha **hecho**	hará
nosotros/as	hacemos	hacíamos	**hicimos**	hemos **hecho**	haremos
vosotros/as	hacéis	hacíais	**hicisteis**	habéis **hecho**	haréis
ellos/ellas/Vds.	hacen	hacían	**hicieron**	han **hecho**	**harán**

Conditional	Present subjunctive	Imperative (do/don't)	Imperfect subjunctive	Gerund
diría	diga		dijera/dijese	diciendo
dirías	digas	di/no digas		
diría	diga	diga/no diga		
diríamos	digamos	digamos		
diríais	digáis	decid/no digáis		
dirían	digan	digan/no digan		
estaría	esté		estuviera/estuviese	estando
estarías	estés	está/no estés		
estaría	esté	esté/no esté		
estaríamos	estemos	estemos		
estaríais	estéis	estad/no estéis		
estarían	estén	estén/no estén		
habría	haya		hubiera/hubiese	habiendo
habrías	hayas			
habría	haya			
habríamos	hayamos			
habríais	hayáis			
habrían	hayan			
habría	haya		hubiera/hubiese	
haría	haga		hiciera/hiciese	haciendo
harías	hagas	haz/no hagas		
haría	haga	haga/no haga		
haríamos	hagamos	hagamos		
haríais	hagáis	haced/no hagáis		
harían	hagan	hagan/no hagan		

¡Viva la gramática!

	Present	Imperfect	Preterite	Perfect	Future
ir *to go*					
yo	**voy**	**iba**	**fui**	he ido	iré
tú	**vas**	**ibas**	**fuiste**	has ido	irás
él/ella/Vd.	**va**	**iba**	**fue**	ha ido	irá
nosotros/as	**vamos**	**íbamos**	**fuimos**	hemos ido	iremos
vosotros/as	**vais**	**ibais**	**fuisteis**	habéis ido	iréis
ellos/ellas/Vds.	**van**	**iban**	**fueron**	han ido	irán
oír *to hear*					
yo	**oigo**	oía	oí	he oído	oiré
tú	**oyes**	oías	oíste	has oído	oirás
él/ella/Vd.	**oye**	oía	**oyó**	ha oído	oirá
nosotros/as	oímos	oíamos	oímos	**hemos oí**do	oiremos
vosotros/as	**oís**	oíais	oísteis	habéis oído	oireis
ellos/ellas/Vds.	**oyen**	oían	**oyeron**	han oído	oirán
poder *to be able, can*					
yo	**puedo**	podía	**pude**	he podido	**podré**
tú	**puedes**	podías	**pudiste**	has podido	**podrás**
él/ella/Vd.	**puede**	podía	**pudo**	ha podido	**podrá**
nosotros/as	podemos	podíamos	**pudimos**	hemos podido	**podremos**
vosotros/as	podéis	podíais	**pudisteis**	habéis podido	**podréis**
ellos/ellas/Vds.	**pueden**	podían	**pudieron**	han podido	**podrán**
poner *to put*					
yo	**pongo**	ponía	**puse**	he **puesto**	**pondré**
tú	pones	ponías	**pusiste**	has **puesto**	**pondrás**
él/ella/Vd.	pone	ponía	**puso**	ha **puesto**	**pondrá**
nosotros/as	ponemos	poníamos	**pusimos**	hemos **puesto**	**pondremos**
vosotros/as	ponéis	poníais	**pusisteis**	habéis **puesto**	**pondréis**
ellos/ellas/Vds.	ponen	ponían	**pusieron**	han **puesto**	**pondrán**
querer *to want, to love*					
yo	**quiero**	quería	**quise**	he querido	**querré**
tú	**quieres**	querías	**quisiste**	has querido	**querrás**
él/ella/Vd.	**quiere**	querías	**quiso**	ha querido	**querrá**
nosotros/as	queremos	queríamos	**quisimos**	hemos querido	**querremos**
vosotros/as	queréis	queríais	**quisisteis**	habéis querido	**querréis**
ellos/ellas/Vds.	**quieren**	querían	**quisieron**	han querido	**querrán**
romper *to break*					
Regular except for				he **roto**, etc.	

264

Conditional	Present subjunctive	Imperative (do/don't)	Imperfect subjunctive	Gerund
iría	vaya		fuera/fuese	yendo
irías	vayas	ve/no vayas		
iría	vaya	vaya/no vaya		
iríamos	vayamos	vamos/no vayamos		
iráis	vayáis	id/no vayáis		
irían	vayan	vayan/no vayan		
oiría	oiga		oyera/oyese	oyendo
oirías	oigas	oye/no oigas		
oiría	oiga	oiga/no oiga		
oiríamos	oigamos	oigamos		
oiríais	oigáis	oíd/no oigáis		
oirían	oigan	oigan/no oigan		
podría	pueda		pudiera/pudiese	pudiendo
podrías	puedas			
podría	pueda			
podríamos	podamos			
podríais	podáis			
podrían	puedan			
pondría	ponga		pusiera/pusiese	poniendo
pondrías	pongas	pon/no pongas		
pondría	ponga	ponga/no ponga		
pondríamos	pongamos	pongamos		
pondríais	pongáis	poned/no pongáis		
pondrían	pongan	pongan/no pongan		
querría	quiera		quisiera/quisiese	queriendo
querrías	quieras	quiere/no quieras		
querría	quiera	quiera/no quiera		
querríamos	queramos	queramos		
querríais	queráis	quered/no queráis		
querrían	quieran	quieran/no quieran		

¡Viva la gramática!

	Present	Imperfect	Preterite	Perfect	Future
saber *to know*					
yo	**sé**	sabía	**supe**	he sabido	**sabré**
tú	sabes	sabía	**supiste**	has sabido	**sabrás**
él/ella/Vd.	sabe	sabía	**supo**	ha sabido	**sabrá**
nosotros/as	sabemos	sabíamos	**supimos**	hemos sabido	**sabremos**
vosotros/as	sabéis	sabíais	**supisteis**	habéis sabido	**sabréis**
ellos/ellas/Vds.	saben	sabían	**supieron**	han sabido	**sabrán**
salir *to go out, come out*					
yo	**salgo**	salía	salí	he salido	**saldré**
tú	sales	salías	saliste	has salido	**saldrás**
él/ella/Vd.	sale	salía	salió	he salido	**saldrá**
nosotros/as	salimos	salíamos	salimos	hemos salido	**saldremos**
vosotros/as	salís	salíais	salisteis	habéis salido	**saldréis**
ellos/ellas/Vds.	salen	salían	salieron	han salido	**saldrán**
ser *to be*					
yo	**soy**	era	**fui** (as for **ir**)	he sido	seré
tú	**eres**	eras	**fuiste**	has sido	serás
él/ella/Vd.	**es**	era	**fue**	ha sido	será
nosotros/as	**somos**	**éramos**	**fuimos**	hemos sido	seremos
vosotros/as	**sois**	erais	**fuisteis**	habéis sido	seréis
ellos/ellas/Vds.	**son**	eran	**fueron**	han sido	serán
tener *to have*					
yo	**tengo**	tenía	**tuve**	he tenido	**tendré**
tú	**tienes**	tenías	**tuviste**	has tenido	**tendrás**
él/ella/Vd.	**tiene**	tenías	**tuvo**	ha tenido	**tendrá**
nosotros/as	tenemos	teníamos	**tuvimos**	hemos tenido	**tendremos**
vosotros/as	tenéis	teníais	**tuvisteis**	habéis tenido	**tendréis**
ellos/ellas/Vds.	**tienen**	tenían	**tuvieron**	han tenido	**tendrán**
traer *to bring*					
yo	**traigo**	traía	**traje**	he traído	traeré
tú	traes	traías	**trajiste**	has traído	traerás
él/ella/Vd.	trae	traía	**trajo**	ha traído	traerá
nosotros/as	traemos	traíamos	**trajimos**	hemos traído	traeremos
vosotros/as	traéis	traíais	**trajisteis**	habéis traído	traeréis
ellos/ellas/Vds.	traen	traían	**trajeron**	han traído	traerán

Conditional	Present subjunctive	Imperative (do/don't)	Imperfect subjunctive	Gerund
sabría	sepa		**supiera/supiese**	sabiendo
sabrías	sepas	sabe/**no sepas**		
sabría	sepa	**sepa/no sepa**		
sabríamos	sepamos	**sepamos**		
sabríais	sepáis	sabed/**no sepáis**		
sabrían	sepan	**sepan/no sepan**		
saldría	salga		**saliera/saliese**	saliendo
saldrías	salgas	**sal/no salgas**		
saldría	salga	**salga/no salga**		
saldríamos	salgamos	**salgamos**		
saldríais	salgáis	salid/**no salgáis**		
saldrían	salgan	**salgan/no salgan**		
sería	**sea**		**fuera/fuese**	siendo
serías	**seas**	**sé/no seas**		
sería	**sea**	**sea/no sea**		
seríamos	**seamos**	**seamos**		
seríais	**seáis**	sed/**no seáis**		
serían	**sean**	**sean/no sean**		
tendría	tenga		**tuviera/tuviese**	teniendo
tendrías	tengas	**ten/no tengas**		
tendría	tenga	**tenga/no tenga**		
tendríamos	tengamos	**tengamos**		
tendríais	tengáis	tened/**no tengáis**		
tendrían	tengan	**tengan/no tengan**		
traería	**traiga**		**trajera/trajese**	**trayendo**
traerías	**traigas**	trae/**no traigas**		
traería	**traiga**	**traiga/no traiga**		
traeríamos	**traigamos**	**traigamos**		
traeríais	**traigáis**	traed/**no traigáis**		
traerían	**traigan**	**traigan/no traigan**		

¡Viva la gramática!

	Present	Imperfect	Preterite	Perfect	Future
venir to come					
yo	**vengo**	venía	**vine**	he venido	**vendré**
tú	**vienes**	venías	**viniste**	has venido	**vendrás**
él/ella/Vd.	**viene**	venía	**vino**	ha venido	**vendrá**
nosotros/as	venimos	veníamos	**vinimos**	hemos venido	**vendremos**
vosotros/as	venís	veníais	**vinisteis**	habéis venido	**vendréis**
ellos/ellas/Vds.	**vienen**	venían	**vinieron**	han venido	**vendrán**
ver to see					
yo	veo	veía	vi	he **visto**	veré
tú	ves	veías	viste	has **visto**	verás
él/ella/Vd.	ve	veía	vio	ha **visto**	verá
nosotros/as	vemos	veíamos	vimos	hemos **visto**	veremos
vosotros/as	veis	veíais	visteis	habéis **visto**	veréis
ellos/ellas/Vds.	ven	veían	vieron	han **visto**	verán
volver to return, *go/come back*					
yo	**vuelvo**	otherwise regular		he **vuelto**	
tú	**vuelves**			has **vuelto**	
él/ella/Vd.	**vuelve**			ha **vuelto**	
nosotros/as	volvemos			hemos **vuelto**	
vosotros/as	volvéis			habéis **vuelto**	
ellos/ellas/Vds.	**vuelven**			han **vuelto**	

Conditional	Present subjunctive	Imperative (do/don't)	Imperfect subjunctive	Gerund
vendría	venga		viniera/viniese	viniendo
vendrías	vengas	ven/no vengas		
vendría	venga	venga/no venga		
vendríamos	vengamos	vengamos		
vendríais	vengáis	venid/no vengáis		
vendrían	vengan	vengan/no vengan		
vería	vea		viera/viese	viendo
verías	veas	ve/no veas		
vería	vea	vea/no vea		
veríamos	veamos	veamos		
veríais	veáis	ved/no veáis		
verían	vean	vean/no vean		
	vuelva			
	vuelvas	vuelve/no vuelvas		
	vuelva	vuelva/no vuelva		
	volvamos	volvamos		
	volváis	volved/no volváis		
	vuelvan	vuelvan/no vuelvan		

45

KEY TO EXERCISES

Chapter 1
1

la salida, la esquina, el espejo, el tocador, el toro, la vaca, la mujer, el hombre, la reunión, el museo, la tienda, la noche, el tomate, el avión, la seguridad, el clima, el lápiz, el bolígrafo, el Canadá, la China.

2

1. (la) goma 2. (el) césped 3. (la) mano 4. (el) día 5. (el) avión

3

dos pares de calcetines, dos cajas de caramelos, dos camisas, dos barras de jabón, dos monederos, dos libros, dos pendientes, dos pulseras, dos relojes, dos cinturones.

4

1. unas 2. unos 3. chuleta 4. quesos 5. la 6. el 7. trucha 8.– 9. postre

Chapter 2
1

un reloj *nuevo*, una camisa *roja*, unos vaqueros *azules*, unas gafas *negras*, unos zapatos *marrones*, una guitarra *española*, una bicicleta *moderna*, una radio *japonesa*, unos pañuelos *blancos*, una chaqueta *de cuero*.

2

1. buen 2. blanca 3. azul 4. fría 5. enfadado 6. ingleses 7. española 8. rica 9. cómodas 10. contenta

3

1g 2d 3a 4b 5i 6j 7c 8e 9f 10h

4

2. El BMW es un coche alemán. 3. Barcelona y Tarragona son ciudades catalanas. 4. El Támesis y el Severn son ríos ingleses. 5. Washington es la capital norteamericana. 6. Mitsubishi es una compañía japonesa. 7. Ben Nevis es una montaña escocesa. 8. Benidorm es una playa española. 9. Francia es un país europeo. 10. Calais es un puerto francés. 11. El café es un producto colombiano. 12. Los canguros son animales australianos.

Chapter 3
1

felizmente afortunadamente alegremente agradablemente cortésmente nuevamente primeramente útilmente válidamente verdaderamente

2

1e 2g 3h 4a 5i 6j 7b 8d 9f 10c

3

1. mal 2. bien 3. rápidamente 4. despacio, a menudo 5. en silencio 6. ruidosamente
7. tristemente 8. con alegría 9. diariamente 10. semanalmente.

Chapter 4

1

Various combinations are possible: consult your teacher.

2

1. Miguel es más bajo que/no es tan alto como/es menos alto que Pablo. 2. ✓ 3. Mi padre es más
gordo que/es menos delgado que/no es tan gordo como mi madre. 4. ✓ 5. La sala de estar es más
grande que la cocina. 6. ✓ 7. ✓ 8. Mi dormitorio es más cómodo que el dormitorio de Pablo.
9. ✓ 10. Mi abuela es más vieja que mi madre.

3

1. Esteban es el chico más/menos vago de la clase. 2. Conchi es la chica más/menos lista de todas.
3. Isabel es la chica más/menos simpática de la clase. 4. Federico es el joven más/menos sobresaliente
de su grupo. 5. Emi es la chica más/menos delgada de mis amigas. 6. La señora Pérez es la
profesora más/menos popular del colegio. 7. Luis es el chico más/menos guapo de la ciudad.
8. Enrique es el chico más/menos deportivo del colegio. 9. Anita es la alumna más/menos
trabajadora. 10. El director es el profesor más/menos estricto del colegio.

Chapter 5

1

1. esta 2. esos 3. aquella 4. aquellos 5. esas

2

1. esta 2. ése 3. éstos 4. este 5. esas 6. Ese 7. ésta 8. ésa 9. aquellos 10. aquella

3

Estos zapatos son más cómodos que *ésos*, pero *aquéllos* son los más cómodos de todos.
Esta chaqueta es más elegante que *ésa* pero *aquélla* es la más elegante de todas.
Este walkman es más moderno que *ése*, pero *aquél* es el más moderno de todos.
Estas joyas son más costosas que *ésas*, pero *aquéllas* son las más costosas de todas.
Esta novela es más interesante que *ésa* pero *aquélla* es la más interesante de todas.
Estos pendientes son más caros que *ésos* pero *aquéllos* son los más caros de todos.
Este coche es más rápido que *ése*, pero *aquél* es el más rápido de todos.
Esta tarta es más rica que *ésa*, pero *aquélla* es la más rica de todas.
Este vino es mejor que *ése*, pero *aquél* es el mejor de todos.
Estas blusas son más baratas que *ésas*, pero *aquéllas* son las más baratas de todas.

4

1. Esta actriz es muy hermosa. 2. Este examen es el más fácil de todos. 3. Estas botas son más caras
que aquéllas. 4. Estos pasteles parecen más deliciosos que ésos. 5. ¿Crees que este casete es más
interesante que aquél? 6. ¿Por qué prefieres esta casa y no aquélla? 7. Este chico es más majo que

ése, pero aquél es el más majo de todos. 8. Esta torre es menos alta que ese edificio. 9. Esta profesora es la menos antipática de todas las de este colegio. 10. Esta vaca es más gorda que ésa, pero aquel cerdo es aun más gordo.

Chapter 6
1

1. mi/tu 2. mis/tus 3. mi/tu 4. mi/tu 5. mis/tus 6. mis/tus 7. mis/tus 8. mis/tus 9. mi/tu 10. mi/tu 11. mis/tus 12. mis/tus 13. mi/tu 14. mi/tu 15. mi/tu

2

1. Mi 2. Su 3. sus 4. nuestras 5. Su 6. sus 7. su 8. tus 9. tu 10. vuestros

3

1. Es de Pepe./Es el perro de Pepe. 2. Es de Pablo./Es el perro de Pablo. 3. Es del profesor./Es el coche del profesor. 4. Es de Marita./Es el balón de Marita. 5. Es de Conchi./Es la foto de Conchi. 6. Son de la profesora./Son los lápices de la profesora. 7. Son del director./Son las gafas del director. 8. Son de Jorge./Son las cartas de Jorge. 9. Son de Pepa./Son los anillos de Pepa. 10. Son de mi madre./Son las llaves de mi madre.

4

1. El mío tiene un mejor equipo de fútbol que el tuyo. 2. La mía tiene unos panoramas más magníficos que la tuya. 3. La mía tiene una piscina más fabulosa que la tuya. 4. La nuestra es más hermosa que la vuestra. 5. Los nuestros son más largos que los vuestros. 6. Las nuestras son mejores que las vuestras. 7. La nuestra es más ancha que la vuestra. 8. Los míos son más simpáticos que los tuyos. 9. Los míos son más generosos que los tuyos. 10. El mío/la mía es más guapo/a que el tuyo/la tuya.

Chapter 7
1

1. 3 2. 17 3. 35 4. 61 5. 72 6. 198 7. 344 8. 544 9. 1.157 10. 2.281

2

1d 2g 3i 4f 5h 6j 7a 8c 9e 10b

3

1. cuatrocientas 2. tercer 3. setecientos 4. mil seiscientos 5. mil quinientos 6. primera 7. cuarta 8. quinto

4

- décimo piso
- noveno piso
- octavo piso
- sétimo piso
- sexto piso
- quinto piso
- cuarto piso
- tercer piso
- segundo piso
- primer piso
- planta baja

Chapter 8

1. (Examples: other measures are often possible). 1 ...tiene ciento veinte (120) metros de largo y noventa (90) metros de ancho. 2 ...tiene (aproximadamente) veinticuatro (24) metros de largo y nueve/once (9/11) metros de ancho. 3 ...tiene (aproximadamente) cuatro (4) metros de alto, nueve (9) metros de largo, y dos coma cinco metros (2,5) de ancho. 4 ...tiene diez (10) centímetros de largo, siete (7) centímetros de ancho y cuatro (4) centímetros de alto. 5 ...tiene veintiocho (28) centímetros de ancho y veintidós (22) centímetros de alto. 6 ...tiene nueve (9) centímetros de ancho y nueve coma cinco (9,5) centímetros de alto. 7 ...tiene (aproximadamente) siete (7) centímetros de diámetro. 8 ...tiene treinta y cinco (35) milímetros de diámetro.

Chapter 9

1

2. A las siete menos cuarto de la mañana 3. A las ocho menos diez de la mañana 4. A las ocho y cinco de la mañana 5. A las ocho y media de la mañana 6. A la una de la tarde 7. A las cinco y cuarto de la tarde 8. A las siete menos diez de la tarde 9. A las ocho menos veinticinco de la tarde 10. A las nueve y diez de la noche 11. A medianoche

2

1. Son las siete de la mañana.	Son las siete
2. Son las ocho y media de la mañana.	Son las ocho treinta.
3. Son las diez y diez de la mañana.	Son las diez (y) diez.
4. Son las doce menos cinco de la mañana.	Son las once cincuenta y cinco.
5. Es la una de la tarde.	Son las trece.
6. Son las seis menos cuarto de la tarde.	Son las diecisiete cuarenta y cinco.
7. Son las ocho y cuarto de la noche.	Son las veinte quince.
8. Son las nueve y veinticinco de la noche.	Son las veintiuna veinticinco.
9. Son las once y cuarto de la noche.	Son las veintitrés quince.
10. Son las doce de la noche. (Es medianoche.)	Son las veinticuatro (horas).

3

1. (el) ocho de enero de mil novecientos noventa y ocho 2. (el) diez de febrero de mil novecientos noventa y nueve 3. (el) tres de marzo de dos mil 4. (el) catorce de abril de dos mil uno 5. (el) veinte de mayo de dos mil cinco 6. (el) veintiuno de junio de mil novecientos ochenta y seis 7. (el) dieciocho de julio de mil novecientos treinta y nueve 8. (el) cuatro de agosto de mil novecientos catorce 9. (el) veinticinco de setiembre de mil novecientos treinta y uno 10. (el) doce de octubre de mil ochocientos noventa y ocho 11. (el) treinta de noviembre de mil cuatrocientos noventa y dos 12. (el) treinta y uno de diciembre de mil ciento nueve

Chapter 10

1

1E 2D 3A 4C 5B 6F

2

1. Es tarde y tengo que coger un taxi. 2. Me parece que va a llover ¿dónde está el paraguas? 3. Mira, llegas tarde: espero desde hace diez minutos. 4. ¡Madre mía, qué frío hace! Voy a ponerme el abrigo. 5. La clase de español empieza pronto tengo mucha prisa. 6. Vamos a esquiar en Sierra Nevada allí hay mucha nieve. 7. Hace mucho sol en Torremolinos y vamos a broncearnos. 8. Hace muy mal tiempo y vamos a quedarnos en casa. 9. Ten cuidado en la carretera, porque hay hielo. 10. Mi amigo murió en un accidente hace dos años.

¡Viva la gramática!

3

1. relámpago 2. calor 3. llovió 4. nevando 5. trueno 6. nubes 7. brillaba 8. bajarán
9. tempestad 10. frente frío

4

1. Tengo / Tienes calor. 2. Está lloviendo. / Va a llover. 3. Hacía sol. 4. Está nevando. / Hay nieve. 5. Tengo / Tienes / Tiene hambre. / calor. / Hace calor. 6. Hace buen tiempo. 7. Tengo / Tienes / Tiene (mucha) hambre. 8. Hay / tormenta / tempestad / relámpago / está relampagueando.
9. Hace (mucho) viento. 10. Tengo / Tienes (mucho) miedo. 11. Tengo / Tienes sueño.
12. Tengo / Tienes suerte. 13. Tengo / Tienes razón. 14. Me hace falta un coche nuevo.
15. Tengo / Tienes (mucha) sed.

Chapter 11

1

yo, tú, él, ella, usted, nosotros, nosotras, vosotros, vosotras, ellos, ellas, ustedes, mí, ti, sí, conmigo, contigo (Falta consigo.)

2

1. La chica nos llamó a nosotros por teléfono. 2. Las que llamaron a la puerta son ellas. 3. Sois vosotros los que llegasteis antes que ellos. 4. Pueden llevar a su hijo consigo si quieren. 5. No sé exactamente lo que usted quiere. 6. Mire usted: yo llegué antes que usted. 7. Por favor, ve tú a la tienda y cómprame unos caramelos para mí. 8. ¿Sabes lo que a mí me enfada?

3

1. Tú 2. Nosotros 3. Ellas 4. yo 5. Ella/Él 6. nosotros 7. conmigo 8. ti 9. usted 10. tú
11. consigo 12. él

Chapter 12

1

1. la voy a llamar/voy a llamarla 2. los quiero comprar/quiero comprarlos 3. las voy a comprar/voy a comprarlas 4. Las he comprado 5. pero no los he comprado 6. la voy a ver/voy a verla esta tarde
7. se las daré en seguida 8. y lo pondrá en la mesa 9. y mi novia se las mostrará 10. Sus padres nos han invitado a cenar, pues iremos a verlos

2

1. Compraron esta casa porque les gusta mucho. 2. Siempre escuchamos las noticias cuando las oímos en la radio. 3. Mis abuelos son muy generosos, y los quiero mucho. 4. No saben dónde está su perro desde que lo perdieron en el parque. 5. Vamos a escribir a María para mandarle nuestras señas. 6. El camarero sabe lo que queremos y nos va a traer café. 7. Si queréis una foto mía, os la daré mañana. 8. Ya sé que me amas y yo te quiero. 9. Mi amiga salió hace dos minutos y no la veo en la calle. 10. Llevo este pantalón porque acabo de comprarlo.

3

1. Antes de bañar a mi perro le doy un caramelo. 2. Esta chica trabaja en el café: la vi ayer. 3. Voy a ofrecerle esta manzana, porque hizo los deberes. 4. Si trabajas mucho te regalaré veinte euros. 5. No sé dónde los perdí. 6. Después de salir por la puerta, siempre la cierro con llave. 7. Mira esta chica, me parece muy guapa. 8. Vi las cartas en la mesa, pero yo no las cogí.

Chapter 13

1

1. que 2. que 3. en el que 4. al que 5. en la que 6. con quien 7. el que 8. Lo que

274

2

1. que 2. el que 3. cuyos 4. el que 5. que 6. que 7. cuya 8. el que 9. que 10. que

Chapter 14

1

1. ¿quién? 2. ¡Cómo! 3. ¿Cuáles? 4. ¿dónde? 5. ¿Por qué?/¿Cuándo? 6. ¿Cuándo? 7. ¡Qué!
8. ¿qué? 9. ¿Cómo? 10. ¡Cuánta!/¡Qué!

Chapter 15

1

1c 2e 3a 4f 5b 6g 7d

2

1. Nunca 2. nadie 3. ningún 4. Tampoco 5. Ni 6. ni 7. a ninguna parte 8. nunca 9. nada
10. nadie 11. ya no

Chapter 16

1

1. en 2. delante de 3. a la derecha de 4. al lado del 5. enfrente del 6. a la izquierda del 7. al
final del 8. en el centro del 9. alrededor de 10. debajo de

2

1. desde 2. hasta 3. en 4. en 5. durante/en 6. antes de 7. entre 8. después de 9. en
10. dentro de 11. Después de 12. después de 13. en 14. en 15. hasta

3

Esta mañana, *al final de* la calle había un grupo *de* personas *alrededor de* un accidente. Cuando llegué allí
vi que un hombre estaba *debajo de* un coche, y *al lado del* coche estaba su bicicleta. El conductor del
coche, un hombre *con* barba, todavía estaba *entre* el coche y las tiendas, hablando *con* dos policías.
Recientemente se cerró el hospital del barrio y ahora estamos *sin* hospital. La ambulancia tuvo que
llevar al ciclista al otro hospital que está bastante *lejos de* aquí.

Chapter 17

1

1. por 2. para 3. por 4. para 5. para 6. por 7. para 8. por 9. por 10. por 11. para
12. por 13. por 14. por 15. por 16. por 17. para 18. por 19. por 20. por 21. para
22. para 23. por 24. por 25. para

Chapter 18

1

1. a 2.– 3. a 4. a 5. al 6. a 7. a 8.– 9. –/al (optional) 10. a

Chapter 19

1

Chicas: Anita, Juanita, Paquita, Rosita, Carmencita, Merceditas
Chicos: Pedrito, Pablito/Pablecito, Miguelito, Rafaelito, Juanito, Carlitos

2

1. Martincito 2. peludo 3. un pelotazo 4. un hombrecillo 5. una mesita 6. barbudo
7. nariguda 8. un manotazo

¡Viva la gramática!

Chapter 20

1

1. Los sábados por la mañana me quedo en la cama hasta las diez. 2. El sábado a mediodía siempre como hamburguesas. 3. Para ir al pueblo subimos al autobús cerca de casa. 4. En una tienda del pueblo compro mis discos. 5. Si hay un partido de fútbol compro una entrada. 6. Los sábados por la noche bailamos en la discoteca. 7. Para volver a casa llamo un taxi.

2

1. habla 2. hablo 3. como 4. gusta 5. bebo 6. charlamos 7. estudiamos 8. nos bañamos 9. compro 10. como

Chapter 21

1 (Examples)

A   jugar, decir, conocer, llover, volver, pensar, poder, dormir, contar, recordar

B   vuelo, sueño, frito, movimiento, nieve, despierto, encuentro, comienzo, salida, juego

2

1. es 2. hay 3. tengo/tenemos 4. Hace 5. vamos 6. preparas 7. saco
8. compro/compras/compramos 9. quieres/queremos 10. podemos 11. podemos 12. tenemos
13. hace 14. bañamos 15. dice 16. prepara 17. va 18. quieren 19. llama 20. trata
21. tiene 22. quedamos

3

1. es 2. puede 3. están 4. ofrece 5. encuentran 6. puede 7. quiere(s) 8. tiene(s)
9. presentan 10. va(s) 11. pasa(s)

4 (Examples)

1. Porque quiero comer. 2. Porque tengo prisa. 3. Me pongo un jersey. 4. Me acuesto. / Voy a la cama. 5. Cojo un taxi. 6. Porque juego al fútbol. 7. Porque estoy enfermo / no me siento bien.
8. Porque la conozco. 9. Porque no sé qué significa esta palabra. 10. Prefiero éste.

Chapter 22

1

1. me peino 2. se ducha 3. te pones el jersey 4. se bañan 5. se levanta 6. nos paseamos 7. se lava 8. te acuestas 9. se viste 10. nos afeitamos

2

1. me 2. se 3. Me 4. se 5. nos 6. se, se, se 7. nos 8. Me 9. se 10. se

3 (Examples)

Yo	me baño	en el cuarto de baño.
Mi madre	se viste	en su dormitorio.
Mi padre	se afeita	en la cocina.
Mis hermanos	se emborrachan	en el cuarto de estar.
Mi hermana	se maquilla	delante del espejo.
Mis abuelos	se broncean	en el patio.
El perro	se pasea	en el jardín.

Chapter 23

1

2. Sí, me gustan. 3. No, no me gusta. 4. Sí, me gusta. 5. No, no me gustan. 6. Sí, me gusta.
7. Sí, me gusta. 8. Sí, me gusta. 9. No, no me gusta. 10. Sí, me gusta.

2
1. duelen 2. gusta 3. gustan 4. gusta 5. duelen 6. encantan 7. duele 8. gusta 9. duelen
10. gustaría

Chapter 24

1

A	empezaré	B	voy a viajar en tren
	cantaremos		¿(lo) vas a comer(lo)?
	trabajarán		van a hablar con papá
	vendréis		(lo) va a hacer(lo) mi amigo
	saldrás		vamos a buscar sitio
	sabrá		¿(os) vais a poner(os) las botas?

2
1. Primero, pagaré todas mis deudas. 2. Iré de vacaciones a Flórida. 3. Viviré en una casa enorme.
4. Aprenderé a conducir. 5. Compraré un coche fenomenal. 6. Abandonaré a mi novio, Jorge, ¡que
es muy feo! 7. Buscaré a un novio más guapo. 8. Seré muy feliz.

3
Hoy, Mariano va a levantarse a las siete.
Va a ducharse / tomar una ducha.
Va a desayunar a las siete y media.
Va a salir de casa a las ocho.
Va a coger el autobús a las ocho y diez.
Va a llegar al cole a las ocho y media.
Va a salir del cole a las cuatro de la tarde.
Va a cenar a las siete de la tarde.
Va a hacer los deberes / estudiar.
Va a acostarse / ir a la cama a las once.

Mañana, Mariano se levantará a las siete.
Se duchará. / Tomará una ducha.
Desayunará a las siete y media.
Saldrá de casa a las ocho.
Cogerá el autobús a las ocho y diez.
Llegará al cole a las ocho y media.
Saldrá del cole a las cuatro de la tarde.
Cenará a las siete de la tarde.
Hará los deberes. / Estudiará.
Se acostará. / Irá a la cama a las once.

Chapter 25

1
1. sería 2. compraría 3. preferiría 4. iríamos 5. esperarían 6. veríamos 7. viajaría
8. gustaría

2
1. Compraría una casa más moderna para mis padres. 2. Daría mil libras a cada uno de mis hermanos.
3. Llevaría a mi familia de vacaciones a Marbella. 4. Me casaría con mi novio/a el año que viene.
5. Pagaría unas bodas magníficas. 6. Invitaría(mos) a todos nuestros amigos y familiares.
7. Organizaría(mos) el banquete en un hotel de lujo. 8. Iríamos a un lugar secreto para la luna de miel.

¡Viva la gramática!

3 (Examples)

1. 2. ¡No, se cortaría la cara! 3. ¡No, arruinaría la cena! 4. ¡No, estropearía la ropa! 5. ¡No, quemaría los pantalones! 6. ¡No, tendría muchos accidentes! 7. ¡No, perdería el/al perro! 8. ¡No, compraría cosas inútiles!

Chapter 26

1

1. iba 2. acompañábamos 3. comíamos 4. dábamos 5. había 6. cantaban y bailaban 7. Era
8. gustaba 9. quería

2

1. La abuela cosía. 2. Angela oía música. 3. Pedro hacía sus deberes del colegio. 4. Mamá cocinaba. 5. Papá se afeitaba. 6. Las gemelas jugaban en el ordenador. 7. Javier y sus compañeros veían un partido de fútbol. 8. Los dos perros dormían delante de la estufa. 9. Mercedes pasaba el aspirador. 10. Montse y yo leíamos una revista.

3a

1. ¿Dónde vivía usted? 2. ¿Cuántos años tenía? 3. ¿Cómo era su piso? 4. ¿Tenía familia?
5. ¿Usted iba al colegio o trabajaba? 6. ¿Qué cosas compraba en las tiendas? 7. ¿Qué comían usted y su familia? 8. ¿Qué periódicos o revistas leía? 9. ¿Había televisión en su casa?

3b

1. ¿Dónde vivías? 2. ¿Cuántos años tenías? 3. ¿Cómo era tu piso? 4. ¿Tenías familia? 5. ¿Tú ibas al colegio o trabajabas? 6. ¿Qué cosas comprabas en las tiendas? 7. ¿Qué comíais tú y tu familia? 8. ¿Qué periódicos o revistas leías? 9. ¿Había televisión en tu casa?

4

1. hacía 2. empezaban 3. llovía 4. era 5. esperaban 6. salíamos 7. íbamos 8. conducía
9. estaba 10. vivían 11. estaban 12. llamaban 13. había 14. encontrábamos 15. venían
16. charlábamos 17. jugábamos 18. divertíamos 19. eran 20. dábamos

Chapter 27

1

A   está comiendo, estamos hablando, están conduciendo, estás dibujando, estáis bebiendo, estoy estudiando, están haciendo, estamos mirando, está poniendo, estoy diciendo

B   estaba comiendo, estábamos hablando, estaban conduciendo, estabas dibujando, estabais bebiendo, estaba estudiando, estaban haciendo, estábamos mirando, estaba poniendo, estaba diciendo

2

Está llegando; se está parando; están bajando; está saliendo; está esperando; se está parando; está hablando; está entregando; está pidiendo; está regalando; está cogiendo; está dando; está subiendo; está bajando; está desapareciendo

3

A 1. está corriendo 2. está estudiando 3. está dibujando 4. está mirando la tele 5. está escribiendo 6. están jugando al tenis 7. están bebiendo 8. se están besando 9. están comiendo
10. están andando

B 1. estaba corriendo 2. estaba estudiando 3. estaba dibujando 4. estaba mirando la tele
5. estaba escribiendo 6. estaban jugando al tenis 7. estaban bebiendo 8. se estaban besando
9. estaban comiendo 10. estaban andando

Chapter 28

1

1. se levantó   2. se duchó   3. desayunó   4. estudió   5. bailó   6. corrió   7. trabajó   8. nadó

2

levanté … salí … llegué … vimos … cogimos … tomamos … compramos … entramos … volvimos … llamé … nos reunimos … bailamos … llevé … llegué …

3

1. decidieron   2. sacaron   3. prepararon   4. olvidaron   5. se acordó   6. buscó   7. salieron
8. compraron   9. llegó   10. empezaron   11. cogieron   12. llegaron   13. bajaron   14. comenzó
15. volvieron   16. pasaron

Chapter 29

1

1. she said   2. we went   3. you know   4. they put   5. you saw   6. hizo   7. quisisteis   8. pagué
9. leyó   10. empecé

2

1. fui   2. busqué   3. tuve   4. vino   5. dieron   6. Dije / Dijimos   7. crucé   8. siguió   9. pagué
10. estuvimos   11. vi / vimos   12. leyó

3 (Examples)

Saqué la llave de mi bolsillo.
¿Viste la tele anoche?
Llegué al cole a las nueve.
Anoche fuimos a la discoteca.
Mi padre me dio un regalo.
Empecé a estudiar español hace dos años.
Mis amigos leyeron este libro.
Mi hermana prefirió ver la tele.
El año pasado estuve dos semanas en Marbella.
¿Hiciste los deberes de matemáticas?
El profe me pidió un chicle.
Mis abuelos durmieron en mi dormitorio.
¿Dónde pusisteis vuestras camisas sucias?
¿Tuviste que pagar mucho?
Vinimos inmediatamente.

Chapter 30

1

miraba – she was looking; leyó – he read; estábamos – we were; viajaron – they travelled; compraban – they were buying; pusiste – you put; leía – he was reading; mire – I looked; viajaba – she was travelling; estuvisteis – you were

2

1. compraste   2. preparaba   3. ponía(n)   4. fueron   5. quitó   6. estaba   7. perdí   8. llamaban
9. sabía   10. cogiste

¡Viva la gramática!

3 (Examples)

1. Tomaba un café cuando entré en el bar. 2. Cuando salí de casa hacía sol. 3. Cuando vio a su amigo llevaba vaqueros. 4. Empezó a llover, mientras buscaba el paraguas. 5. Empezó a llorar mientras oía las malas noticias. 6. Cuando recibió la carta hablaba con su padre. 7. El padre aparcó el coche cuando llegó a casa. 8. Cuando estaba en Londres, vi a la reina.

Chapter 31

1

1. visitado 2. ido 3. visto 4. jugado 5. pasado 6. comido 7. tomado, puesto 8. escrito 9. enviado 10. roto, comprado

2

1. hemos pasado 2. han hecho, han preparado 3. ha viajado, ha tenido 4. han pasado, han trabajado, han ayudado, han recibido 5. ha jugado 6. han sido 7. hemos aprendido 8. habéis hecho, os habéis instalado, habéis probado.

3

1. Sí, señor, lo he llenado / he llenado el congelador de pescado.
2. Sí, señor, las he puesto / he puesto las latas de judías en los estantes.
3. Sí, señor, los he traído / he traído los paquetes de café.
4. Sí, señor, las he puesto / he puesto las etiquetas con los precios.
5. Sí, señor, las he contado / he contado las botellas de leche.
6. Sí, señor, lo he lavado / he lavado el mostrador de tabacos.
7. Sí, señor, las he arreglado / he arreglado las carretillas.
8. Sí, señor, lo he barrido / he barrido el suelo.
9. Sí, señor, los he limpiado / he limpiado los asientos de los cajeros.
10. Sí, señor, lo he terminado / he terminado mi trabajo.

4

1. Enrique acaba de comer. 2. El camarero acaba de traer las bebidas. 3. Antonio y yo acabamos de casarnos. 4. Los Domínguez acaban de llegar a su hotel. 5. Yo acabo de leer una novela muy larga.

Chapter 32

1

1d 2f 3i 4e 5h 6a 7c 8b 9j 10g

2

1. habré aprobado 2. habrá visitado 3. habrá cambiado 4. habrá crecido 5. habremos ido 6. habrán venido 7. habréis hecho

Chapter 33

1

volviendo – returning; vuelto – returned; vendido – sold; sorprendido – surprised; vendiendo – selling; puesto – put; oyendo – hearing; sufrido – suffered; estudiando – studying; encontrado – found; poniendo – putting; oído – heard

2 (Examples)

1. Comprando un billete de lotería. 2. Marcando goles. 3. Cortando pan. 4. Estudiando el español. 5. Comprando una entrada. 6. Dándole un ramo de flores todos los días. 7. Lavando el coche o trabajando en el jardín. 8. Cogiendo un avión.

3

A   (patatas) fritas – freír; (el cielo) cubierto – cubrir; abierto – abrir/cerrado – cerrar; satisfecho – satisfacer; la permisión – permitir; la puesta (del sol) – poner

B   entrar – la entrada; parecer – (el) parecido; ir – la ida; ver – la vista; caer – la caída; variar – la variedad/variado

Chapter 34

1

1. escribir 2. poner 3. vivir 4. dibujar 5. escuchar 6. volver 7. pagar 8. comprar
9. considerar 10. subir 11. acabar 12. salir 13. soler 14. poner 15. mentir

2

1. Coger seis huevos y dos kilos de patatas. 2. Pelar las patatas y cortarlas en trozos. 3. Poner cuatro cucharadas de aceite en una sartén. 4. Calentar el aceite y freír las patatas. 5. Batir los huevos en una fuente, y añadir las patatas: mezclarlos bien. 6. Poner los huevos y las patatas en la sartén, y freírlos bien. 7. Usando un plato, dar la vuelta a la tortilla para freír el otro lado. 8. Terminar de freír la tortilla. 9. Sacar la tortilla de la sartén, y dejarla enfriar. 10. Servir en forma de pinchos con un vasito de vino.

3

1. ir 2. tener 3. participar 4. jugar 5. poder 6. escuchar 7. salir 8. comprar 9. encontrar
10. ver 11. buscar 12. pasar

Chapter 35

1

1. puedo 2. debo 3. Tengo 4. debemos 5. sé 6. sé 7. saben 8. deberían 9. Deberían 10. Hay que

2

1f 2d 3g 4j 5i 6a 7h 8c 9e 10b

Chapter 36

1

1. ¡Ten cuidado! 2. Deme un paquete de éstos. 3. Cómprale un regalo. 4. Coge un taxi.
5. Cómete un bocadillo. 6. Dame un panecillo. 7. Abre la puerta. 8. Vete a buscar la aspiradora.

2

1. Cierra la ventana. 2. Enchufa el aparato con cuidado. 3. Lava y abre los mejillones. 4. No tires basura a la calle. 5. No toques los modelos. 6. Lleve la derecha. 7. En casos de urgencia llame a la policía. 8. Abróchese el cinturón. 9. No deje artículos de valor en las habitaciones. 10. No lleve las sillas al jardín.

1. Cerrad la ventana. 2. Enchufad el aparato con cuidado. 3. Lavad y abrid los mejillones. 4. No tiréis basura a la calle. 5. No toquéis los modelos. 6. Lleven la derecha. 7. En casos de urgencia llamen a la policía. 8. Abróchense el cinturón. 9. No dejen artículos de valor en las habitaciones.
10. No lleven las sillas al jardín.

Chapter 37

1

1. está; es 2. son; están 3. estaba; era 4. estoy; soy 5. somos; estamos 6. serán; estarán

2

1. estamos 2. eres 3. estamos 4. es 5. es 6. es 7. está 8. estás 9. es 10. estamos

¡Viva la gramática!

Chapter 38

1

1252:	las murallas fueron construidas por el rey
1540:	el puente fue construido sobre el río
1864:	la fábrica de lana fue fundada
1937:	el Ayuntamiento fue destruido por una bomba
1953:	el nuevo Ayuntamiento / Ayuntamiento nuevo fue abierto por la reina
1966:	la estación de trenes fue cerrada
1993:	el polideportivo fue abierto por el alcalde
1995:	las calles fueron peatonalizadas por el Ayuntamiento
1995:	los coches fueron prohibidos en el centro

El año que viene: una nueva piscina / piscina nueva será abierta

2

1. fue 2. está/estaba 3. Fue 4. fue 5. Fue 6. estaban 7. estaban 8. fueron 9. fue 10. Está
11. son

Chapter 39

1

2. se construyó 3. se fundó 4. se destruyó 5. se abrió 6. se cerró 7. se abrió 8. se
peatonalizaron 9. se prohibieron 10. se terminó

2

1. A Montse le escribieron una postal. 2. A Javier le mandaron una carta. 3. A Ana le dieron un
reloj. 4. A Ramón le dijeron la verdad. 5. A Rosario la vieron en la discoteca. 6. A Gerardo le
oyeron llegar. 7. A Pili la prohibieron entrar.

Chapter 40

1

1. vayas 2. hagas 3. coma 4. limpie 5. oigas 6. salgas 7. te quedes 8. saques 9. hables
10. estés

2

1. vaya 2. trabaje 3. juegue 4. visiten 5. termine 6. tenga 7. quiera 8. aprobemos
9. suspendáis 10. haya

3

1a. tuvo 1b. tenga 2a. reciba 2b. recibí 3a. contestó 3b. conteste 4a. lleguemos
4b. llegamos

Chapter 41

1

1. fuera 2. hiciera 3. comiera 4. limpiara 5. oyera 6. saliera 7. se quedara 8. sacara
9. hablara 10. estuviera

2

1. fuéramos / fuésemos 2. trabajara / trabajase 3. jugara / jugase 4. visitaran / visitasen
5. terminara / terminase 6. tuviera / tuviese 7. quisiera / quisiese 8. aprobáramos / aprobásemos
9. suspendierais / suspendieseis 10. hubiera / hubiese